THE ORIGINS OF EUROPE'S
NEW STOCK MARKETS

Dear Michelle,
I wish you all
the best,

Elliot

Elliot Posner

The Origins of Europe's New Stock Markets

HARVARD UNIVERSITY PRESS
Cambridge, Massachusetts, and London, England   2009

Library of Congress Cataloging-in-Publication Data

Posner, Elliot, 1965–
  The origins of Europe's new stock markets / Elliot Posner.
      p.   cm.
  Includes bibliographical references and index.
  ISBN 978-0-674-03171-5 (cloth : alk. paper)
  1. Stock exchanges—Europe.   2. Capital market—Europe.   3. Finance—Europe.   I. Title.

HG5422.P67 2008
332.64'24—dc22   2008013948

To Gillian

Contents

List of Tables and Figures

Acknowledgments

In the years it took to complete this book, I did research in six countries, moved into five separate dwellings, switched offices thrice, said "I do," changed thousands of diapers, and flew back and forth between Washington, D.C., and Cleveland for five years, until landing, happily, in this lakefront city of classical music, huge houses, and great beer. Writing a book during such an odyssey would not have been possible without the assistance of a large number of people and institutions.

For their funding, I thank the American Consortium on European Union Studies (ACES), the Institute for European, Russian, and Eurasian Studies (IERES) at George Washington University's Elliott School of International Affairs, the GW Center for the Study of Globalization (GWCSG), University of California, Berkeley's Institute of European Studies (IES) and Center for German and European Studies (CGES), the University of California's Institute on Global Conflict and Cooperation (IGCC), and the John D. and Catherine T. MacArthur Foundation.

This book's roots lie in Berkeley, California, where I benefited from the ideas, comments, and support of Vinod Aggarwal, Aaron Belkin, Nikolaos Biziouras, Kiren Chaudhry, David Collier, Ruth Collier, Beverly Crawford, Neil Fligstein, Andrew Janos, Martin Kenney, Bronwyn Leebaw, David Leonard, Jonah Levy, Rita Parhad, Robert Powell, Robert Price, Kirsten Rodine, Beth Simmons, Steven Vogel, J. Nicholas Ziegler, and the much-missed Ernst Haas. AnnaLee Saxenian was a consistent source of support, and John Zysman, many of whose ideas percolate through these pages, provided invaluable advice. I owe an especially large debt to Steven Weber. This book grew out of our joint project, and his influence is everywhere.

I benefited immeasurably from five stimulating years at George Washington University. My colleagues there gave valuable feedback and encouragement. I especially thank Deborah Avant, Alasdair Bowie, Maurice East, Henry Farrell, Harvey Feigenbaum, Martha Finnemore, James Goldgeier, Henry Hale, Steven

Kelts, Gina Lambright, Kristin Lord, Kimberly Morgan, Henry Nau, Chad Rector, Melissa Schwartzberg, Amy Searight, Susan Sell, John Sides, Emmanuel Teitelbaum, and Erik Voeten. I was lucky to have three superb research assistants: Maryam Zarnegar Deloffre, Joel Mathen, and Scott Roecker. Karen Beckwith, Justin Buchler, Brian Gran, Kathryn Lavelle, Kelly McMann, Peter Moore, and Joseph White—new colleagues at Case Western Reserve University—offered helpful comments in the final months of writing.

For reading and commenting on sections of the manuscript at various stages, I thank Tiberiu Dragu, Julia Lynch, Craig Parsons, Kristin Smith Diwan, and Nicolas Jabko. Several individuals deserve special mention in this category: Kathleen McNamara, Abraham Newman, Gillian Weiss, and Jonathan Zeitlin. I also appreciate conversations with David Bach, Tim Büthe, Marios Camhis, Melani Cammett, John W. Cioffi, Orfeo Fioretos, Emiliano Grossman, Kathryn Lavelle, Jonah Levy, Evan Lieberman, Lauren Morris MacLean, Angelo Manioudakis, Wayne Sandholtz, Nicolas Véron, Steven Vogel, Scott Wallsten, and Daniel Ziblatt.

Parts of the book were first delivered at conferences. I was fortunate to receive comments from Robert Bates, Mark Blyth, Tania A. Börzel, Brian Burgoon, Philip G. Cerny, Roy Ginsberg, Harold James, Paulette Kurzer, Sophie Meunier, James Morone, Daniel Mügge, Louis W. Pauly, Mark Pollack, Vivien Schmidt, Michael E. Smith, Jonathan Story, Amy Verdun, Nigel Wicks, Anastasia Xenia, and Alasdair R. Young.

In sections of this book, I use material adapted from my "Sources of Institutional Change: The Supranational Origins of Europe's New Stock Markets," *World Politics* 58 (October 2005); 1–40, and by permission of Oxford University Press, from my "Stock Exchange Competition and the Nasdaq Bargain in Europe," in *With US or against US? European Trends in American Perspective* in *State of the European Union*, vol. 7, ed. N. Jabko and C. Parsons (2005). In Chapter 7, also by permission of Oxford University Press, I modified and updated sections from my "Financial Transformation in the EU," in *Making History: European Integration and Institutional Change at Fifty* in *State of the European Union*, vol. 8, ed. S. Meunier and K. R. McNamara (2007).

Many generous individuals proved instrumental to my research: in London and Brussels, Katie Morris; in Paris, Catherine Lubochinsky and Marc Sounigo; in Frankfurt, Ellen Thalman; and in Geneva, Eugene Schulman and Andrew Sundberg. I am also extremely grateful to the many busy executives, officials, and academics who took the time to speak with me in person or on the telephone, write responses to my questions, or assist my research in other ways: Paul Arlman, Peter Baines, Stefan Bergheim, Jean-Louis Berton, Reinhard Biebel, Sébastien Boitreaud, Vincent Boland, Peter Clifford, Ronald Cohen, Martin A.

Donges, Fabrice Demarigny, Javier Echarri, Hassan Elmasry, José María Fombellida, Pierre de Fouquet, Reto Francioni, Jonathan Freeman, Giancarlo Giudici, Anita Gradin, J. David Germany, Paul Goldschmidt, Hillary Hedges, Karel van Hulle, Daniël Janssens, Matthew King, Susan Koski-Grafer, Karel Lannoo, Philip Laskawy, Dominique Leblanc, Johannes H. Lucas, Thomas Krantz, L. D. M. Mackenzie, Judith Mayhew, Amy Houpt Medearis, Nicole de Montricher, P. J. Charles Moray, Denis Mortier, Albrecht Mulfinger, Eric Müller, Daniel F. Muzyka, David Naudé, Clive Pedder, Jos B. Peeters, Jacques Putzey, Olli Rehn, Peter Roosenboom, George Ross, Paul Rutteman, Stephen Ryan, Alexander Schaub, William Stevens, Dominique Strauss-Kahn, Alex Tamlyn, Martin Taylor, Robert Thys, Lynn E. Turner, Marc Verlinden, James Wallar, Theresa Wallis, Crispin Waymouth, and Stanislas M. Yassukovich. I also thank my editor Michael Aronson of Harvard University Press, for making the publication process seem so easy.

Several friends helped make the research and writing enjoyable. For their hospitality, housing, and other forms of camaraderie, I thank Jim Biek, Dinah Diwan, Gina Diwan, Roger Diwan, Lise Morjé Howard, Marc Morjé Howard, Jen Sermoneta, Rachel Sherman, Victor Tanner, and Scott Wallsten. Kathleen McNamara and Susan Sell gently steered me in the right direction from time to time. Dean Mathiowetz and Ben Read contributed endlessly to my thinking and graciously put up with a decade of late-night stock market discussions. Abraham Newman never stopped giving thoughtful responses, even as the questions became increasingly minute. Steven Weber helped me balance intellectual experience with life's other pursuits.

I am also deeply grateful to my family: to my brother Jeff for buying me a printer; to my sister Tammy for always checking up on me; to my *beaux-parents* Carol and Norman for babysitting; to my late grandmother Gay for encouraging me to pursue a scholarly career; to my son Oliver for finding joy in garbage trucks and closets; and to my parents Bill and Lil for supporting this book and everything that led to it.

Lastly, I dedicate this book to my life partner, Gillian Weiss, not merely because she read and edited every page of every draft through to the notes. For most of the last decade, we have traveled together, even when physically apart. Her companionship, above all, has inspired me throughout the journey.

List of Abbreviations

AFIC	Association Française des Investisseurs en Capital
AFSB	Association Française des Sociétés de Bourse
AIB	Association of Independent Businesses
AIM	Alternative Investment Market
APCIMS	Association of Private Client Investment Managers and Stock Brokers
BVCA	British Venture Capital Association
CBI	Confederation of British Industry
CEC	Commission of the European Communities
CESR	Committee of European Securities Regulators
CEU	Council of the European Union
CISCO	City Group for Smaller Companies
COB	Commission des Opérations de Bourse
DG	directorate general
DTB	Deutsche Terminbörse
DTI	Department of Trade and Industry
EASD	European Association of Securities Dealers
EC	European Community
ECB	European Central Bank
ECJ	European Court of Justice
ECN	electronic communication network
Ecofin	Economic and Financial Affairs Council
ECU	European currency unit
EEC	European Economic Community
EEMEC	European Electronic Market for Entrepreneurial Companies
EMS	European Monetary System
EP	European Parliament
ESC	European Securities Committee
EVCA	European Private Equity Venture Capital and Association (formerly European Venture Capital Association)

ERM	Exchange Rate Mechanism
ESM	European Securities Market
EU	European Union
FASB	Financial Accounting Standards Board
FESE	Federation of European Securities (formerly Stock) Exchanges
FIBV	Fédération Internationale des Bourses de Valeurs (now World Federation of Exchanges)
FSAP	Financial Services Action Plan
FSA	Financial Services Authority (UK)
IAS	International Accounting Standards
IASB	International Accounting Standards Board
IASC	International Accounting Standards Committee
IFRS	International Financial Reporting Standards
IMF	International Monetary Fund
IOSCO	International Organization of Securities Commissions
IPO	initial public offering
ISD	Investment Services Directive
LIFFE	London International Financial Futures and Options Exchange
LSE	London Stock Exchange
MATIF	Le Marché à Terme International de France
MESEC	Marché Européen des Sociétés Entrepreneuriales de Croissance
NASD	National Association of Securities Dealers
NTBF	new techonology-based firms
NYSE	New York Stock Exchange
OFT	Office of Fair Trading (UK)
OTC	over the counter
RIE	Registered Investment Exchange
ROIE	Registered Overseas Investment Exchange
SBF	Société des Bourses Françaises
SFE	Scottish Financial Enterprise
SEA	Single European Act
SEAQ	Stock Exchange Automated Quotations System
SEC	Securities and Exchange Commission (U.S.)
SIB	Securities and Investment Board
SME	small and medium-size enterprises
SPRINT	Strategic Programme for Innovation and Technology Transfer
UCITS	Undertakings for Collective Investment in Transferable Securities
U.S. GAAP	U. S. generally accepted accounting principles
USM	Unlisted Securities Market

THE ORIGINS OF EUROPE'S
NEW STOCK MARKETS

CHAPTER 1

Europe's New Stock Markets

In 2006 two giants of American capital markets, the New York Stock Exchange (NYSE) and the Nasdaq Stock Market, entered a competitive buying spree for their European counterparts. Nasdaq made the first move with a March bid for the London Stock Exchange (LSE). Acquiring a 25 percent share was enough to block its U.S. rival from purchasing the UK entity, even though the takeover failed. In June the NYSE responded with a successful offer for Euronext, the pan-European exchange, and threatened to create a new London market to compete with the LSE's.[1]

The extension of this American rivalry to the Atlantic's other shore is an extraordinary paradox. On the Continent, the dominance of bank financing left capital markets underdeveloped in the postwar decades, and in Britain seventy-odd years of effort failed to improve market-based financing for entrepreneurial companies.[2] Yet six years into the new millennium, the NYSE apparently considered Europe to be one of this century's next frontiers. Sitting at the nexus between America's cutting-edge industries and risk capital, moreover, Nasdaq still saw competitive advantage in gaining a foothold in the United Kingdom. The twists in this story extend beyond the exchanges, which were merely the latest American financial players to flock to Europe.[3] U.S. investment banks had long ranked among the top performers across most categories of the European securities sectors, and the largest broker-dealers at the century's end depended on Europe for approximately 20 percent of their net revenues. Private equity and hedge-fund capital with U.S. origins had been flowing into the Continent since the mid-1990s, and Americans were among the most active in mergers and acquisitions.[4]

What drew American finance to Europe? Part of the answer lies in regulatory change in the United States. The Sarbanes-Oxley Act of 2002 increased the costs of raising capital on American soil and modestly helped Europe outpace the United States in some financial services categories, most notably international initial public offerings (IPOs). Business lobbies and New York politicians seeking regulatory rollback blamed Sarbanes-Oxley for Europe's relative financial rise, but Washington's stiffer rules were more triggers than causes of the Nasdaq and the NYSE turn toward Europe.[5]

This book addresses the other part of the answer. Arguably, Europe's appeal as a global financial center has more to do with internal developments than U.S. reforms. In the euro's wake, Europe underwent a financial transformation.[6] Even for the world of finance, where markets and regulatory regimes had been in uninterrupted flux for thirty years, recent developments in the region were exceptional. They included the creation of regionally integrated money, bond, and other wholesale markets, and a legal overhaul that shifted financial regulation significantly from the national level to the European Union (EU), the fifty-year-old polity that binds twenty-seven national economies.[7] This transformation represents one of the most significant contemporary changes in global finance, creating new expectations among firms from the United States and elsewhere and bolstering the positions of European officials in international arenas. Inside Europe, these changes are moving the EU closer to one of its early goals: a single financial market.

The underlying causes of European financial transformation are the subject of this book. Explaining change in the arrangements that allocate capital is challenging, because powerful interests, close finance-government ties, and the sector's centrality to all areas of the economy typically work against reform, let alone overhaul. Using new stock markets for smaller companies as the main illustration, the following pages show that the origins of financial change in Europe predate the single currency's advent, which quickened the pace of reform but was not its principal cause. The chapters that follow also demonstrate that the transformation represents more than an offshoot of global processes or government-to-government agreements. My investigation traces Europe's financial transformation to a powerful, though underestimated and slow-moving, internal force for fundamental change—the continued development of the EU.

Ascribing causation to Europe's regional polity and the integration project it embodies runs headlong into a venerable problem for analysts of international affairs: how to explain the metamorphosis of an international arrangement, like the EU, from a vehicle for intergovernmental cooperation and economic integration into an entity greater than its constituent parts and sufficiently independent to cause change in them.[8] Recent and past scholarship points to multiple routes by which such elemental change occurs. This book explores the importance of one such route, the day-to-day activity of supranational bureaucrats.

The empirical chapters account for why and how the presence of skilled civil servants working for the European Commission, the EU's main bureaucracy, contributed to the creation of new stock markets for smaller companies. Market formation is a variant of what social scientists label institutional change.[9] In explaining the origins of Europe's new markets, I therefore engage in scholarly debates about the origination and change of governance arrangements in a generic sense.

The incremental accumulation of routine activities by Brussels civil servants over a fifteen-year period carved out a political space for challenging established market arrangements. These bureaucrats had little effect on smaller-company finance in the 1980s, when their efforts were still relatively sparse. Reforms instead followed distinct national patterns driven by domestic financial establishments. By the mid-1990s, however, the European Commission officials had crafted several new political facts, most notably, a venture capitalist interest group supporting a pan-European market, setting the stage for a political clash with national finance-government coalitions over the scope, regulation, and purpose of markets. The unintended result was competitive mimesis and experimentation, yielding a dozen Nasdaq-like stock markets, then several others based on a British variety, and drawing an inflow of mobile capital into Europe's smaller companies and unprecedented levels of venture capital.

In sum, by explaining how Europe became friendly terrain to the fleet-footed species of capitalism and evolved into a rival financial hub that gives its officials new international clout, this book addresses two issues central to the global political economy. The first concerns the EU and, by extension, other international arrangements. Analysis of the origins of the EU and the forces behind its grand bargains is plentiful. But comparatively few studies provide a basis for treating the regional polity, its supranational actors, and their interventions as independent forces capable of effecting domestic and international change. This book, using the new market story, helps fill the gap. The second issue involves market formation and its relationship to politics, culture, and economic opportunism. Traditionally, political scientists and sociologists have been more interested in understanding the constraints and stabilization processes that impede market formation than in explaining how politically weak challengers overcome formidable obstacles in the first place.

The following chapters take up this subject and draw attention to the role of the EU's supranational bureaucracy as a source of motivated political actors capable of generating competing conceptions of markets, thereby strengthening the influence of some financial interests and loosening the hold of others. What emerges is a paradoxical image of market formation and, more broadly, institutional innovation contingent on a bureaucrat-driven, incremental, and cumulative process.

Gateways for Global Finance

For three decades smaller companies—especially entrepreneurial ones in high-technology sectors—stood at the center of public debates in Europe about how to revitalize national economies.[10] Identifying such firms as the seedbeds of future innovation, wealth, jobs, and international competitiveness in the post–Bretton Woods era, policymakers saw limited financing options as an impediment to these companies' development. Multiple efforts to borrow the American solution of opening stock markets to small and untested companies (allowing them to sell publicly traded ownership shares in exchange for capital) never generated much support from national financial gatekeepers. As a result, smaller enterprises remained largely shut out of corporate capital markets (see Table 1.1).

Table 1.1 Proposals for smaller-company stock markets in Europe, 1977–2005

Year	Name of Market and Owner	Principle
1977	Compartiment Spécial, Fr Exchange	National Feeder
1978	Mercato Ristretto/Expandi (2005), It Exchange	National Feeder
1980	Unlisted Securities Market, UK Exchange	National Feeder
1982	Aktiemarked III, Den Exchange	National Feeder
1982	Officiele Parallel Markt, Ne Exchange	National Feeder
1982	Segundo Mercado, Barcelona Exchange	National Feeder
1982	Swedish OTC Market, Swe Exchange	National Feeder
1983	Second Marché I, Fr Exchange	National Feeder
1984	Bors II, Nor Exchange	National Feeder
1984	Second Marché, Be Exchange	National Feeder
1985	*ECU-EASD, Private Actors*	*Pan-European Nasdaq*
1986	Segundo Mercado, Bilbao Exchange	National Feeder
1986	Segundo Mercado, Madrid Exchange	National Feeder
1986	*Segundo Mercado, Valencia Exchange*	*National Feeder*

Year	Name of Market and Owner	Principle
1987	Geregelter Markt, Ger Exchange	National Feeder
1987	Third Market, UK Exchange	National Feeder
1989	*EASDAQ I, UK (Scotland), Private Actors*	*National Nasdaq*
1989	*European OTC Market, Private Actors*	*Pan-European Nasdaq*
1989	*European Securities Market, Private Actors*	*Pan-European Nasdaq*
1992	Dutch Participation Exchange, Ne Exchange/Private	National AIM
1992	*European Private Equity Exchange, UK Private Actors*	*Pan-European AIM*
1992	*Mercato Locale Del Nord Ovest, Turin Exchange*	*National AIM*
1993	*EASDAQ-UK, Private Actors*	*National Nasdaq*
1993	*ECASE, UK Private Actors*	*National Nasdaq*
1993	*The Enterprise Market, UK Exchange/Private*	*National Nasdaq*
1993	*The National Market, UK Exchange/Private*	*National AIM*
1993	Second Marché II, Fr Exchange	National Feeder
1994	*MESEC, Fr Exchange*	*Pan-European Nasdaq*
1995	Alternative Investment Market (AIM), UK Exchange	National AIM
1995	*Electronic Share Interchange, Private Actors*	*National AIM*
1996	EASDAQ, Private Actors	Pan-European Nasdaq
1996	Nouveau Marché, Fr Exchange	National Nasdaq
1997	Euro.NM Belgium, Be Exchange	National Nasdaq
1997	Euro.NM Amsterdam, Ne Exchange	National Nasdaq
1997	Neuer Markt, Ger Exchange	National Nasdaq
1998	Nya Marknaden, Swe Exchange	National Feeder
1999	SWX New Market, Swz Exchange	National Nasdaq
1999	NM-List, Fin Exchange	National Nasdaq
1999	Techmark, UK Exchange	National Nasdaq
1999	Nuovo Mercato, It Exchange	National Nasdaq
1999	SMAX, Ger Exchange	National Nasdaq
1999	Austrian Growth Market, Aust Exchange	National Nasdaq
2000	Nuevo Mercado, Sp Exchange	National Nasdaq
2000	KVX Growth Market, Den Exchange	National Nasdaq
2000	ITEQ, Ir Exchange	National Nasdaq
2000	*iX-Nasdaq Merger, UK-Ger Exchanges*	*Binational Nasdaq*
2001	Nasdaq Europe, U.S. Exchange	Pan-European Nasdaq
2002	NextEconomy/NextPrime, Euronext	Multinational Nasdaq
2003	Prime Standard, Ger Exchange	National Nasdaq
2005	Alternext, Euronext	Multinational AIM
2005	Entry Standard, Ger Exchange	National AIM
2005	IEX, Ir Exchange	National AIM
2005	First North, OMX	Multinational AIM

Note: Unrealized proposals are set in italics.

That changed in the mid-1990s. Between 1995 and 2006, financial elites in more than a dozen western European countries engaged in a frenzied cross-border battle to create some twenty new stock markets, most of which in the initial years were explicitly modeled on an iconic American institution, the Nasdaq (see Table 1.1). As of 2007, the most successful survivor of the ongoing competition was London's Alternative Investment Market (AIM), with a homegrown organizational form. With almost 1,700 listed companies and a market capitalization of over 100 billion pounds, AIM reversed decades of failure to become a core mechanism for allocating financial resources to smaller firms.[11] AIM's record in raising capital for international companies was a key factor behind the Nasdaq's interest in the LSE. Although several new markets based on the U.S. form—like Paris' Nouveau Marché and Frankfurt's Neuer Markt—eventually failed, they were household names during the turn-of-the-millennium boom and bust in international corporate share prices. While the exchanges put AIM imitations in the place of the failed Nasdaq look-alikes in 2005, the rise and fall of these market experiments are important developments for a region sometimes depicted as averse to risk and U.S.-style capitalism.

Arrangements for distributing capital, even when based on markets, are political institutions. They tell us who controls the price of capital, as well as who is able to obtain it.[12] Aftershocks from the new stock markets still reverberate across European societies—a reminder that financial markets are not neutral, impersonal allocation mechanisms.

The organizational form of capital markets influences the balance of obligations and risks between citizens and their governments. The specific rules of a stock market determine which firms may tap into giant pools of investor capital and what specific hurdles firms must surmount to do so.[13] Differences in the rules—and the underlying organizational principles—encourage certain patterns of investment, savings, and entrepreneurial activity and discourage others, creating winners and losers among societal groups and economic sectors.

The Nasdaq principle, for instance, is a bargain by which companies exchange information for access to capital.[14] Even untested firms with relatively short histories, if willing to reveal high levels of information about their operations, may seek financing from corporate capital markets. In the United States, giving enterprises access to stock markets helps create an incentive structure that encourages risk-taking behaviors, such as venture capital investment in start-up companies. Such access also shapes some of the uncertainties with which Americans live: the ways they save for retirement, the places they work, their job security and ability to buy homes, and the disparity between rich and poor.

In the post–World War II decades, European financial systems rested on different principles—even in the United Kingdom, where arrangements are sometimes labeled Anglo-American. The high-risk, high-reward world of the U.S. market is antithetical to the social compacts that led European governments to protect citizens from the extremes of capitalism.[15] Keeping smaller firms away from the constraints of financial markets was part of the glue holding these national compromises together. Allocating capital through banks and public programs, as opposed to markets, made it easier for governments and societies to use the economy as an instrument of political and social aims. It helped to perpetuate family control over companies, lock in national labor regimes and entitlement programs, and protect citizens from the unwanted gyrations of a capitalist economy. One result, to repeat a refrain European financiers often uttered even as recently as the early 1990s, was that risk taking simply did not pay.

The new markets facilitate wealth creation. But they also chip away at the European social compacts, opening the door of smaller-company finance to the broad trend of marketization and its bounties and subjecting Europeans to exacerbated swings of global capital. Twelve years after their introduction, these market experiments have spawned several observable effects typical of the U.S. political economy.

First, at core, the new markets unlocked a source of capital on favorable terms to sometimes unproven companies with relatively short track records, a class of firms with historically restricted financing alternatives in Europe. Approximately 3,500 newly listed companies raised over 100 billion euros between 1996 and 2006.[16] These figures start from an almost zero base, representing a significant reallocation of financial resources.

Second, the new markets rolled out novel assets in the European setting (that is, equity shares in chancy companies). They look like ones long available in the United States and similarly attract mobile capital, sometimes the retirement savings of Americans.[17] Global institutional investors, however, were neither the only buyers nor the most voracious in the early years. Once given the opportunity, households in the United Kingdom, France, and Germany poured their savings into these stocks, belying conventional wisdom that Europeans are risk averse because they lack a so-called equity culture. Largely sheltered from the perils of global finance in the postwar decades,

European households were among the biggest beneficiaries when valuations reached frothy levels at the end of the 1990s. In the aftermath of the March 2000 international market crash, these households bore the costs.[18]

Finally, the new markets have given venture capitalists a sturdy foothold in Europe. Until their introduction, venture capitalism, at least of the U.S. variety, hardly existed on the Continent or in Britain, despite a multitude of national efforts to establish it. With the new markets, the outlook of these financiers changed: they began to believe that investing in start-ups would reap profits commensurate to those made by their U.S. counterparts.[19] Venture capitalists turn a profit by divesting from a risky investment in a young enterprise at a higher price than they paid. Selling shares to the public through a stock market is the preferred mechanism for doing so. This is why the new markets changed venture capitalists' expectations about taking chances in Europe.

As illustrated in Figure 1.1, with the announcement of the first new markets in 1994, 1995, and 1996, these financial intermediaries were able to convince asset managers (pension funds, insurance companies, banks, universities, private corporations, and governments) to invest in funds devoted to European early stage companies.

The unprecedented level of American-style venture capitalism opens European firms to another category of footloose investors, as outsiders gain new opportunities to buy shares of formerly cosseted smaller companies, some owned and tightly controlled by families and entrepreneurs.[20] The geographic origins of the capital pouring into venture capital investment funds, like that of private equity funds in general, became significantly more international (especially American) from the mid-1990s on. Non-European countries, for instance, made up a larger percentage than nondomestic European sources of capital in every year between 1997 and 2005. The United Kingdom remains the preferred domicile for fund managers. In 2006, for example, British-based private equity funds attracted more than half of all incoming investment capital. Yet less than a third originated in the United Kingdom, and roughly half was invested in other European countries.[21] Further internationalization occurs after initial public offerings, moreover, when venture capitalists and the other owners of smaller companies sell shares on one of the new markets to foreign as well as local buyers.

Venture capitalists are not merely on-the-ground nodes of global investors but a challenge to some of the underpinnings of European social-democratic capitalism. The business model of venture capitalists is premised on a calculation that some 70 to 90 percent of investments in young compa-

nies will fail. No one should expect a replication of U.S. entrepreneurial capitalism in Europe, and a dozen years after the launching of the first new
market, the ultimate implications of all this venture capital slushing around
the Continent remains largely unknown.[22] Much will depend on previous
national particularities and the nature of other simultaneous and subsequent EU reforms, which are discussed in Chapter 7 and the Conclusion.
Still, it is hard to imagine a scenario without an increase in firm openings
and closures, more frequent firings and hirings, and the accompanying social
dislocation—the very types of reforms that many Europeans consider anath-
ema to their values and have long resisted.

Unexpected Market Innovation

These social and economic effects are not the only reason Europe's new markets are important and interesting. Looking into the future from the early
1990s, even the most seasoned observer of European finance would not have

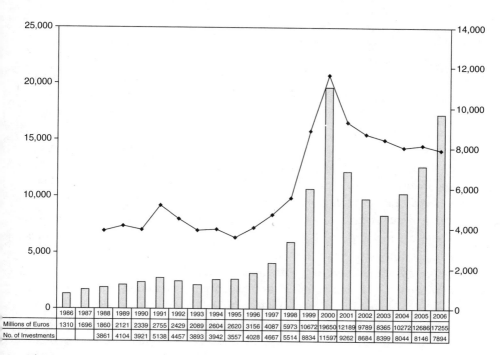

Figure 1.1. Venture capital investments, Europe. Venture capital includes
seed, start-up, and expansion investments. *Source:* EVCA.

anticipated the outburst of market innovation that ensued. This book's historical chapters thus answer three main questions: First, why did European-level competition erupt over smaller-company stock markets in a sector characterized by protected national financial systems? Second, why did the exchanges adopt an American principle for organizing new markets after rejecting it for more than a decade and then create a second round of markets based on a British model? And, third, why did this rash of market mimicry occur in the middle of the 1990s, twenty years after the Nasdaq debut?

The outbreak of competition in a formerly protected sector surprised everyone, even the exchanges themselves. As recently as 1993 and 1994, financial elites of the various European capitals were making independent decisions about smaller-company stock markets, with little concern about what their foreign counterparts were doing or what Brussels bureaucrats envisioned. The elites' first experiments with these markets had failed. Governments, regulators, industry groups, and stock exchanges revisited the issue and came to decisions that reflected national differences and independent policymaking.

These separate processes and decisions exemplify the continued fragmentation of finance in the early 1990s, despite the relative ease of investing across borders.[23] In December 1992, the LSE announced the closure of the Thatcher-era Unlisted Securities Market (USM). With implicit support from the UK Treasury, the exchange fought off a public campaign by local financial services companies to pressure it into creating new markets and in April 1994 reiterated its intention to end the decade-long experiment in smaller-company markets. In 1993 the Paris exchange implemented a series of reforms to the Second Marché, originally part of French president François Mitterrand's post–U-turn financial package.[24] The changes followed recommendations from a two-year review that ignored efforts by venture capitalists and others to create a new market based on the Nasdaq. By May 1994, the national securities authority and stock exchange were lauding the success of the revamped Second Marché. With little widespread perception of a smaller-company financing problem in Germany, the Frankfurt exchange left its existing smaller-company markets largely untouched.

In smaller-company finance, as these distinctly national decision-making processes exemplify, no one even imagined that competition was just around the corner. National elites continued to make policy as they had for decades. Years of national and EU financial regulatory reforms had not dislodged entrenched relations between established domestic financial communities and their governments, which protected local firms and exchanges from foreign rivals. Finance ministries, treasuries, and securities supervisors cared about the financing problems of smaller companies, but only to the extent that solutions not undermine the competitiveness of national financial services industries in the run-up to "Europe 1992," the slogan for the EU's late-1980s push to consolidate the Common Market. The result was the maintenance of stock exchanges' privileged positions. The typical methods of spurring regional competition—EU laws and decisions by supranational antitrust authorities and judges—were decidedly absent. The lack of progress by Europe's policymakers in the financial sectors was nowhere more evident than in investment services, especially surrounding the issue of cross-border competition among national stock exchanges.[25] In fact, when governments in 1993 finally agreed to weak European-level legislation that guaranteed much of the old national discretion, finance ministers still refused to delegate implementation authority to Brussels, as they had in other areas of financial services.[26]

The emergence of 1990s competition is all the more enigmatic because it began as a contest over copying the Nasdaq principle, the adoption of which the exchanges and other national financial policymakers had actively opposed for more than fifteen years. The U.S. form was well known in Europe in the 1980s. National financial policymaking elites considered and rejected it as part of the discussions leading to the creation of the 1980s markets, and the history of smaller-company markets in Europe is littered with failed proposals for Nasdaq look-alikes (see Table 1.1).

Opposition from financial elites, usually spearheaded by exchanges and backed by national treasuries, had not subsided by the late 1980s and early 1990s.[27] German banks, the primary owners of the Frankfurt exchange, were the most ardent opponents of the European Securities Market (ESM), a 1989 proposal to create a pan-European Nasdaq copy. In 1993, the LSE rejected plans for a Nasdaq copy, the Enterprise Market, and in Paris in 1994, the bourse did not give support to the proposed Marché Européen des Sociétés Entrepreneuriales de Croissance (MESEC).

Multiple factors lay behind the opposition. Without experience in American-style entrepreneurial finance or the necessary risk capital, banks and other financial firms feared that foreigners, especially U.S. firms, would dominate the new sectors. There was also petty resistance to new ways of doing things, as well as concern among the exchanges that a Nasdaq copy would draw activity from their main markets, reducing all-around liquidity and members' revenues. Aside from protectionist reactions and knee-jerk hostility to change, opposition also stemmed from principled objections. Some financiers and policymakers simply believed that Europe in the 1980s and early 1990s was poor soil for the U.S. form. They argued that tightly held smaller companies, without a tradition of disclosure (nor a willingness to absorb the costs of providing greater transparency), would not want to list their shares; that Europe lacked both institutional investors with the right incentives for buying risky stocks and an equity culture able to draw household buyers; and that the markets would ultimately fail due to the absence of an enforcement and regulatory regime appropriate for U.S.-style entrepreneurial finance. The fact that these critics were vindicated by the Neuer Markt's and Nouveau Marché's demise and the success of AIM, the least Nasdaq-like of the bunch, only added to the new markets' puzzles. If the Nasdaq form did not represent an economically more efficient model for organizing a stock market in Europe, why did reluctant exchanges seek to copy it?

Finally, there is the question of timing. The issue is not only that national financial communities had completed independent deliberations over smaller-company markets only months beforehand, with none deciding to create new ones, let alone ones based on the American principle. The Nasdaq Stock Market opened for trading in 1971 and became a sensation in Europe by the early 1980s because of its function as the financing mechanism for the likes of Apple Computers and Microsoft. Europeans did not copy the U.S. form in the first twenty-five years of its existence. As Chapter 7 discusses, they waited until the mid-1990s, when the U.S. icon of capitalism was under investigation by the U.S. Department of Justice and the Securities and Exchange Commission (SEC) for collusion among its members.

Explaining Convergence across Borders

Questions about institutional convergence across borders, like the ones I ask with respect to Europe's new stock markets, are classic subjects of social science inquiry.[28] Yet when the phenomenon occurs in contemporary Europe, it poses a conundrum for proponents of the standard repertoire of explanations. Most analysts agree that the processes of globalization are somehow implicated when countries adopt the same social and economic models. They disagree, however, over what globalization entails and whether it plays a background or determining role in spreading similar forms. These differences lead some observers to emphasize the immediacy of common global pressures brought to bear by high levels of cross-border capital mobility or the allure of ideas disseminating from leading nations; other observers highlight local context, the domestic politics of adjustment and state-to-state negotiations. A long tradition of bifurcating causes into global and national categories makes it difficult to imagine that regional realms of supranational rules, procedures, politics, and bureaucracy may function as independent forces of change.

If convergence and, more broadly, domestic institutional change have roots in regional phenomena anywhere, the EU—the most advanced experiment in cross-border rule making—should be a font of such effects. In a wide range of public policy domains (including almost all areas of exchange, agriculture, environmental protection, data privacy, consumer health and safety, monetary policy, gender equity, and foreign policy, in addition to finance), reform within countries can no longer be understood without reference to European-level legislation, procedures, processes, politics, and actors. Such observations are so prevalent in the EU context that many experts simply accept that the regional polity acts as an exogenous causal force in their investigations into variegated national responses—without peering behind the assumption.[29] In a very real sense, the EU as a producer of public policy and change has reached critical mass.[30] Political economy theory, outside the cadre of EU specialists, has lagged behind.

Compared with many nation states and the processes of globalization, the EU is a relatively recent phenomenon. Its penetration of social, political, and economic domains has grown gradually, unevenly, and sometimes subtly. There is, however, a more fundamental reason for why students of international and comparative politics have been slow to incorporate its effects into their analyses. The priori bases for treating the European polity as an autonomous entity, rather than an agreement among states or a microcosm of globalization, remain contested and underdeveloped. The ambitions of this book thus extend beyond explaining an important instance of innovation in European systems for allocating capital, and even beyond identifying a missing explanatory variable in approaches to domestic change. This book contributes to scholarly debate about how to conceive of the EU and other supranational arrangements as independent sources of effects and agents of change.

I focus on one fairly common aspect of the international realm: the presence of supranational bureaucracies and civil servants whose daily activities help to shape, over time and sometimes behind the scenes, the parameters of public debate, the array of relevant interests, and the opportunities available to policy entrepreneurs.[31] The European Commission acts as the official initiator of European-level legislation and "guardian" of the treaties.[32] Its formal responsibilities, shared with the Council of the European Union, the European Parliament (EP), and the European Court of Justice (ECJ), include a mix of legislative, executive, and regulatory functions derived from treaties and secondary Europe-wide laws. The bureaucracy is organized, horizontally, into fairly autonomous directorates general that specialize in policy domains and, vertically, between the college of commissioners (appointed by governments) and the main body of administrators, comprised during the 1980s and 1990s of roughly 20,000 mostly career civil servants.[33]

Compared with national administrations, the European Commission lacks material resources, numbers of career employees, and formal powers within the political system to which it belongs. These weaknesses raise questions of when, why, and how its supranational bureaucrats, who must rely heavily on national-level authorities to implement EU legislation, act as independent political actors.[34] Frequently invoked answers come from principal-agent analysis, which rarely expects bureaucratic autonomy from legislative officials and then only when they see benefit in giving civil servants wide areas of discretion in a policy domain.[35] The stock market story shows how this approach can systematically underestimate bureaucratic influence in the EU context. By relying on too narrow an understanding of what bureaucrats typically do and where they are most likely to leave their mark, the principal-agent perspective is unlikely to capture the importance of incremental interventions that increasingly matter as they accumulate over time.

This book turns our attention to the role of Brussels civil servants in shaping political discourse, framing debates, crafting new interests, mobilizing coalitions, and otherwise reconstituting the social and political world in which these civil servants and other political actors operate.[36] Building on insights from the fields of international relations, EU studies, American political development, and the sociology of markets, my approach takes such bureaucratic activity to be a normal aspect of political life in the EU. Similar to civil servants elsewhere, Brussels officials develop independent goals, have resources at their disposal, and alter policymaking processes through their actions. With limited legal authorities, technical expertise, and other conventional resources, they pursue aims tied to the European integration project by making what they do seem useful and legitimate to others. Most important, these officials create autonomy from member governments (and more recently, the European Parliament) by embedding themselves in supportive coalitions, sometimes of their own making. They carry out these tasks with political skill and campaigns of incremental intervention that over long periods reshape political facts in unpredictable ways, which are sometimes favorable to sudden waves of institutional innovation.

Taking the seemingly mundane activities of Brussels civil servants seriously forces us to rethink what we mean by and where to look for bureaucratic influence. Rather than as supranational entrepreneurs deftly shaping bargains among governments, this book's protagonists emerge as actors who are enterprising mainly in retrospect, after tallying the often inadvertent effects of more than a decade-long slog to avert opposition and avoid the limelight. Their relatively bold intervention is what set off the process of market innovation examined in these pages. Yet I emphasize the way EU officials create opportunities, not how talented leaders pounce on them. In contrast to accounts that depict the European Commission as a hierarchy and focus on particular figures, here I show active civil servants pursuing consistent goals that outlasted top personnel and presidents and that continuously drew resistance from counterparts working in other parts of the organization. To be sure, the Brussels bureaucracy as a structure can be supportive of schemes to overcome nationally fragmented markets. The focus in the following chapters, however, is on when, why, and how civil servants effect change in the face of internal conflicts and leaders consumed by other priorities.

Finally, this book is about a particular type of institutional change: market formation. I take markets as institutional expressions of politics, though not necessarily of the national variety, and I expect political actors and actions, not merely economic opportunists and global forces, to drive market creation. The analytical hurdle I tackle is identifying where overlapping layers of political actors and rules are likely to breed clashing conceptions of markets, who within that context have motives and capabilities to upset established patterns of exchange and governance, and under what conditions they are likely to do so. This study provides answers to these questions by highlighting the significant degree to which the EU is a market-creating enterprise. The roles of supranational civil servants, the accumulative effects of their actions, and the political battles they foment rank among the most important factors behind market formation and change in the EU. In much of Europe during the last twenty-five years, officials in Brussels were a source of opposition to established ideas about the scope, regulation, and purpose of markets as well as who has the right to create them. Seeking regional as opposed to nationally bounded markets, they were instigators of struggles over markets and thereby catalysts of institutional innovation.

The history of Europe's smaller-company stock markets illustrates why and how the cumulative effects of actions by Brussels civil servants can spark such political battles. Based on a close examination of a quarter century of stock market experimentation, this study, concentrating on developments in the United Kingdom and France, links the surge of cross-border competition and copying to European Commission officials, whose actions forged a political arena for challenging status quo financial arrangements. Venture capital firms, stock exchanges, smaller-company lobbies, banks, government ministries, and especially entrepreneurial individuals contributed to the creation of the new markets. The book's argument is not intended to demote the importance of the capital, skills, and toil of these organizations and individuals. Rather, it brings to the fore the complex political and social contexts that support capital markets and the crucial role Brussels bureaucrats played in creating such an environment.

These conclusions are derived from a controlled comparison of the newest markets to one another, to previous ones, and to proposals that never saw the light of day. I develop the historical record from original research based on multiple sources, including the financial press, private- and public-sector reports and, most important, research and interviews that I conducted (unless otherwise noted) in eight European countries.[37] Because governments jealously protect their national sovereignty over financial regulation, Europe's new market story is a "hard" case for an argument that emphasizes the independent effects of supranational actors.[38] My findings strongly suggest that in underestimating the EU as an agent of change, we overlook a major driving force in European and global politics and economics; and in ignoring slow-moving cumulative processes, we miss a potential cause of sudden bursts of change in Europe and beyond.

Organization of the Book

By making new political space for challenging established financial arrangements, the actions of European Commission bureaucrats led to the creation of new types of stock markets in Europe. The historical chapters support this argument by establishing not only that a Brussels-crafted political arena—replete with a well-organized interest group, competing political discourses, and a permissive interpretation of EU laws—accounts for the cross-border competition, mimicry, and market innovation in the 1990s but also that the absence in the 1980s of this kind of environment helped to undermine the efforts of potential challengers to the status quo. In other words, I show that variance over time in the presence and concentration of Brussels-orchestrated political conditions explains the pattern of change in the types of smaller-company markets that Europeans created.

Column three of Table 1.1 (page 4) documents this pattern, and Figure 1.2 illustrates my explanation schematically. Beginning in the late 1970s, Commission civil servants began to develop policy ideas, promoting a regional venture capitalism industry and thereby clashing with established financial interests that thrived on nationally fragmented arrangements. By the early 1980s, the Brussels officials were fostering a pan-European interest group that would advocate these policies, especially a regional stock market. By mid-decade, they experimented with political discourses and frames that might broaden the appeal for such a market. These included efforts to associate a pan-European stock market for smaller companies with the European currency unit (ECU) and the advancement of European integration, with the promotion of subnational regions, and ultimately with the Nasdaq form as a means for solving Europe's unemployment problem. But these small-scale endeavors seemed to matter little in financial reform processes during these years. Instead, national financial elites easily blocked schemes

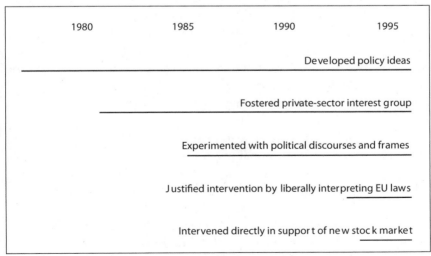

Figure 1.2. The European Commission and the creation of a supranational political arena.

from Brussels, using their relations with governments and supportive units within the supranational bureaucracy to protect their interests in the status quo and slow the pace of change. They prevented Commission officials from exerting influence, kept U.S. forms of finance at bay, and carried out stock market–creation processes with little concern about cross-border competition, venture capitalist preferences, or Brussels' plans. Only in 1994, when the officials used an EU law to justify a direct intervention in support of a particular market proposal, did the accumulated effects of these measures spark competition and a turning point, observable in Table 1.1, in the kinds of smaller-company stock markets created across Europe.

After elaborating on the thirty-year market-creation pattern, Chapter 2 reviews alternative explanations before expanding on my approach to institutional change and market formation. Chapters 3–5 chronicle developments from the late 1970s to 1993, when Commission officials were gradually crafting political conditions that would later set the stage for market innovation. It is also the period when national exchanges created smaller-company stock markets that reflected the great differences among domestic financial systems. Chapter 3 traces the origins of European Commission interest in entrepreneurial companies and venture capitalism during the period, uncovers their role in creating a pan-European venture capitalist interest group and in experimenting with political discourses and frames that might legitimize their policy ideas, and shows the inability of Brussels officials to affect domestic financial markets. Chapter 4 covers British and French developments in smaller-company finance, showing that experimentation in stock markets followed distinctive national trajectories in the 1980s. Chapter 5 demonstrates the inability of domestic venture capitalists, as recently as the early 1990s, to influence market-creation processes on their own—despite the relative ease of attracting international capital to their funds and investing across borders.

Chapter 6 shows that fifteen years of small-scale actions by Brussels bureaucrats created a supranational political space for contesting established arrangements and made smaller-company finance in Europe amenable to rapid market innovation. Government-finance coalitions against change are a mainstay of rich countries. By 1994, however, Commission officials had put in place conditions conducive to destabilizing the sector. The centerpiece of the civil servants' program was a pan-European stock market for smaller companies. Having framed their proposal with a political discourse that tied job creation to Nasdaq-like stock markets, catalyzed national venture capitalists into a European pressure group, and justified an intervention by liberally interpreting European Community law, the bureaucrats managed to circumvent opposition with a final act: they backed a 1994 venture capitalist plan for a pan-European Nasdaq copy. The European Commission's intervention had intended and unintended effects. Instead of a single new market, the possibility of a pan-European competitor drew the national stock exchanges into a contest over which would supply the future Nasdaq of Europe. The exchanges and supporters in their respective governments were able to claw back some control. By enforcing the previous norm about the inappropriateness of direct Brussels interventions in financial markets, these nationally-oriented elites temporarily ended debate about who could create capital markets and later elevated the issue (along with the question of how to manage cross-border competition) to the EU legislative level. They also undermined the new pan-European challenge by channeling domestic financial activities to their own new markets. Nevertheless, the national financial establishments could not roll back the new competitive pressures. The chapter thus explains why and how a Brussels intervention ignited a regional competition that resulted in national rival markets modeled largely on the U.S. form and in an innovation process that ultimately attracted the NYSE and Nasdaq.

Chapter 7 uses these conclusions to assess alternative explanations. It then returns to the book's main themes and examines their applicability for understanding three other aspects of the EU's sweeping financial transformation: the Financial Services Action Plan (FSAP), a comprehensive legislative program for promoting cross-border regulatory harmonization; legislation mandating the convergence of national accounting standards for listed companies; and the Lamfalussy process, new procedures that shift much of financial rule-making from the national to the EU-level. The Conclusion locates the development of Europe's new stock markets within regional and transatlantic developments and draws implications for European societies, the legitimacy of EU financial rule-making, and international imbalances and financial governance.

CHAPTER 2

Markets, Politics, and Bureaucrats

The new stock markets of the nineties and the early years of the twenty-first century represent a curious turn in European finance. The very insiders who created them, for the most part national stock exchanges, had for a decade blocked market innovation of this kind and continued to receive government support in opposing it. The high stakes surrounding financial arrangements and their general resilience to change—not just in Europe but across the globe in developed and developing nations alike—add to the empirical conundrum. What was behind the regional competition? Why did the national exchanges initially copy an American principle for organizing the new markets and then turn to a British form? And what explains the timing of this creative spate of cross-border mimicry?

I attribute the battle over Europe's new markets, their organizational forms, and the timing of change primarily to the intended and unintended consequences of bureaucratic action, carried out over a fifteen-year period by officials working for the European Commission. This chapter peers beneath the argument's surface to provide a framework for the historical narrative that follows. First, I take a closer look at the observable patterns of change that I set out to explain: from the creation of the eclectic group of 1980s stock markets produced by protected national financial communities to the introduction of Nasdaq look-alikes fostered in an atmosphere of intense cross-border competition to an emergent trend toward a model based on the Alternative Investment Market (AIM), London's 1995 market.[1] Second, this chapter explores alternative perspectives for explaining institutional change. Social science strives to improve the understanding of phenomena in part by identifying where to look for causes. Political economy explanations tend to highlight firms responding to economic internationalization, global advocates spreading liberalism, and nationally oriented politicians and officials adjusting to new external constraints. Thus implicit in my claim that EU political actors were the primary agents responsible for the new markets is a critique of basic assumptions underpinning these traditional analyses. Third, this chapter explains my rationale for treating EU-related phenomena, and supranational bureaucratic action in particular, as independent causes. I maintain that the independent causal status rests on firm theoretical ground, by drawing on an eclectic range of scholarly traditions. The final section details how activity carried out by Brussels bureaucrats played out in the case of Europe's new stock markets.

Stock Market Forms and a Pattern of Change

Markets have become an increasingly dominant mechanism for allocating capital to firms, governments, and households. Though the trend is global, the timing of change, its intensity, and its impact have depended on political context.[2] In Europe, years of privatizations and other national and EU regulatory reforms opened up a range of market-based alternatives to public and private bank financing. Until the mid-1990s, however, corporate capital markets had almost exclusively benefited large enterprises. The financing of smaller companies remained the preserve of national banks, sealed off from international competition and poorly suited to the financing of many types of enterprises, especially in the range of technology sectors that were flourishing in the United States.[3]

The continuity of these financial arrangements to a large extent reflected a failure of political will to extend market opportunities to young firms. Europeans, in fact, were no strangers to stock markets for smaller firms in the eighties and early nineties (see Table 1.1, page 4). During the post–Bretton Woods economic crises, as mentioned in Chapter 1, policymakers focused the spotlight on these companies and their difficulty in obtaining capital, identifying them as a source of innovation, job creation, economic growth, and enhanced international competitiveness.[4] One widespread response in the 1980s was to cajole the national stock exchanges to improve financing options for smaller companies by creating new stock markets.

I use three dimensions to distinguish among smaller-company stock markets created in Europe over the last thirty years: barriers to quoting, informational standards, and independence.[5] They tell us about access (that is, which companies can raise capital directly from investors) and control (that is, which financial intermediaries control trading flows).[6] Tables 2.1 and 2.2 (pages 24, 26) show some of the important barriers to quoting and informational standards for stock markets in France, Germany, and the United Kingdom. The barriers to quoting company shares on stock markets include minimum company size, minimum number of years in existence, and minimum shares or amount of capital an enterprise must sell to the public. Company informational standards for quoting shares on stock markets determine the extent to which firms must supply an accurate portrayal of their finances to the public, not just to financial insiders. Table 2.2 specifies the type of accounting standards (that is, national or international), frequency and language of reporting, and other disclosure-related requirements. Independence refers to whether a smaller-company stock market serves as a permanent platform for quoted companies or as a stepping-stone to a market for larger firms. Using these political dimensions, I identify three main types of smaller-company stock markets during the period under investigation.

Feeder Markets of the 1980s

In response to political pressure, the national exchanges created feeder markets in the 1980s. Rules of the main national stock markets had prevented most smaller and younger firms from listing shares. The feeder markets ostensibly made it easier by lowering barriers such as minimum levels of market capitalization and number of years in existence, as well as informational standards. Companies on the London exchange's 1980 Unlisted Securities Market, for example, had to have only a three-year record (compared with the five-year requirement for the main market) and to meet less rigorous informational standards (see Tables 2.1 and 2.2). The Paris bourse's 1983 Second Marché similarly reduced the necessary number of years a company had to be in operation (from three to zero) and required only lax informational standards, compared with those of the main stock market. In conjunction with a lack of independence (the smaller-company markets were designed to feed the main national markets fresh young companies once they matured), these rules appeared to deter investors, the presence of whom is an obvious condition for improving capital-raising prospects, and ensured that the markets would retain many of the idiosyncratic features embedded in national financial systems. In large part because of these design defects, the feeder markets failed to alter financing patterns significantly.[7]

In every case, the national exchanges rejected designs that would purportedly lure internationally mobile investors, as had the Nasdaq, which had channeled capital to young enterprises in the United States. There, by requiring companies to reveal high levels of information according to widely accepted accounting standards, investors were able, at least in theory, to calculate the high risks of young-firm shares and invest accordingly. The European exchanges instead merely lowered the bar that smaller companies had to meet in order to list shares, all the while maintaining control over trading flows.

The flawed setup was not an accident. Throughout the 1980s, the national exchanges, owned by financial intermediaries who lacked economic incentive for promoting and supporting the feeder markets, operated in the absence of cross-border competition for investors and listing firms. The exchanges sought to preserve protectionist arrangements, whereby national financial services firms relied on revenues from larger-company stock markets and intimate lending relations with smaller enterprises. This is why the 1980s feeder markets embodied a perverse set of incentives that prompted investors to wait until the best young companies graduated upward. In the end, the feeders were appendages of sheltered domestic industries that left smaller-company finance in the hands of domestic banks, brokers, accountants, and other service providers. Not surprisingly, the 1980s markets withered as the exchanges and local intermediaries found fewer and fewer reasons over time to promote them.

Nasdaq Copies of the 1990s

Energetically promoted and designed by the national exchanges to attract mobile capital under the control of international asset managers, most of the new stock markets of the 1990s differed starkly from their predecessors. Namely, they required companies wanting capital to disclose high levels of financial information and thus mimicked the Nasdaq's main principle and underlying bargain. By "copying" the Nasdaq Stock Market, I do not mean that Europe's exchanges borrowed either its mechanism for determining prices (which was different from that of the New York Stock Exchange but not new to Europeans) or its electronic technologies, introduced in 1971 to improve transparency in the over-the-counter market. Rather, the exchanges mimicked Nasdaq's underlying principle, which requires companies to reveal high levels of information about their finances and operations in exchange for capital from investors.

Table 2.1 Barriers to quoting company shares on stockmarkets

		Minimum Capitalization, Assets, Equity Capital
France	Main Market	None, 2005
		None, 1994
	Alternext 2005	None
	Nouveau Marché 1996	€1.5 million in shareholder equity prior to listing
	Second Marché	None, in practice
		FF 50 million, 1993
		None, 1983
Germany	Prime Standard 2003 (Regulated Market)	Liable equity of €750,000
	Main Market 2000	2.5 million DM with flexibility
	Entry Standard 2005	None
	Neuer Markt 1997	€1.5 million
	Geregelter Markt 1987	500,000 DM
	Freiverkehr	None
United Kingdom	Main Market	£700,000 (scientific companies, £20 million pounds), 1992
		£700,000, 1990
		£500,000, 1980
	Techmark 1999	£50 million with flexibility
	AIM 1995	None
	Third Market 1987	None
	USM	None, 1990
		None, 1980

Sources: Hartmut Schmidt, *Special Stock Market Segments for Small Company Shares: Capital Raising Mechanism and Exit Route for Investors in New Technology-Based Firms,* EUR 9235 EN, Commission of the European Communities, DG Information Market and Innovation (Brussels, 1984); Schmidt, *Advantages and Disadvantages of an Integrated Market Compared with a Fragmented Market, March 1977,* Commission of the European Communities, Competition—Approximation of Legislation Series, no. 30 (Brussels, 1977); ELBAssociates and Consultex, "The Feasibility of Creating ECU-EASD: A European Association of Securities Dealers to Trade over the Counter in ECU-Denominated Shares," Geneva, 1985; COB, "Le Second Marché," Paris, 1992;

History of Company Accounts, Trading Record	Minimum Number and Amounts of Shares in Public Hands
3 years of accounts	25%
5 years of trading record, 3 years of accounts	25% with flexibility, 600,000 shares if shares over FF 30 million
2 years of accounts	Minimum float of €2.5 million
None	20%, 100,000 shares, €5 million value
2 years of accounts	10%
None	10%
3 years of accounts	Minimum float of 10,000 shares
3 years of accounts	25% with flexibility, €1.25 million
None	None
3 years of accounts with flexibility	20% with flexibility and a float of €5 million, only common stock, 100,000 minimum shares
None	None
None	None
3 years (with exceptions)	25%
3 years	25%
5 years	25%
1 year (with flexibility)	25% and at least £20 million
None	None
1 year	None
2 years	10%
3 years	10%

Graham Bannock, "European Second-Tier Markets for NTBFs," Graham Bannock and Partners, London, 1994; Nikko Research Center, *Nikko Monthly Bulletin: New Stock Markets and Venture Capital in Europe* (London, June 1995); Coopers & Lybrand, *EASDAQ, The Nouveau Marché, AIM: An Update 1996* (London, 1996); BVCA and DLA, *A Guide to the Stockmarkets* (London, 2000 and 2002); Simon Johnson, "Which Rules Matter? Evidence from Germany's Neuer Markt," unpublished, 2000; and Web sites of the exchanges.

Table 2.2 Company informational standards for quoting shares on stock markets

		International (U.S. GAAP, LAS/IFRS, or National with Reconciliation) or National Accounting Standards?
France	Main Market	IFRS, 2005 French GAAP, IAS, or U.S. GAAP with reconciliation, 2000
	Alternext 2005	Either International or National (EEA companies), or IFRS or U.S. GAAP (non-EEA companies)
	NextEconomy 2005	IFRS
	Nouveau Marché 1996	French GAAP, IAS, or U.S. GAAP with reconciliation
	Second Marché	National, 1993 National, 1983
Germany	Prime Standard 2003 (Regulated Market)	IFRS or U.S. GAAP
	Main Market	IFRS, 2004 National
	Entry Standard 2005	IFRS (EEA companies) or National (non-EEA companies)
	Neuer Markt 1997	International
	Geregelter Markt 1987	National
United Kingdom	Main Market 2004	IFRS Either International or National
	Techmark	IFRS, 2004 Either International or National
	AIM	IFRS (EEA companies), or choice of IFRS, U.S. GAAP, or four other sets of standards (non-EEA companies), 2007 Either International or National, 1995
	USM 1980	National

Sources: Hartmut Schmidt, *Special Stock Market Segments for Small Company Shares: Capital Raising Mechanism and Exit Route for Investors in New Technology-Based Firms,* EUR 9235 EN, Commission of the European Communities, DG Information Market and Innovation (Brussels, 1984); Schmidt, *Advantages and Disadvantages of an Integrated Market Compared with a Fragmented Market, March 1977,* Commission of the European Communities, Competition—Approximation of Legislation Series, no. 30 (Brussels: 1977); ELB

Quarterly Reports?	English: Optional, Required, or Neither?	Ad Hoc Disclosure of Significant News?
Yes	Required	Yes
Turnover only	Optional with French summary	Yes
No	Optional	Yes
Yes	Required	Yes
Yes	Optional with French summary	Yes
No	Optional with French summary	Yes
No	Optional with French summary	Yes
Yes	Required	Yes
Yes	Required	Yes
No	Optional	Yes
No	Optional	Yes
Yes	Required	Yes
No	Neither	Yes
Yes	Required	Yes
No	Required	Yes
Yes	Required	Yes
Yes	Required	Yes
No	Required	Yes
No	Required	Yes
No	Required	Yes

Associates and Consultex, "The Feasibility of Creating ECU-EASD: A European Association of Securities Dealers to Trade over the Counter in ECU-Denominated Shares," Geneva, 1985; COB, "Le Second Marché," Paris, 1992; Graham Bannock, "European Second-Tier Markets for NTBFs," Graham Bannock and Partners, London, 1994; Nikko Research Center, *Nikko Monthly Bulletin: New Stock Markets and Venture Capital in Europe* (London, June 1995); Coopers & Lybrand, *EASDAQ, the Nouveau Marché, AIM: An Update 1996* (London, 1996); BVCA and DLA, *A Guide to the Stockmarkets* (London, 2000 and 2002); Simon Johnson, "Which Rules Matter? Evidence from Germany's Neuer Markt," unpublished, 2000; "AIM Rules for Companies, 2007," www.londonstockexchange.com; and Web sites of the exchanges.

Despite significant variation, the exchanges in most cases devised new informational requirements that far exceeded the minimum domestic regulations. Table 2.2 isolates this trend in France, Germany, and the United Kingdom. Frankfurt's Deutsche Boerse, for example, was particularly ambitious. Companies listed on the Neuer Markt had to present public information in English, supply quarterly reports, and provide accounts in accordance with standards considered rigorous and transparent by international investors (that is, U.S. Generally Accepted Accounting Principles, or U.S. GAAP; International Accounting Standards, or IAS; or national standards with reconciliation). At the time, not even the most established corporations on the main stock markets had to follow such rigorous requirements.[8]

Until stock prices tumbled in the 2000 international bear market, some of the Nasdaq copies were spectacularly successful capital-raising mechanisms for Europe's smaller companies. The high-flying Neuer Markt, with a peak of almost 350 listed companies and a market capitalization of 234 billion euros, was by far the leader and for many the EU's answer to the original Nasdaq, which had begun to attract some European companies. But the next-largest market, the Nouveau Marché, with roughly 200 companies and a smaller market capitalization, performed well too.[9] Nonetheless, for reasons discussed in Chapter 7, the Frankfurt and Paris markets and many of the other Nasdaq copies did not survive the international downturn.[10]

AIM Copies and Cross-Border Competition

London's Alternative Investment Market, created in 1995, was the exception to the 1990s trends. Notably, it survived and prospered after the price collapse. Rather than copy the Nasdaq principle, the LSE gave AIM a home-grown form, which other exchanges, including Euronext and Deutsche Boerse, began to replicate in 2005.[11]

The AIM form combines some of the low regulatory aspects of the feeder markets with a mechanism for screening potential companies and attracting investors. It has intermediaries back newly listed firms and thereby send signals to investors. Unlike the feeders, AIM is an independent market, not a staging area for young companies. Rather than expect, as per the Nasdaq idea, that stringent informational standards act as a filter, allowing investors to make informed decisions, under the AIM model the screening mechanisms are exchange-approved financial services firms whose reputations would be damaged (at least in theory) by bringing poorly performing companies to market. The AIM form thus seeks to attract investors not through transparency but through independence and intermediaries whose fortunes depend on the quality of relatively unknown companies. Like their eponym, the AIM copies were able to maintain relatively low levels of regulation by existing largely outside the posteuro rigorous and Europeanized regime governing listings, trading, and oversight of official EU-regulated markets.

Table 1.1 (page 4), illustrates the 1977–2005 pattern from feeder to Nasdaq look-alike to AIM copy, with one turning point in the early 1990s and another around 2005. A second pattern, not captured in this table, suggests the first inflection point is important for another reason. In the last decade of the twentieth century and early in the twenty-first, market experiments, unlike their predecessors, were created in the context of lively competition among Europe's stock exchanges.

Before the early 1990s, as Chapter 1 demonstrated, national financial elites made market-formation decisions without serious consideration of what their foreign counterparts were doing. National exchanges did not perceive themselves in cross-border competition over smaller quoted companies, investors, and intermediaries. AIM was the first market created under the new conditions. The LSE introduced it to thwart the possibility that a proposal for a privately owned pan-European market, Easdaq, might succeed. The Paris bourse created the Nouveau Marché in response. These two early efforts set off a contest to become the center of entrepreneurial finance in Europe that soon afterward consumed exchanges in most of the other financial centers.

The Neuer Markt's stunning early success prompted foreign exchanges to make adjustments to their own markets.[12] For instance, fearing reforms to AIM would prove insufficient to prevent Frankfurt's dominance, in November 1999 the London exchange created another market, Techmark. At first the Paris exchange attempted to manage competition and combine forces with the other continental exchanges, in part to prevent the feared domination by London, the historic leader of European equity finance. Euro.NM, a federated network of the Paris, Frankfurt, Amsterdam, Brussels, and Milan new markets, however, fell apart once executives at the German exchange began to believe the Neuer Markt could make it alone.

The rivalry among exchanges did not abate after the 2000 downturn. Despite the failures of the Nasdaq copies, non-European exchanges entered an intensified European battle over smaller-company stock markets. AIM, which only a few years prior had appeared a laggard, found itself at the center of events as it replaced the Neuer Markt as the leading market. The survival of

London's junior market was in large part accidental. The LSE had transferred mining and other nontechnology companies from its 1980s feeder to AIM. Together with attractive tax incentives for investors, these measures helped London's market weather the downturn, which saw global investors lose interest in technology sectors. AIM's paradoxical survival notwithstanding, both Euronext and the Deutsche Boerse responded to the new leader by creating new markets to replace the closed ones.

On the other side of the Atlantic, the Nasdaq Stock Market, in particular, felt competitive pressure from AIM, which, as mentioned in Chapter 1, was one of the exchange's main motivations behind its bids for the LSE and OMX. At first, the competition was over potential listings from the likes of Israel, China, Canada, Russia, and India, but by 2006 AIM was also attracting companies from the United States itself.[13] The Nasdaq was not the only American exchange to show interest in AIM and the LSE. There was speculation that the NYSE would use its 2006 purchase of Archipelago (an upstart computerized trading system, known in the financial world as an electronic communications network, or ECN) to offer "the equivalent of AIM on Wall Street," and after the 2007 merger with Euronext, the U.S. exchange aggressively promoted Alternext as an alternative to AIM. By 2007 the cross-Atlantic competition was palpable at the World Economic Forum in Davos when John Thain, NYSE chief executive, made sniping remarks about AIM's regulatory regime. And this was merely the most public example of the onslaught of acrimonious accusations made by U.S. exchange executives and securities regulators.[14]

In sum, experimentation in smaller-company stock markets followed a pattern with three main characteristics: a shift from nationally protected markets to, at first, regionally circumscribed and then international competition; a move from the feeder form to foreign organizational principles; and a critical inflection point in the early 1990s.[15]

Three Views of Institutional Convergence

Few political economists outside the circles of EU experts contemplate regional factors as potential causes of domestic change.[16] This is the main reason standard perspectives from the globalization literature do not offer satisfactory accounts of the pattern of institutional convergence and market formation described above.[17] This section briefly identifies this shortcoming in three prominent approaches.

Internationally Mobile Capital and Venture Capitalists

The most widely invoked explanation for converging domestic financial arrangements emphasizes the causal role of higher levels of capital mobility and its impact on the policy preferences and influence of relatively mobile firms.[18] My study echoes a widely invoked critique of the perspective. The return of internationally mobile capital at the end of the twentieth century is an indisputable factor behind Europe's new stock markets. Regional competition among exchanges for investors and listing companies could not have occurred without the inexpensive movement of financial assets across national borders. Nevertheless, as an explanation for domestic change, capital mobility is insufficient, unable to account for the timing, nature, speed, and extent of liberalization and re-regulation of domestic financial services industries.[19] Versions of the approach applied to the EU context, whereby the European Commission acts on behalf of nationally based firms, are no exception.[20] The perspective simply misses the degree to which allocation of financial resources is an extension of politics.

Diverse types of evidence suggest that change in political setting, not in levels of capital mobility, was primarily responsible for the thirty-year pattern in European smaller-company stock markets. First, the timing of market formation does not match the pattern of change in the levels of international capital flows, an indicator of capital mobility. Second, venture capitalists, local nodes of international capital, and the financial firms most relevant to the new market story formed unified policy preferences only after a political intervention, not in response to higher levels of capital mobility. Third, only an artificially truncated analysis, limited to the events of 1993–1995, would conclude that venture capitalists were leading agents of change alongside Brussels officials who had pushed for new markets since the mid-1980s. Fourth, until a multiyear political process produced an alternate market conducive to their business, venture capitalists—despite their ability to move assets across borders—could not credibly threaten to exit and thereby had little influence over local stock exchanges. Finally, the relative success of AIM and failure of the Nasdaq copies undermine the proposition that competitive forces, borne from higher levels of capital mobility, drove venture capitalists and political actors, who preferred the U.S. model, toward a more economically efficient form.

The Diffusion of Ideas

A competing explanation locates causation in the sociological process of diffusing ideas across borders.[21] Cultural dissemination contributed to the pattern of European market creation but, like capital mobility, did not determine it. If American ideas about how to organize a financial system had not made their way to Europe, institutional convergence would most likely have followed a very different path. Yet the historical record raises doubts about the immediate relevance of spreading norms as a convincing explanation for the pattern of change.

Brussels civil servants, the main agents in the new market history, acted as protectors of the European integration project, not as "norm entrepreneurs" committed to specific technical beliefs.[22] A political calculus to overcome opposition to their agenda of creating a pan-European market, more than a logic of appropriateness, motivated their promotion of the Nasdaq model.[23] National exchanges, moreover, innovated because they faced competitive pressure, not because they had been persuaded of the U.S. form's merits. Many European policymakers and financiers long considered the Nasdaq model an uncontroversial success in the United States. But the brief moment of ideational consensus about its suitability for solving local problems and about reputational costs for not following it was an effect, not a cause, of the 1990s round of market building.[24]

Domestic Variables and State-to-State Negotiations

A final set of explanations locates the fundamental causes of convergence at the domestic and state-to-state levels rather than in global processes and emphasizes country-specific pressures and constraints, strategies of national adjustment to an altered international environment, and intergovernmental bargaining.[25] The domestic approach captures the pattern of change well through the early 1990s, as the feeder markets and their failure reflected distinct national adjustments to commonly felt problems.[26] Limited to national political settings while treating the EU political arena as an afterthought, this perspective succeeds in explaining national elite attempts to stabilize and co-opt competition in the nineties and early in the twenty-first century, but does not explain the genesis, direction, and timing of cross-border competition and mimicry. Nor did failures with previous experiments and uncertainties about what to do next lead to satisficing—the selection of solutions that appear to have worked well in leading countries.[27]

The state-to-state view maintains that cross-border competition and convergence in domestic arrangements stem from political bargains that are struck between participating governments and ultimately driven by domestic economic interests of the biggest member countries.[28] My findings resonate with the criticisms of others. While certainly capturing one path to major domestic change and innovation in Europe, this view misses alternate routes.[29] Formal (and informal) agreements among governments were not responsible for the 1990s and 2000s episodes of market creation. During fifteen years of constructing a foundation that proved in 1994 amenable to innovation, Brussels civil servants acted without legal authority from governments or legitimacy in the eyes of market participants to intervene in smaller-company stock markets. A 1993 EU law governing stock exchange competition proved important because European Commission officials interpreted it liberally, confounding national ministers of finance who had refused to extend implementation powers to the Brussels bureaucracy.

The Argument

Instead of substantiating these mainstream perspectives on domestic institutional change, the historical record shows that market innovation sprung from the incremental evolution of the EU polity: the accumulation of interventions by European Commission civil servants was the most important cause of the cross-border competition that spawned Europe's new markets, their forms, and the timing of innovative change. By assigning causation to Brussels, I counter long-standing conventions that reduce regional-level phenomena to the interests and actions of states, transnational firms, and global actors spreading U.S. forms of liberalism. From the narrow vantage of the globalization debates that pit national against international causes of institutional change, my EU-as-cause explanation will no doubt appear to make heroic assumptions and claims. Seen through a different lens, however, the argument reflects and builds on well-developed ideas, even if political economists have been slow to incorporate them.

Treating supranational rules, procedures, and actors as autonomous phenomena is a prevalent theme of the constructivist school of international politics.[30] Traditional approaches to the subject assume that politics takes place primarily within national borders and that the global political arena, lacking a world government, is a stark sphere of action, typified by official state-to-state interactions. Constructivists, in contrast, relax these assumptions, envisioning supranational clusters of institutionalized space populated by an array of actors of whom states are merely among the most important. Applied to the global political economy, this view provides a complex picture of regularized exchange embedded in formal and informal rules and, ultimately, in a world or supranational areas of political culture. Such institutionalized space, by this conception, resembles domestic political life and leads constructivists to expect similar types of politics. This is the reasoning behind recent work that treats international organizations as bureaucracies that shape global politics:[31] Bureaucracy affects supranational arrangements, according to this view, just as it does modern domestic governance, and supranational bureaucrats behave in ways similar to their domestic counterparts. If acting with relative autonomy from legislative authorities at the domestic level, by extension civil servants would be prime candidates for autonomous action in the EU, the densest area of supranational rule-making.[32]

Research on the European integration experiment shows the relevance of these insights in the EU context. From the earliest work, analysts demonstrated that state-to-state cooperation engenders autonomous political and economic processes that contribute to the deepening and widening of the regional polity.[33] Generations of scholars advanced endogenous-change propositions, most recently employing concepts from the historical institutionalist branch of comparative politics, such as "feedback loops" and "path dependencies."[34] Whereas this literature is primarily focused on the development of the polity itself and regards the integration process as a cause, the argument of this book represents a recent scholarly turn that uses the same cause to explain domestic change within member countries.[35]

My claims about the specific roles of supranational civil servants build on research concerned with the ins and outs of EU governance. This literature provides theoretical reasons for treating the quotidian actions of Brussels officials as causes of change. Three relevant themes run through this diverse body of work. First, at a day-to-day level, Commission civil servants, like their counterparts in other organizations, apply political skills to establish legitimacy and authority and to circumvent perceived obstacles to their goals;[36] second, their influence is often incremental and cumulative;[37] and, third, because of the European Commission's fragmented and open internal structure and role within the regional body, politics within the Brussels bureaucracy is likely to instigate (and reflect) general EU political contests.[38]

European Commission functionaries, like their counterparts in other bureaucracies, enhance relatively weak material and legal powers by making their actions and goals seem, in the minds of others, like legitimate solutions to widely felt problems.[39] They employ political skills to garner support for preferred policies and do this by creating focal points, changing minds, getting others to defer to them, interpreting rules, defining debates, and forging new interests. These actions tend to take place in the background of the main political arena because Brussels bureaucrats are not likely to win in head-to-head contests against legislative authorities and powerful corporations. Without the legitimacy that comes with legal authority over a given policy domain, these functionaries pursue their aims in ways that cover their tracks, make it seem as if others are leading, and ensure that their own interventions appear to be responses to someone else's demands.[40]

Three types of action have been widely observed and are part of the everyday fabric of EU policymaking: the forging of interests and political voices that may later be used to form supportive coalitions; the promulgation of discourses and causal linkages that favorably frame issues; and the reinterpretation of rules that push change in selected directions. In the first type of action, Brussels bureaucrats create their own bases of support by constituting new interests at the European level and mobilizing them into coalitions and expert networks.[41] They hold conferences, introduce counterparts from different countries, put forth agendas for action, and subsidize new Brussels-based organizations. Once in place, the new political voices are in a position to spearhead the agenda, giving the civil servants' actions an aura of legitimacy (in the eyes of their new constituency and democratically elected governments) by seemingly responding to societal demands. In this way, Brussels bureaucrats create autonomy for themselves from governments (and more recently the European Parliament) by embedding themselves in homemade networks.

In the second type of action, Commission officials promote political discourses that frame problems and solutions in ways that justify their preferred policies.[42] Here, Brussels officials promulgate a favorable interpretation of problems and solutions through a constant flow of in-house and outsourced reports, statistics, and other forms of Europe-wide information about the industry or policy area. Finally, Commission officials, like civil servants elsewhere, frequently use the passage of new legislation and other formal rules made by others to advance their own agendas.[43] Interpreting rules is a common mode of bureaucratic action, enabling functionaries to make rules in the absence of legal authority. New laws are always incomplete, breed uncertainty about future interpretations, and thereby supply endless opportunities for attentive Brussels civil servants willing to take legislation in preferred directions, even in ways unintended by its creators.

Contrary to high-profile interventions at discrete moments when European Commission leaders, like Jacques Delors, seem to change the course of history, the types of bureaucratic actions emphasized here become causes of observable change only over extended durations. Forging political voices with the organizational wherewithal to affect policy and shaping political discourses and frames take time. The impact of any particular bureaucratic measure, moreover, is dependent on preceding acts and therefore likely to be greater where officials remain in the same post or unit for long periods and the internal organizational structure of the European Commission has been stable, both characteristic features of the Brussels bureaucracy. Contingent processes are also unlikely to follow predictable linear paths, making temporal analysis—that is, an investigation over multiple years—crucial to uncovering the effects of bureaucratic activity.[44]

Finally, the conditional nature of bureaucrat-shaped processes implies that the content of preferred policies (and whether they are attained) is secondary to the presence of independently held goals that motivate civil servants to act in the first place. Even so, arguments attributing change to bureaucrats, even if their actions produce unintended effects, must still establish political autonomy—and in particular independent preferences—from other political actors.[45] Most Brussels civil servants, according to past and recent studies on the European Commission, share supranational norms that motivate their behavior, and observers sometimes depict these functionaries as loyal devotees to their official mission of defending the regional integration project.[46] Treating the European Commission as a unitary or hierarchical organization can nevertheless be misleading. Within sometimes ill-defined common norms, the fairly autonomous and functionally specific directorates general of the bureaucracy tend to have distinct interpretations of goals and means for achieving them and to develop their own coalitions, networks, and constituencies.[47] As the lines between once-separate policy domains overlap over time, this fragmented and open structure lends itself to classic bureaucratic politics, turf wars, and "dysfunctional" behavior.[48]

Bureaucratic politics within the European Commission, as some EU watchers note, may also upset an existing order and propel institutional change.[49] While the actions of some Brussels officials will promote prevailing arrangements, the incremental activity of others will eventually cross old policy divisions and challenge the status quo. Because of the porous walls of the Brussels bureaucracy, the conflicts that arise do not always remain internal. Instead, they take the form of clashing coalitions, with revisionists and incumbents on different sides, and set the stage for both a shakeup of extant arrangements as well as political and economic reaction.

Limitations of Bureaucratic Influence

A countervailing view to this perspective of the European Commission takes its cue from principal-agent analysis.[50] By overlooking the temporal, incremental, and contingent character of bureaucratic influence, the principal-agent approach underemphasizes the impact of the Brussels bureaucracy. Analysts in this tradition argue that delegated authority and the mechanisms put in place to control "agency slack" provide a useful guide to bureaucratic behavior and set the general parameters within which to expect political autonomy from legislative authorities, especially member governments. Accordingly, the degree to which Brussels civil servants are able to realize independent agendas is more or less confined to "discretion zones" set by politicians, who weigh the costs and benefits of delegating tasks to the European Commission. On the one hand, allocating power allows legislative authorities to achieve goals that might otherwise be too expensive or elusive. On the other hand, delegation comes with costs, including the possibility that bureaucrats might pursue an agenda unintended by the principals, and the expenditures associated with efforts to prevent them from doing so. Commission officials, these analysts reason, have no monopoly over policy entrepreneurship; are normally outmatched in most skills, resources, and attributes necessary for opportunistic behavior in the public arena; and therefore adjust their actions accordingly. The conclusion of these studies is that supranational autonomy, while important at times, is a rare phenomenon.[51]

There are well-known practical difficulties associated with applying the principal-agent approach to a fragmented and open bureaucracy in which internal units report to different and sometimes multiple principals and develop their own bases of support.[52] The contrasting perspective developed in the earlier sections of this chapter encompassed an additional critique. If bureaucrats refashion the political landscape gradually in ways amenable to policy entrepreneurship, institutional change, and innovation, then their actions over time take change processes beyond discretion zones, expand those zones, and create frequent instances of political autonomy within them.[53]

First, investigating background processes, as opposed to conflicts fought in the public arena, broadens the meaning of influence. Civil servants tend to devote much energy to keeping their interventions out of the limelight and fostering a sense of legitimacy for their actions. Almost by definition, the principal-agent approach paints an incomplete picture, by sidestepping the legitimacy-enhancing efforts of bureaucrats taking place away from the public's view. Looking at *ex ante* preferences and asking who, in the final policy or legislative outcome, got what they wanted excludes processes wherein Commission officials typically make their mark, especially in destabilizing previous arrangements.[54] An assessment of influence ought to weigh who wins in the public spotlight against the impact of civil servants working in the background.

Second, following change processes over time unveils otherwise undetectable effects of Europe's civil servants and leads to further recalibration of bureaucratic influence. From a vantage point of ten, fifteen, or twenty years, the details of particular policy outcomes often pale in importance to the sequence of contingent acts and events that produced them. The very fact that an issue reaches the central EU political arena and has an array of vested participants may represent so great an alteration to the status quo as to render the final outcome of minor importance. What was deemed a bureaucratic defeat in the late 1990s through the principal-agent lens may in fact be rather inconsequential compared with the changes of the 1970s and 1980s that set the stage for the contest.

Finally, taking into account background and temporal processes also challenges the principal-agent view over when European Commission leaders are likely to succeed in public disputes. Critics have long complained that the principal-agent approach has relatively little to say about the purposeful behavior of supranational bureaucrats and, in particular, cannot account for variance in European Commission action within the broad parameters of discretion zones, even though the results may significantly affect the lives of ordinary Europeans.[55] In response, to explain variance in bureaucratic influence within discretion zones, principal-agent promoters (and some critics) emphasize exogenous opportunity "structures" created by crises, new legislation, and changing preferences of member governments. All are said to provide ripe conditions for policy entrepreneurship, fostering uncertainty about the future and favoring the informational advantages of the Brussels leadership and its ability to catalyze coalitions and table proposals expeditiously when timing is of the essence.[56]

Seemingly exogenous opportunity "structures" at one point in time, however, may be the product of previous bureaucratic action. Brussels officials do not merely respond to externally induced crises. They themselves transform economic problems, new legislation, and political change into crises in need of urgent attention and ripe for action. Opportunistic interventions associated with the entrepreneurial skills of European Commission leaders, by this logic, may punctuate long periods of incremental interventions carried out by career civil servants. Thus even in a narrow analysis of bureaucratic influence over a highly publicized policy conflict at a discrete moment in time, the principal-agent framework is likely to underestimate bureaucratic autonomy.

Despite these shortcomings, such a perspective does turn attention to potential problems and limitations of arguments based on the causal role of the European Commission. As principal-agent analysts point out, it is easy to mistake the subtle influences of legislative authorities for bureaucratic autonomy. Claims of independent bureaucratic behavior must be carefully substantiated with empirical evidence submitted to rigorous analysis. In this sense, the approach raises the bar for deriving conclusions about bureaucratic autonomy.

Furthermore, the European Commission may be the hub of EU policy-making and an important source of domestic institutional change in Europe. But its officials are by no means the only EU political actors with the capacities to effect change through the formal political arena or background processes. Principal-agent scholars emphasize the role of actors with formal legal authorities, reminding us of their immense powers to restructure the political environment in which bureaucrats operate. New political facts that Brussels officials create, such as interest groups and discourses, may not be reversible. But government ministers, the EP, and the ECJ are capable of derailing, redirecting, co-opting, and slowing Brussels-driven processes. For example, in the late 1990s, as discussed in Chapter 7, the EP and the Council were able to reduce the repertoire of actions available to Brussels civil servants and minimized the impact of internal bureaucratic politics by formalizing procedures and opening decision-making processes to the public. Other analysts, moreover, stress the informal roles of political actors other than the European Commission. They include regional networks of national regulators, ECJ judges, and lobbyists, to give a few obvious examples.[57]

The Origins of Europe's New Stock Markets

Attuned to these potential pitfalls, this book's argument extends ideas about Brussels-driven causal processes to explain domestic institutional change and, specifically, market formation in the context of the EU. In many areas of the economy, such as finance, entrenched relationships between incumbent firms and governments ensure a strong bias in favor of existing arrangements.[58] Why and how, then, do challenges to the status quo (especially from upstart industries) succeed in bringing about change? Politics is likely to be a destabilizing force, alongside technological change and economic opportunism. Nowhere is this truer than in the EU, whose purpose is partially to recast domestic markets at the supranational level. Because of the centrality of markets and the fact that the integration project is still a work in progress, the rules and principles constituting and governing markets are among the most contested within the EU. In the constant wrangling over the building of a common market, Europeans leave few aspects of these institutions unexamined. They clash over the basic purpose and geographical reach of markets, the regulations about which entities can compete and what they can exchange, the rules covering access to financial resources, and the actors possessing the right to create new markets. The EU has several built-in mechanisms that generate challenges to extant market arrangements.[59] The cumulative effects of bureaucratic actions are among the least explored.

In the case of smaller-company stock markets, Brussels officials from a few directorates shared a view, widely held inside and outside the European Commission, that nationally segmented markets were a source of Europe's unemployment, slow growth, and lagging international competitiveness. However, years of working within the directorates' narrow policy domains—technological innovation and small and medium enterprises—by the mid-1980s led to a particular solution that challenged established market arrangements and set off turf wars with directorates officially charged with financial policy. Their objective was a Europe-wide stock market for high-risk companies that would rival the U.S. Nasdaq and be a locus of entrepreneurial activity, venture capital financing, and technological innovation.

The civil servants held little sway over the creation of the 1980s feeder markets. National elites—established financial interests and their governments—dominated the direction of market change during this period and persistently opposed U.S.-style pan-European models promoted by the Brussels officials and others. Yet ten years later, interventions by bureaucrats from the same directorates sparked competitive market-making that neither national insiders nor Commission officials anticipated.

These relatively low-level civil servants insinuated themselves into this crucial role in unassuming ways over a fifteen-year period. They mobilized eager but marginalized venture capitalists to support this agenda and leveraged these private actors to carry out projects in a sphere where supranational officials were seen as meddling and acting without a mandate. These civil servants promoted a political discourse about the Nasdaq and job creation in the United States, framed debates around these themes to win support for their preferred policies, and exploited the legitimacy of American institutions and the sense of urgency surrounding economic problems. In short, by crafting supportive interests and political frames, these bureaucrats opened a new supranational political space for challenging established financial arrangements and simultaneously made them more susceptible to institutional innovation.[60]

Convinced that conditions were in place for effective intervention, the Commission officials used the 1993 passage of the Investment Services Directive (an intergovernmental agreement to integrate the sector through managed competition) as justification to make their move.[61] Behind the scenes, they backed plans for a pan-European Nasdaq copy called Easdaq, which the bureaucrats hoped would create a regionwide sector of entrepreneurial finance and challenge the national monopolies of established stock exchanges. The result was market innovation but not of the kind they had envisioned. In contrast to the past, the civil servants were able to outmaneuver detractors from European Commission directorates allied with national financial interests and treasuries. But the possibility of losing out to an upstart rival prompted the national exchanges to react by creating Nasdaq copies of their own, drew them into a cross-border competition, and ultimately led them to reinvent what it meant to be a supplier of stock markets at the turn of the millennium. Exchanges took these actions despite their previous opposition and their belief that Europe of the 1990s lacked the regulatory and social foundations necessary for U.S.-style markets. When the Nasdaq model lost some of its cache after the international stock market crash, the exchanges continued the competitive mimicry by copying the new smaller-company leader, AIM.

The intrusion of Brussels civil servants into what had been the exclusive policymaking domain of established domestic financial communities and governments thus set off a spiral of competition and copying that significantly altered the financing terrain for smaller companies and Europe's position in global finance. With the European Commission intervention, the issue quickly entered the public political arena. No one did or could have anticipated the events that followed. The bureaucrats achieved significantly less than what they wanted. Nevertheless, they had a profound impact. Without their actions, while some type of institutional change might have eventually occurred, it is unlikely the national exchanges would have engaged in cross-border competition and created new stock markets for smaller firms, designed them to attract international investors by borrowing the U.S. form and then a British model, and done so starting in the middle of the 1990s.

CHAPTER **3**

The Early History of a
Brussels Initiative

By the end of the 1970s, the idea that smaller companies might play a vital economic role in Europe moved to the forefront of political debates about how to redress unemployment, stagnation, and technological backwardness. National and European Community policymakers envisioned these firms as motors of economic revitalization and hubs of innovation in the postindustrial economy and shared similar beliefs about the financing problems they faced. If smaller companies were to be the seedbeds of job creation and growth, they needed easier access to inexpensive capital. Stock markets offered one logical solution.

This chapter chronicles the early interest of Brussels civil servants in technological innovation and their promotion of venture capitalism and a pan-European stock market as remedies for perceived decline. It documents their inconspicuous actions in the 1970s and 1980s, actions that by the mid-1990s, as later chapters will show, gradually reconfigured the political landscape in ways conducive to competitive market experimentation. Laying out the historical record from the early decades helps to establish the causal significance of these bureaucratic activities and their cumulative nature. During this period, as Figure 1.2 (page 17) depicts graphically, the vision of stock markets held by some Brussels functionaries began to clash with those of national financial elites. Without strong private-sector support, let alone persuasive arguments for how proposed new markets would solve urgent economic problems or justification for immediate intervention, these civil servants lacked the political context and resources that would later embolden them to circumvent opposition. The chapter thus details the failure of European Commission officials to win battles over audacious market schemes in the 1980s, while unwittingly laying the foundations for a future intervention that would alter perceptions about the feasibility of cross-border competition and thereby radically change smaller-company financing arrangements in Europe.

Political Origins of Europe-wide Venture Capitalism

Despite the Treaty of Rome and other foundational agreements for creating a regional economy and regulatory apparatus, finance in Europe during the 1970s and 1980s remained a distinctly national affair embedded in domestic political economies. Only in the aftermath of two 1986 events, the passage of the Single European Act (SEA) and London's Big Bang, does it make sense to speak of incipient stages of a regional financial system.[1] Even compared with the generally modest levels of cross-border financial integration, however, smaller-company finance stands out from other areas of the financial services industry. The sector was all but immune not only to competition within the region but also to securitization and other international trends. It was against this backdrop that a group of Commission officials working in a division devoted to technological innovation, not financial regulation, saw the future in a pan-European financial infrastructure conducive to venture capitalism.[2]

The history of the Europe's new stock markets starts in the late 1970s, when this bureaucratic enclave began to endorse venture capital as a solution to Europe's technological gap with the United States and Japan, a gap that was believed to be causing economic problems.[3] Such an interest in innovation policy (the label coined for public efforts supporting the commercial exploitation of new technologies) grew out of the Commission's mission, which was specified in the Treaty of Rome, to promote the dissemination of information among member countries as a means to achieve economic integration. By 1980, Directorate General (DG) 13, the Commission division housing these functionaries, was renamed "Information Market and Innovation."[4]

As they explored the role of finance in innovation, DG13 officials developed expertise in the problems faced by European new-technology–based firms (NTBFs) in seeking investment capital.[5] Technological research and development within smaller enterprises was widely understood as a key to solving European economic problems. "Tomorrow's technologies," officials wrote, "are today's innovations—and these are often born and developed by entrepreneurs in small and medium-sized industrial firms."[6] The problem, in these civil servants' eyes, was that industrial policies existed to help large established companies (for example, national champions) develop showcase technologies such as computers, aircraft, and nuclear power; the policies were not created to overcome the problems inherent in financing NTBFs: unusually high risks that investors in young companies have to accept. Once officials' thinking reached this point, the answer seemed obvious. Europe needed what the United States had: a vibrant venture capital industry.

Supranational bureaucrats were not alone in making these connections. Indeed, as Chapter 4 shows, some national government officials made many of the same linkages and began to promote venture capitalism as a solution to economic problems. By 1979 nearly every country in Europe boasted one sort of venture capital scheme or another. Despite a wide variety of approaches, however, most policies shared a single theme: the promotion of national venture capital industries. The Commission's efforts, in contrast, fostered an integrated European venture capital industry.[7]

At the time, the difference between national and European approaches and Commission or national government leadership seemed to matter little, as policies aimed to promote venture capital largely failed everywhere in Europe or were so modest as to have only a slight effect. National and Brussels initiatives faced similar obstacles. Europe was poor soil for American-style venture capitalism, which at least in its country of origin rested on favorable tax laws, pension systems, and stock markets.[8] National financial elites who controlled the regulatory environment either had little or no contact with these types of financiers, were unaware of their needs, and perceived their proposals as threats to established practices and revenue streams. Aspiring to bolster national financial capitals and industries, governments supported venture capital (usually through interventionist industrial policy), only to the extent that it did not encroach on the perceived interests of established financial services industries (protected by finance ministries, treasuries, and central banks). The result, even in the United Kingdom, was a failure to create an environment conducive to venture capitalism.

The efforts of DG13 officials ran into similar resistance. While they did not have to manage cross-cutting goals, they sometimes faced fierce opposition from national financial communities, which could rely on national government support to undermine initiatives that trespassed too far into sensitive financial matters. By 1980, these communities could also count on another division inside the European Commission, DG15 (Financial Institutions and Taxation), to represent their views.[9]

The European Commission and Its Officials

An eclectic array of policymakers considered venture capitalism to be a potential solution to Europe's economic problems. But it was not at all clear in the late 1970s and early 1980s how to go about fostering an American-style venture capital industry in societies built on political bargains designed to keep this sort of high-risk activity at bay. How then did the DG13 officials arrive at their version of pan-European policies, especially the creation of a Europe-wide stock market for smaller companies? The agendas they pursued reflect a predisposition toward regionally integrated markets, a permissive Commission leadership, and a fortuitous location within the fragmented structure of the bureaucracy. Most of all, however, their policies evolved organically through day-to-day operations. Assigned to the narrow task of spurring innovation and motivated by the prospects of fixing Europe's problems and improving its international competitiveness, these civil servants gradually developed a network of venture capitalists and embedded themselves within it.

European Commission specialists, for the most part, expect Brussels officials to prefer initiatives that shift markets, regulation, and authority to the European level.[10] An abundance of research shows Commission officials of all ranks inclined to blame problems on fragmented national economies and see solutions in further European integration.[11] This study is no exception. Two decades of reports, proposals, policies, and studies, as well as personal interviews, substantiate these patterns in the history of Europe's smaller-company stock markets.[12] DG13 civil servants interpreted the problems facing venture capitalists as EU scholars might expect: these officials considered nationally divided economies too small for a flourishing industry. They saw the absence of an integrated financial market as the biggest barrier to fixing Europe's venture capital deficit. From their first proposals to their most recent, these officials found solutions in policies designed to create a supranational foundation for supporting a European venture capital industry. This pursuit of policies with a European scope—still evident fifteen years later—thus reflects a predilection among employees of the Brussels bureaucracy, who after all, entered the European Commission knowing that their jobs would be to protect and enhance the regional integration project.[13]

Some EU researchers assume that the European Commission behaves as a unit.[14] While referring to Commission policies and strategies is useful in some contexts, doing so here would overlook pervasive internal conflicts driving behavior and ultimately market innovation.[15] As the budding dispute between DG13 and DG15 suggests, sharing broad supranational norms or objectives does not translate directly into similar policy preferences.[16] The officials opposed to the venture capital promoters never argued against the integration of European financial markets. Rather, as detailed later in this chapter, they had a different view of Brussels' role in the process and questioned the feasibility of successful interventions, given that governments had not agreed on terms for cross-border competition.[17] Venture capitalism, moreover, became a political priority of the European Commission only in 1996, when David Wright, a career civil servant and advisor to President Jacques Santer (1995–1999), took an interest and elevated the issue area to the highest strata of the bureaucracy.[18] The politically appointed commissioners finally reached a consensus in favor of the promotion of European venture capitalism in 1998, after two decades of internal tensions.[19] Thus the presence of a common bias toward further regional integration did not preclude internal strife and bureaucratic politics. If we look merely at the 1980s, these differences may not seem crucial. In the aftermath of the 1994 Brussels intervention, as Chapter 6 demonstrates, the internal policy cleavages were a central dynamic behind the 1990s pattern of market making.

In some respects, the civil servants in DG13 (and later their allies in other DGs) operated in an accommodating environment. The structure of the Brussels bureaucracy gave the functionally differentiated DGs significant autonomy to develop subcultures and policy preferences.[20] In addition, the specific program to enhance European venture capitalism followed a trend toward market-oriented strategies embraced by the European Commission leadership in the post-Keynesian era.[21] At various times between 1978 and 1994, DG13's policy ideas found strong support from particular Commission leaders. In the early years, for example, DG13 fell under activist commissioner Etienne Davignon's portfolio, upon his first appointment in 1979. Commission president Jacques Delors (1985–1995), the exemplar of supranational entrepreneurs, personally endorsed a proposed pan-European Nasdaq copy in 1985.[22] In the late 1980s and early 1990s, several commissioners, including Able Matutes, Raniero Vanni d'Archirafi, and Christos Papoutsis, actively promoted venture capital as part of the new set of SME programs.[23]

The support of these leaders notwithstanding, it makes little sense to reduce policies pursued for two decades within a small group of civil servants (or actions they motivated) to these political appointees or any one Commission presidency. The promotion and development of venture capital policies predated and outlived Delors' attention, which in the area of finance instead turned to the liberalization of capital controls, the imposition of mutual-recognition regimes, and the adoption of a single currency. Ironically, DG13's program, as noted, was elevated to the top of the Commission's political agenda several years after the 1994 intervention by low-level bureaucrats, even though their actions made perhaps the most significant Brussels contribution to a regional venture capital industry. DG13's ideas and strategies for carrying them out evolved gradually within the division and later in conjunction with other DGs, spanned presidencies and the tenures of a host of commissioners and even outlasted several directors general, the top civil servants. This pattern suggests a relatively autonomous preference-formation process at the lower levels of the bureaucracy.

Conflict between DGs stems to some extent from the differing policy tasks, which prompted thinking along separate evolutionary paths. But this conflict also reflects asymmetrical degrees of autonomy, rooted in which government representatives monitored which DGs and activities.[24] Arguably, officials inside DG15 were just as inclined as their DG13 colleagues to integrate European financial systems but by the early 1980s not nearly as free to advocate bold supranational designs. On the one hand, finance ministers and stock exchanges kept DG15 on a tight leash. Since it was transformed in 1980, this grouping had become the service charged with the legal harmonization of domestic financial services regulation. The ministers were wary of Brussels' meddling in capital markets, especially after DG15 showed interest in a pan-European stock exchange.[25] The ministers' caution continued well into the 1990s, when Ecofin, the Economic and Financial Affairs Council (comprised of finance ministers from member governments) refused to extend implementation powers to the European Commission in the 1993 Investment Services Directive (ISD), as Chapter 6 discusses. On the other hand, government representatives with nonfinancial portfolios oversaw the general activities of DG13 (and its future allies in other divisions). The absence of a European political voice for venture capitalists was an opportunity for these DGs to create their own supportive coalition. The result was to give them more latitude (and cover) to develop pro-European and interventionist policies. DG13's encroachment into contentious financial matters in the name of innovation apparently raised few red flags among government representatives in the Industry Council or among venture capitalists, whereas more-powerful finance ministers saw it as illegitimate interference.[26]

A Pan-European Stock Market as Policy

The particular initiative to create a pan-European stock market exemplifies the gradual evolution of DG13's policy preferences. The officials saw a stock market as a possible solution to the venture capital problem only after several years of incremental successes, failures, and learning by doing. Their first impulse, in the spirit of the service's interventionist reputation, was to mirror the industrial policies for supporting large companies. But by 1980, with neoliberal economic ideas ascendant, the ideological tide had already ebbed away from direct bureaucratic intrusions, at least at the European Community level, where the United Kingdom now had a veto. DG13's earliest venture capital proposals were unable to get past Ecofin.[27] Community funds were to be directly invested and lent to companies (through the European Venture Capital Fund Project and the European Innovation Loan Fund, respectively), a dirigiste scheme that no longer seemed appropriate by the start of the 1980s.

These early policy programs and the ideas they contained differed from those that officials in DG13, DG16 (Regional Policy),[28] DG18 (Financial Operations),[29] and DG23 (Enterprise/SMEs) would advocate fifteen years later. The European Venture Capital Pilot Scheme of 1980–1984, the one short-lived investigative program that did receive Council approval, contrasted sharply with the market-based Easdaq initiative of 1994. The scheme revolved around small grants given directly to companies. In the ill-fated European Venture Capital Fund Project, to cite another example, the proposed European fund would not have invested in risky businesses, and the fund's managers would not have hands-on relationships with those firms in which they invested—two of the key characteristics of contemporary venture capitalist firms.[30] This type of Commission thinking in the 1970s and early 1980s echoed a phenomenon discussed in later chapters: European "venture capital" at this time referred to a very different set of activities than we associate with it today. Rather than being out of touch with trends in the private sector, the bureaucrats had worked closely with the leading "venture capital" firms, which during this period had roots in national government efforts to stimulate the industry.

Having failed to win support for its first proposals, DG13 gradually turned to "industrial" policies more consistent with the prevailing set of economic ideas. Instead of filling the venture capital gap with funds under its discretion (alone or in partnership with private firms), it used its political resources to catalyze venture capitalists into taking the lead in overcoming structural barriers and creating the necessary infrastructure, including equity markets.

Creating a European Voice for Venture Capitalists

DG13's role in creating the European Venture Capital Association (EVCA) in 1983 represents the directorate general's earliest achievement, however modest it appeared at the time. In 1979, officials from the service had begun to sponsor regular symposia, bringing together the European Community's venture capitalists.[31] The functionaries wanted national venture capitalist firms to begin a dialogue with their cross-border counterparts, to recognize that they faced similar problems, and to think of themselves as part of a single European industry. Also, the officials had political goals closely associated with their bias toward seeing European integration as a solution. They were well aware that they could not effect change on their own. In a political climate hostile to direct intervention, Commission officials could not appear to be initiators—especially in financial matters in which the reigning stream of thought characterized political actors as obstacles to the natural harmony of market forces.

To be effective, the policy efforts of Brussels civil servants would have to look as if the venture capitalists were driving them. To achieve this goal, the financiers needed a voice in the European political arena and an identifiable policy network, preferably a malleable one. This was a primary impetus behind the symposia the Commission officials organized in the early 1980s and ultimately behind the creation of EVCA, an industry organization that would claim with a degree of legitimacy to represent venture capitalists' aggregated interests. Brussels officials a decade later would indeed use EVCA as the primary vehicle for initiating and carrying forward a plan to build a pan-European Nasdaq copy.

An Intervention Blocked in 1985

Events in 1985 show that creating EVCA, a significant milestone in hindsight, did not automatically or even more easily transform what Commission bureaucrats considered urgently needed and reasonable proposals into policies. In some respects, in fact, the EVCA-creation process, because it drew little if any resistance, lulled officials into a false sense of the prospects for future successes. Political realities became abundantly clear in 1985, when a proposal for a pan-European Nasdaq copy, despite the endorsement of Jacques Delors, died quickly due to opposition from national financial elites and to a lack of organizational capacity inside EVCA.

The proposal began with an American's simple idea. Observing the European venture capital industry from his newly adopted home in Geneva, Eugene Schulman, formerly a Beverly Hills stockbroker, arrived at what he thought a logical conclusion: Europe needed a Nasdaq stock market of its own. He enlisted one friend as a partner, Rhodes scholar Andrew Sundberg, and solicited financing from another friend, Sam Goodner, to research, write, and promote an independent multiclient study.[32]

Far removed from the financial world in 1985, Schulman and Sundberg saw themselves as men of ideas. While they aimed to pay back Goodner and make a profit from selling the study at 12,000 Swiss francs apiece, they were primarily concerned with widely circulating the idea—a goal they met.[33] By the end of the year, they had sold the study to European and American banks, stock exchanges, and EVCA (whose chairman, Richard Onians, strongly supported the proposed market in EVCA's newsletter); visited financial communities in Paris, Frankfurt, Milan, and Amsterdam; and received coverage in the financial press.[34]

Wanting to attract Commission support for the proposal and specifically to interest its president, Schulman and Sundberg deliberately framed their market scheme around the ECU (European currency unit). Not only would the Schulman-Sundberg market, named "ECU-EASD" (see Table 1.1, page 4), mirror the Nasdaq form and function, it would also trade company shares denominated in the single currency.[35] At first, the strategy seemed to work, as it offered a feasible mechanism for expanding the European project. Delors endorsed it and circulated the study within the Commission and at EVCA, which quickly became one of the proposal's sponsors.

The officials in DG13 also embraced it. From their perspective, the Schulman-Sundberg market was the natural extension of the officials' own efforts to stimulate venture capital in Europe. Officials in this and other services had already identified secondary stock markets as a key problem in financing innovation.[36] DG13 adopted the pan-European market as a policy goal, one that would long outlive the specific 1985 proposal. Officials were aware that venture capitalists could not make profits commensurate with high risks unless they could sell their investments in young companies through an appropriate stock market. Already in the mid-1980s, the newly created national feeder markets (discussed in the next chapter), had begun to falter and, against the seemingly limitless success of the American Nasdaq in financing entrepreneurial companies, appeared to be no more than small puddles of capital for national firms. The proposal for a pan-European Nasdaq, by contrast, had the potential to overcome the fragmentation of national markets and provide venture capitalists with the benefits of a much larger pool of investors. At one point, Commission officials even indicated that they were on the brink of offering several million dollars for start-up funding.[37]

But somewhere on the avenues between the Commission's Berlaymont Building and EVCA's offices, the proposal died.[38] Within the EU bureaucracy, there was opposition from other services. DG15, whose constituents included national stock exchanges with the ears of their respective finance ministries and treasuries, had been working closely with the exchanges in integration projects of its own and gained a reputation for supporting "market-led" as opposed to interventionist policies. Its efforts, focused on writing legislative proposals, tended to follow an intergovernmentalist logic of managed ties between separate national markets, coordinated cross-border information systems, and mutual recognition of national regulatory regimes, with harmonized minimal standards.[39] No one, at this point, knew what an independent pan-European market would mean, but the exchanges and their owners had little appetite for an experiment that intruded on their market-making autonomy.[40] Because of the threat posed to the exchanges and the widely held perception that Europe's nationally fragmented regulatory regimes rendered such a market unfeasible, it is not surprising that Commission officials, most likely from DG15, became a source of significant resistance to the pan-European Nasdaq idea—a role DG15 maintained well into the 1990s.

Officials in DG13 and other services, by contrast, would have liked to intervene but were poorly positioned to overcome the opposition. The ECU-EASD proposal had become a highly public initiative, whose success depended largely on the political and framing skills of its backers. The endorsement by Delors—who was familiar with smaller-company financing issues because of his involvement in the 1983 introduction of a dedicated market for smaller companies in France (discussed in Chapter 4)—had drawn broad coverage from the financial press. Given the widely held perception during the Reagan-Thatcher decade that policymakers interfere with politically neutral financial markets, a Commission intervention in support of ECU-EASD would have needed to be carefully finessed.[41] But an obvious source of political cover was absent in 1985. EVCA, an industry organization, seemed the perfect instrument in principle. With its strong backing, the

Commission might have argued that Brussels was merely responding to a market-led initiative spearheaded by European venture capitalists. But EVCA, still relatively new, suffered from low levels of organizational capacity and few resources. Individual venture capitalists in Europe, moreover, were too marginal politically and financially to be effective advocates without a strong industry organization. In addition, the ECU-EASD promoters in the Commission had yet to find a persuasive political argument for a pan-European Nasdaq copy that would make it difficult for national governments and national financial communities to oppose such a market. Schulman and Sundberg had tried to do this by using the ECU to tie the proposal to the single-market project. As a strategy, however, the currency framing did not readily evoke a solution to significant problems articulated in the political discourse of the mid-1980s. It simply lacked resonance.

For pragmatic reasons tied to the minimal levels of regulatory harmonization in European finance, DG13 and other Brussels officials were probably unwilling to expend their own political capital within the bureaucracy. The ECU-EASD proposal came before its time and likely would have faced legal and practical difficulties, if not impasses. Regional regulatory integration in finance hardly existed and was almost certainly not developed enough for a stock market based on cross-border trading. The pan-European Nasdaq proposal still preceded the post–Single European Act initiatives for a European passport for investment services firms, banks, and insurance companies and the liberalization of capital restrictions. In other words, some of the arguments from the exchanges were hard to refute. The promarket officials could not make a convincing case that a legal framework invited or even enabled pan-European equity markets. Schulman and Sundberg wrote about the complex array of national obstacles to cross-border financial activity and hoped the adoption of the ECU would alleviate some of them. But from a pragmatic perspective, a pan-European market most likely required a firmer foundation of European-level rules to support cross-border competition in financial services—a development still eight years away.[42]

More Hesitancy in 1989

In 1989, the Schulman-Sundberg proposal reemerged. In the wake of the Single European Act and the run-up to 1992, the date designated for completing the single European market, the idea of a pan-European smaller-company stock market again circulated in several corners of the Brussels bureaucracy.[43] The seed planted by the Geneva team had sprung roots, an unsurprising development, because a pan-European market corresponded well with the goals of many European policymakers imbued with the spirit of the single-market program. This time Commission officials initiated the process when they asked Schulman and Sundberg, who had by then moved on to other projects, to update their proposal and meet with Commission officials about getting it off the ground. At one point in 1989, the officials again intimated that they were willing to provide large sums of funding for setup costs.[44]

The renewed initiative came from an inter-DG working group, overseen by the Commission's secretariat general's office and organized to explore ways to push along the single-market project.[45] Over the course of 1989, the working group solicited three separate proposals (see Table 1.1, page 4), two of which involved Schulman and Sundberg. The first was called the European Over-the-Counter Market (EOTC) and merely summarized the 1985 study and proposal. On the behest of the working group, Schulman and Sundberg created a second proposal, this time teaming up with the Scottish Financial Enterprise (SFE), a lobby representing the Scottish financial services industry, which was concerned about the decades-long centralization of British finance in London. The SFE, which submitted that same year a similar proposal called EASDAQ—not to be confused with the 1996 market of the same name (see Table 1.1)—had been working closely with DG16 (Regional Policy) and other regional industry organizations. The Scottish lobby saw in a pan-European electronic over-the-counter market modeled on the Nasdaq a means for promoting Europe's local financial centers in places like Glasgow, Lyon, Copenhagen, Bremen, and Turin. In the combined proposal, the new consortium renamed the planned market the European Securities Market (ESM) and couched it as a policy for supporting regional (that is, subnational) financial centers.[46]

The ESM, like its 1985 predecessor, failed largely because at the end of the day an unpropitious political context made Commission officials unwilling to provide support. DG13, still interested in promoting venture capital, was again active in the process but now had new allies.[47] The newly created DG23 (Enterprise/SMEs) also interpreted the financing obstacles faced by smaller enterprises as one of the biggest reasons for Europe's high unemployment rates, slow growth, and innovation problems. And like their counterparts in DG13, officials in the new service believed a pan-European market could be a solution to the problem. DG16 supported the creation of a pan-European Nasdaq because of the potential of such a market to preserve the importance of smaller financial centers, which were on the losing end of a decades-long process that had centralized financial activity in London, Paris, Frankfurt, and other national financial capitals.[48]

Resistance again, this time on the record, came from DG15, which was still working closely with national exchanges and national governments to get negotiations under way for the delayed legislation on the integration of investment services.[49] Reflecting the views of its negotiating partners—especially the German universal banks, majority owners of the Frankfurt exchange—the DG15 representative argued, "If [a pan-European market for entrepreneurial firms] was economically viable, then the market would create it itself and pay for it."[50] He also voiced skepticism about both the timing (arguing that a pan-European market would remain premature until EC securities legislation was in place) and the independence of the proposed market (maintaining that a model that gave a big role to national exchanges would be better suited to the needs of smaller companies).

The promarket coalition once again failed to overcome the opposition. The reasons in 1989 resembled what they had been in 1985. While the proposals did not make a big splash in the financial press, the process was highly political, as in 1985. This time the clashes took place at the inter-DG level, which became a microcosm for broader disputes about the scope, governance, and purposes of financial markets and the role of Brussels in creating them. Each of the six participating DGs had its own constituencies, policy networks, interpretations, and policy approaches. Despite a broad base of support, officials promoting the market were again vulnerable to the substantive objections of DG15. While no one knew for certain how much or what kind of regulatory integration would sustain a pan-European stock market for smaller companies, it was still too soon to put forth a convincing argument that the threshold had been reached in 1989.[51] In addition, the civil servants favoring the market were keenly aware that to succeed, they would have to gain private-sector support and frame the proposal in terms with broad appeal. EVCA continued, however, to be a weak organization, financially sustained by EU programs and, as Chapters 6 and 7 show, divided on whether venture capitalists should work with or against national exchanges.

Finally, private-sector interest groups that were organized around the issue of regions proved no match for financial interests from Frankfurt, London, Paris, Milan, and Amsterdam. These financial elites and their national governments were primarily concerned about future cross-border competition. They tended to believe the best way to ensure the preservation of a prominent national financial-services industry in an integrated European market was through increased scale—centralizing finance in a single national center that could then contend with the other leading financial cities. A pan-European stock market, promoting local financial industries, ran against this logic and posed a threat to those interests, like the main national stock exchanges, with a stake in the centralization process. The promarket officials tried to make the case that the demise of small financial centers was an urgent problem that the pan-European market would solve—which is why they pressured Schulman and Sundberg into teaming up with the SFE. But the issue had no more bite than the framing of the 1985 proposal around the ECU. The regions angle lacked the kind of political salience that would generate widespread support throughout Europe. The plight of regional financial centers was especially unlikely to persuade major financial actors and their national governments, whose positions mattered most.

In sum, from the late 1970s to 1989 Brussels civil servants incrementally developed an agenda for building an environment supportive of a European venture capital industry. One of their pet policies, to support a pan-European stock market for smaller companies, met stiff resistance from within and without the European Commission in 1985 and 1989. Despite creating a political voice for venture capitalists and experimenting with arguments about why Europe needed such a market, the political terrain remained infertile, leaving the civil servants with few tools for circumventing opposition from Europe's financial capitals. In consequence, Brussels refrained from introducing radical stock market experiments and, as the next two chapters illustrate, had little influence over smaller-company market making, which remained under the control of established financial interests and their governments.

CHAPTER 4

Creating Feeder Markets in the United Kingdom and France, 1977–1987

As a platform for challenging the status quo in finance, Europe's regional polity of the 1980s had little to offer. Despite the efforts of the supranational bureaucrats described in the last chapter, the European Economic Community (EEC) lacked a concentration of interest-group activity, of forums for articulating and contesting policy arguments, and of rules open to interpretation. This political context afforded European Commission officials only meager autonomy from national financial establishments, undermining the civil servants' sometimes ambitious agenda.

Later chapters show that in the mid-1990s a more developed political space bolstered Brussels' efforts to shape national market arrangements. This chapter demonstrates the converse. A barren arena in the 1980s left the locus of debate and power in traditional national political forums. Domestic policymakers in Britain and France were able to control reform processes, largely unencumbered by direct or indirect European Commission intrusions. Financial policymakers across Europe, like their counterparts in Brussels, saw new specialized stock markets for smaller companies as a solution to economic problems. Such markets, however, implied reform of national arrangements that rested on close government-finance relations. Even though many individuals in government and the private sector were genuinely motivated by the potential public benefits of healthy smaller companies, powerful financial elites shaped reforms to favor vested interests—that is, equity markets supporting existing lucrative businesses and protecting traditional intermediaries from domestic and foreign competition. Entrenched financial systems thus set the scene for the often contentious politics that surrounded proposals for new stock markets, shaping the conservative pattern of market reform during the 1980s and early 1990s and producing significant cross-border variance based on national traditions.

Feeder Stock Markets in the United Kingdom

In the postwar decades, British government officials, industrialists, and financiers broadly agreed on the importance of smaller companies to the overall well-being of the British economy, portraying them as incubators of innovation and growth. Smaller-enterprise matters featured prominently in public debates about how to revitalize the economy. One persistent problem, first exposed through the 1931 MacMillan Committee Report, became known as the "MacMillan gap" or the "equity gap." The phrase referred to the relative difficulty of smaller firms in obtaining finance in general and equity finance in particular. The issue never disappeared; it resurfaced in the 1971 Bolton Committee Report and again in the late 1970s in the many volumes produced by the Wilson Committee.[1] Indeed, the widespread perception of an equity gap in the 1970s initiated a process of institutional change, gained momentum with Margaret Thatcher's interest in smaller companies and enterprise, and eventually led to the 1980 creation of the USM, the United Kingdom's first stock market for smaller companies. The market-creation process was deeply embedded in the particulars of the British financial system and domestic politics, and the outcomes reflected the preferences of the most powerful actors within them. The incipient EU financial system, detectable in modest EEC legislation and the (sometimes lofty) proposals of Brussels civil servants, in contrast, scarcely affected decisions.

A Public Policy Problem

The London Stock Exchange in the postwar decades reserved access to its equity market for the most established and largest companies. Its leadership argued that the exchange had two obligations to investors: to ensure that admitted companies provided high levels of information so that investors could make appropriate investment decisions; and to protect investors against the high risks associated with certain classes of companies. Reflecting the paternalist attitude implied in the second obligation, the LSE's market exemplified the Anglo-American large-company equity market model.

During these years, western Europe had two types of stock markets. The continental large-company markets, by 2007 close to extinction, had only marginal roles in the financing of national firms. They were sideshows to credit-based financial systems dominated by governments or cartels of parapublic and private banks. The same actors who had discretion over the allocation of credit also controlled these markets, either by owning the stock exchanges or by limiting their autonomy.[2] For national financial insiders, continental large-company markets represented power by other means. In Germany, to use Susanne Lütz's words, "issuing and trading customers' shares were only a further element of the close relationship between house banks and industry."[3] In France, writes John Zysman, "in raising funds on the securities market a firm [did] not escape the influence of the major financial institutions—particularly the banks—and the government."[4]

The continental large-company form and its underlying principle of preserving control in the hands of financial insiders reveal the marginal role of these markets. The empowered financial intermediaries gave access to a relatively small group of highly select firms. Listing was as much about prestige and facilitating negotiated transfers of ownership as about raising capital. High, though flexible and informal, barriers to quoting and the opacity of low informational standards gave the cartels of financial intermediaries power to anoint only the firms they selected for listing.

In contrast, the Anglo-American large-company model, epitomized in the LSE's Official List, represents a social bargain between government and financiers that stems from the relative importance of capital markets in financing national firms.[5] The exchanges centralized trading activity, to reduce informational fragmentation and improve price formation; monitored against price manipulation and fraud; standardized assets and procedures, to reduce costs; and provided clearing services and protections against counterparty risk.[6] In return, governments gave securities brokers a degree of official or informal protection from unfettered competition, as well as autonomy over the supervision of trading activity and market participants, and the selection of market forms and regulations.

In contrast to the continental model, here member-owners depended heavily on stock markets for revenue and placed great importance on their ability to attract investors and maintain markets as centers of liquidity. The exchanges thus devised selection mechanisms for creating expectations of markets that housed well-performing companies.[7] First, the exchanges required companies to publish accurate financial information so that investors could make informed decisions. The knowledge that investors have an inside view of business operations and therefore accurately value shares, in theory, deters poorly performing companies from seeking public listings and creates a market of profitable enterprises. Second, exchanges imposed high barriers to quoting to protect investors from certain classes of risky firms, such as smaller companies. Without protection from these risks, went the rationale, savers would shy away from investing in stocks, companies would lose a key financing option at the heart of the economy, and brokers would lose their primary source of revenue.

The LSE's high barriers to quoting, in particular, ensured that only established corporations could seek quotations. The obligation to protect investors against firm risk, enshrined in a five-year history of company accounts and a capitalization of 500,000 pounds (see Table 2.1, page 24), prevented most smaller enterprises from qualifying for an official listing. Quotation was not for start-ups or rapidly growing young companies.[8]

In the late 1970s, the difficulty smaller companies faced in gaining access to capital markets through the LSE had worsened because of a shift in the profile of investors. Wealthy individuals and families had traditionally been the dominant category of British investors in shares of national companies, and they had long showed a propensity to invest in stocks of smaller listed companies, albeit established ones presenting relatively low risk. By the end of the decade, asset managers, overseeing pension funds and unit trusts, had replaced individuals as the dominant decision-makers investing in British shares. Asset managers, unlike wealthy households, were not as inclined to invest in smaller companies, because of the pressures to follow indices of larger companies, the need for high levels of liquidity and large numbers of available shares, and the higher costs per company of financial analysis. The overall effect was a dampening in demand for the smaller-company shares quoted on the LSE, relatively lower valuations, and consequently higher costs for smaller companies wanting to raise equity finance through the capital markets.

At the time, participants and analysts understood the shift in savings patterns and its effects on smaller companies.[9] Less clear were the reasons why these firms had not obtained other sources of external financing. Relatively few of them received debt and equity financing from new or improved government programs or private banks.[10] According to the Wilson Committee Reports, commercial banks and government programs had improved the availability of external capital to smaller companies since the early 1970s.

Private and government financial intermediaries reported the lack of demand for funds. There was not a shortage of external capital available but a shortage at terms acceptable to smaller-business owners. Apparently, the key problem for British smaller firms lay in a fear of losing control. High interest rates and a 3 percent high-risk premium made bank loans to smaller companies expensive. But even smaller-enterprise advocacy groups did not question that the costs were commensurate with the higher risks. What made bank lending and other types of financing unacceptable were the covenants and collateral that had the potential to jeopardize the owner's control.[11]

The Stock Market Solution

Two industry groups that testified before the Wilson Committee, the Confederation of British Industry (CBI) and the Association of Independent Businesses (AIB), touted the expansion of the United Kingdom's tiny over-the-counter (OTC) market as a solution to the "control" problem. Their vision of OTC markets had two somewhat idealized sources. First was the international exemplar of the decades-old American OTC market, overhauled in 1971 to include an electronic quotation system and renamed NASDAQ (National Association of Securities Dealers Automated Quotation) and later the Nasdaq Stock Market. AIB argued that smaller companies preferred equity financing to debt financing because of difficulty meeting interest payments during economic downturns. Of the various forms of equity financing, AIB favored stock market quotation because of its alleged ability to ensure that the new outside owners of a company would remain decentralized and distanced at arm's length. Thus wanting a special market dedicated to the shares of smaller companies, these witnesses turned to the United States for a model. They maintained that the American OTC market allowed entrepreneurs to raise funds from capital markets without the threat of losing control. The presence in the United States of a vibrant market of decentralized buyers of smaller-company shares made the difference by reducing the chances of an unwanted takeover.[12]

Interestingly, the AIB's 1977 assessment fails to mention a critical characteristic of the American OTC market. To offer shares to the public in the United States, all companies, including those traded over the counter, were (at least in principle) required to disclose investor-friendly financial information. Investors had been willing to buy shares in large part because of these highly transparent statutory informational standards. There was a flip side of the coin, however. The founders of publicly quoted companies in the United States had to give up, at least to some extent, the use of clandestine financial operations as a tool for preserving control, an implication that did not make its way into the British industry perceptions of the times.

The OTC market idea had already surfaced in public policy discussions in Brussels and London. Earlier in 1977, for example, the European Commission had released a study (conducted by Hartmut Schmidt of the University of Hamburg) that offered an alternative to the prevailing ideas of harmonizing and integrating domestic equity markets as a solution to the financing inefficiencies faced by European companies. To the dismay of the Brussels officials who commissioned the study, instead of cross-border harmonization and integration, Schmidt advocated the creation of national market segments that would meet the special needs of different types of national companies.[13] Rather than accepting the then-standard view that optimal efficiency could be reached only through a single market for company shares, Schmidt made the efficiency case for market fragmentation.[14] The arguments of the CBI and AIB echoed Schmidt's logic (though it is not clear the extent to which they were directly influenced by it). By the time of the Wilson Committee testimony, the industry groups had already been conducting a lobbying campaign to pressure the LSE into creating a second-tier stock market for smaller companies.

The LSE's Co-opting of the Process

It is not surprising that several years earlier these industry advocate groups had turned to the LSE to supply a new market for smaller companies. Financial, industrial, and political power in the United Kingdom during this period, to borrow an idea from Zysman, inhabited separate worlds.[15] This arrangement meant that few in government or industry had expertise in finance. While business leaders and public officials knew they wanted smaller companies to have cheaper and easier access to the capital markets, they did not have the legal right or the knowledge base to create them. The division of authority also gave rise to an attendant regulatory ideology that assigned the details of market-making to the relevant financial actors themselves.[16]

From legal and practical perspectives, innovation in the form of equity markets could come only from the LSE. Having in the early 1970s subsumed regional British stock exchanges, the LSE was now the only option. The

British financial system and regulatory regime vested formidable powers in the pre–Big Bang LSE, first and foremost providing it with a legal monopoly in regulated share trading and settlement. The LSE supplied the only regulated market and the only clearing system for the settling of officially regulated transactions of equities. Under the principle of self-regulation, the exchange policed its own members, who alone could trade or settle shares, and its rules forbade them from dealing on other markets, except under specified conditions. The exchange even determined the rate of fixed commissions for executing transactions. The LSE, moreover, had discretion over the procedures companies followed to raise capital and list shares. The exchange thus had exclusive discretion over its markets' form—that is, barriers to quoting and informational requirements. Finally, the LSE also represented the interests of its member firms, which comprised nearly all stock market participants in the City.

The London exchange had used its resources over several years to resist pressures to create new markets under its own umbrella. But now the smaller-company lobby groups were positing a more ambitious idea, the expansion of the British OTC market, outside the LSE's channels. As part of the Wilson Committee investigation, the exchange, under the chairmanship of Nicholas Goodison, submitted a special report on smaller companies, in which it strongly opposed the proposal and attempted to dissuade the committee from adopting it.[17]

The LSE made three arguments in 1978 and 1979 submissions to the Wilson Committee, all connected by a single protectionist undercurrent: that the stock exchange should have monopoly control over access to equity financing. First, the LSE argued it had the obligation to protect investors from the high risks of most smaller companies. Second, the LSE emphasized the role of its members in supplying risk capital to companies active in the exploration of the North Sea and suggested that this mechanism could also be used by smaller firms seeking capital for expansion.

Finally, and most importantly, the exchange protested the expansion of an OTC market outside its purview. The LSE argued that the United Kingdom was too small and concentrated for an American-style market and that the growth of the British OTC market would create duplication. Here, the exchange maintained that it had long offered an infrequent trading facility, which with a little promotion could easily be transformed into the solution that smaller companies desired. Under LSE rule 163(2), member firms could match orders of unquoted company shares with case-by-case permission.

While the trading facility did not provide a continuous market and the LSE did not have a regulatory relationship with the unquoted companies, investors had the protection of its compensation fund. In addition, the LSE claimed that in the current British OTC market a single firm had a monopoly. In the United States, the OTC market was based on the competition of at least two securities dealers for the shares of each company. In Britain, single firms handled all orders alone.

Perceived Domestic Competition

The American experience with an OTC market apparently left an indelible impression on the London exchange's stance and arguments. LSE members had watched the Nasdaq grow into a competitor to the NYSE in less than a decade and no doubt wondered whether the same might occur in the LSE's backyard. Rather than a model worth copying, the Nasdaq symbolized the LSE's worst-case scenario. The Nasdaq's rise fostered a mind-set among LSE members to see competition even where it remained a remote possibility. This exaggerated sense of vulnerability had throughout the 1970s drawn the LSE into a series of attempts to thwart London's over-the-counter markets from encroaching into its near monopoly.

Private financial firms (licensed dealers) had begun to create markets for shares of companies not traded on the LSE. In 1972, M. J. H. Nightingale and Company (later known as Granville and Company) turned itself into a specialized secondary equity market for firms unwilling or unable to list on the LSE. Nightingale assisted firms raising capital by placing shares in the hands of carefully selected investors. The company then provided a trading service for a commission by matching buyers and sellers; eighty to ninety were leading British financial firms.[18]

A second development in the British OTC market created more serious fears of competition among LSE members. In 1973, Harvard Securities Limited, founded by Canadian M. J. Glickman, dealt in the shares of American OTC companies. Then, after 1977, Harvard Securities began raising capital for and trading the shares of British smaller companies. It attracted much controversy within the financial establishment. Not only did the company offer an alternative to the LSE for trading and raising capital, but following the American market-maker model, Harvard Securities Limited also risked its own capital and dealt directly with private clients—demonstrating that British private investors, like their American counterparts, would invest in high-risk OTC stocks.[19] Eventually, Harvard Securities' controversial activities and success (abetted by the Wilson Report's support and publicity) lured other licensed dealers into the new American-style OTC market.

With Nasdaq's emergence in the air, the LSE's executives perceived the increased activity on the OTC market as a potential threat that needed an immediate response. But there are good reasons to doubt whether Britain's OTC market would have followed the same trajectory as the United States'. The introduction of an electronic quotation system marked the latest step since the landmark 1930s legislation to protect investors participating in the United States' OTC market.[20] The United Kingdom of the 1970s, however, lacked a similar regulatory environment outside the LSE's rigid regime, which precluded the kinds of smaller firms that were raising capital from the public in the United States. The level of information smaller companies should be required to divulge was very much in question and remained unsettled through the 1990s. In the burgeoning British OTC market of the 1970s, investors relied not on a national regulatory regime but on the reputation of financial intermediaries like Nightingale and Harvard Securities, which produced information on their client companies. Providing information as such imposed serious constraints on the potential scale of the market. OTC companies could sell shares to the public without registering as public firms. Only after the passage of the British Companies Act of 1980 did nonlisted enterprises with public company status have to submit accounts to national authorities. But this regime did not affect the OTC market, where companies could remain private. In the clubby City financial circles of the 1970s, in consequence, few financial intermediaries were willing to risk their reputation by providing equity finance services to smaller companies. So at the time of the Wilson Committee's recommendation to promote the development of Britain's OTC market in 1980, very few financial intermediaries had committed themselves to the existing market or appeared about to do so.

Nonetheless, the LSE leadership apparently perceived this modicum of activity on the OTC market as a threat with potential costs (that is, competition in the equities trading business) that could easily outweigh the risks of providing a market for smaller company shares. The exchange thus attempted to redirect these financial activities toward its own markets and members. When the Wilson Committee seemed on the verge of recommending the expansion of the OTC market in 1979, the exchange moved by proposing the USM's creation.

The Thatcher Government and the Creation of a Stock Market

The LSE's first effort had failed to bring the OTC market under its control. In December 1977, the exchange circulated a brochure to promote Rule 163(2) of the LSE's rule book, which permitted members to match trades of unlisted companies with specific approval.[21] The Wilson Committee had just released its interim report of 1977, which mentioned the broad-based support for innovation in smaller-company markets, including an expanded OTC market, from industry and government (specifically, the Department of Industry).[22] The report lent widespread publicity to the OTC market. The LSE's promotion of Rule 163(2) was a reaction, aimed to assert the exchange's control over any new trading activity, even if it did not fall under LSE's existing regulatory umbrella.[23] (The OTC firms normally had private company status, did not publish accounts, and did not have to meet any of the exchange's disclosure provisions.) Increasing the use of the rule by LSE members was also an attempt to preempt the committee from recommending an expanded OTC market.

Within two years, however, the exchange again returned to the smaller-company question. Its strategies had failed to silence political calls for an OTC market outside LSE control or to reduce the perceived threat of competition. Equally important, the Conservative Party's return to power in May 1979 affected the LSE in two new ways. First, the LSE wanted the new government to be more sympathetic than the previous one to the exchange's ongoing attempt to escape the clutches of the Office of Fair Trading (OFT). The OFT's director general had tried to use a new statutory instrument to oblige the LSE to place its rule book under the control of the Restrictive Practices Court, a measure that would have significantly reduced the LSE's traditional autonomy.[24] To ingratiate itself to Thatcher's new government, the exchange sought to avoid the impression that it posed an obstacle to new programs promoting entrepreneurial activity and that it adopted the cause of small companies. The prime minister had appointed the first ministerial appointment for small business and developed a series of programs for small companies (for example, Business Expansion Scheme, or BES, and Loan Guarantee Schemes).[25] The exchange feared the government would interpret LSE opposition to the OTC proposals as an obstacle to the promotion of entrepreneurship in general. Second, the new government and political climate increased the chances of an emboldened Wilson Committee, willing to recommend public intervention to remove the impediments to an enlarged OTC market. In December of 1979, perceiving this possibility, the LSE sprung into action with a much bolder initiative.

In an attempt to co-opt the process of institutional change and ensure its discretion over the supply of stock markets and trading activity, the exchange introduced a proposal for a smaller-company second-tier market, owned and regulated by the LSE—a model very close to what Hartmut Schmidt had recommended a few years earlier. Rather than risk the growth of the British OTC market, over which it may not have much control, the LSE tried to preempt the effort by abandoning its claim that smaller-company finance fell outside its purview.

Using the increased "unregulated activity" as the rationale, in December 1979 the LSE circulated a Green Paper that led directly to the creation of the USM, a second-tier market completely under the LSE umbrella. The exchange claimed to be concerned about potential scandal.[26] The LSE could argue Rule 163(2) was proving an inadequate instrument for imposing its control over the budding market, as exchange members comprised only a portion of the active firms. The higher levels of activity, while still a trickle compared with United States' OTC volumes, increased the risks to the LSE's status as overseer of orderly markets. As a self-regulatory organization, the LSE was supposed to police its members and guarantee fair trading. In the OTC market, however, populated with secretive private companies and opaque dealings, the LSE could do neither. Pointing to the activity levels of the late 1970s, the LSE argued that the OTC market had the potential to damage the City's reputation. The answer was a smaller-company market, under LSE control, that would promote entrepreneurial activity by lowering the barriers to quoting.

Other factors, in addition to perceived competition, contributed to the USM's creation. Some members were also eager to find a solution to the depressed new issues (that is, initial public offerings, or IPO) market. In the late 1960s and early 1970s, the LSE attracted approximately fifty new companies a year. Between 1972 and 1979, the numbers fell by more than 50 percent.[27] The flow of newly listed companies affects the general well-being of any stock exchange, which needs to offset the normal exodus from mergers, acquisitions, and delistings. But the 1970s decline in new issues particularly hit the pocketbooks of those firms whose revenues depended on new companies coming to market. The poor conditions for listing on an equity market, created by the deep 1970s recession in industrialized countries, caused the decline, a fact supported by the renewed flow of new listings in the 1980s. At the time, however, some LSE members found it convenient to accept the government and industry arguments about the high barriers to quoting. They hoped lowering barriers was the answer to the slowdown of new issues.

After resisting government and industry demands for five years, the LSE created the USM in 1980. Heightened perception of competition—exacerbated by the new Conservative government's agenda, the Wilson Committee recommendations, and the depressed new issues market—prompted the exchange to abandon its long-held positions about supplying and regulating markets for quoting and trading smaller, riskier company shares. Rather than global pressures, regional agreements among European governments, cross-border competition, or the actions of Brussels bureaucrats, domestic politics shaped the market-creation process. Existing national arrangements bestowed enormous political and market power on the LSE. The process began with national perceptions of a problem and ended with solutions dominated by the most powerful actor in the sector. The LSE did not simply meet the demands for change initiated by industry lobbies and government; it was able to co-opt the process. After staving off pressure for half a decade, the exchange finally acted when it saw in the USM a way to redirect the OTC activity toward its members and trading systems. As detailed in the next sections of this chapter, the LSE managed to achieve its own goals, even when they differed from those of government and industry.

The USM's Feeder Form

Different organizational forms of stock markets cater to the goals of different actors. In the 1970s, the effects of variant designs were largely unknown, even in the United Kingdom, with its history of equity financing for large companies. This uncertainty, combined with a lack of expertise in government and industry, meant that the USM's organizational form generated limited debate and ultimately favored the LSE. The leadership of the LSE understood better than others how some forms diverted trade flows away from the exchange and otherwise affected its members' businesses. Smaller companies and the industry groups representing them, in contrast, did not envision how their goals might be reached through a particular design. As a result, these groups limited their lobbying to a few simple and uncontroversial dimensions—primarily that the form would make access to capital markets as easy as possible for smaller companies. A decade later, as Chapters 5 and 6 show, discussions about smaller-company markets would include more-nuanced and conflict-ridden disputes about investor risks.

At the end of the 1970s, however, the USM discussions focused on an un-bundled notion of risk: balancing the trade-off between the LSE's responsi-bility to minimize investor exposure to chancy ventures and the public policy goal of lowering requirements and costs of quotation to maximize access for smaller firms. The critical factor of informational standards (the U.S. mechanism for ensuring that investors could assess the risks they might take) did not emerge as a separate issue from the overall regulatory require-ments, and the question of control (the degree to which a new market should fall under the LSE umbrella) never entered the USM debates. In fact, once the LSE proposed creating the USM, the idea of a separate market outside the LSE all but disappeared. It quickly became a given to all involved that the LSE would own, control, and regulate a new smaller-company market. This meant that in selecting a form for the USM, the exchange would have to negotiate details only at the margins, not over its main concerns.

On November 10, 1980, one year after circulating the Green Paper, the LSE opened trading on the USM.[28] Although the USM's ultimate form did not precisely mirror the LSE's original plan, the form largely reflected the plan's two specific goals of diverting trading activity in smaller-company shares away from the OTC market and guaranteeing that the new market did not compete with the Official List but rather serve it as a source of high-quality new companies. A 1981 circular to exchange members suggested that the USM's design was not in itself sufficient for achieving the first goal. The circular instructed members to urge companies with actively traded OTC shares to list on the USM by December 1981, threatening to prevent members from "taking a position" in Rule 163(2) shares after that date. In the view of smaller companies with unlisted shares, the circular aimed to kill the active market in OTC shares.[29] At the same time as it introduced the USM, the LSE changed Rule 163(2) to Rule 535(2). According to one ob-server, "The Stock Exchange view clearly was that the so-called third-tier equity market under Rule 535(2) was only a temporary measure and that the introduction of USM would see an end to dealings under the rule."[30] Moreover, once the USM opened, the LSE gave companies incentives to sell shares right away, by waving some of the expensive quoting requirements.

The LSE's original Green Paper of December 1979 articulates clearly how the USM's form would secure the second goal, that of guaranteeing that the new market did not compete with the Official List. The USM was to be an

intermediate market segment, between official listing and the existing transactions marketed under Rule 163(2). Firms with the most actively traded
shares under Rule 163(2) would move up to the new USM. The USM would
then become a stepping stone—a feeder mechanism—to the Official List.
The LSE made a few minor concessions here. For instance, after negotiating
with CBI, the exchange dropped its original proposal to automatically graduate a company to full listing as soon as its capitalization exceeded 10 million pounds.[31]

The details of the final rules, published in October 1980, show how the
LSE made it easier and less expensive for companies to quote shares on the
USM than on the Official List (see Tables 2.1 and 2.2, pages 24, 26).[32] Other
than in exceptional cases, there were no minimum capitalization requirements equivalent to the Official List's half a million pounds. USM companies
needed a track record of only three years instead of five. They had to fulfill
the accounting provisions of the Companies Act of 1948 (section 38) for all
firms selling shares to the public. They did not, however, have to submit an
accountant's report to the exchange, where sponsors, conscious of their reputation and expecting a thorough investigation, would enlist the most pres-
tigious accounting firms.[33] In fact, because USM companies were covered
only by the UK Companies Act regime but not the more rigorous regimen of
the LSE's Official List, they did not have to undergo any prevetting of
prospectuses by the exchange, and they did not have to include a clause
stating that nothing material (that is, significant) would be omitted. These
disclosure requirements were significantly lower than those for the Official
List. Finally, the USM companies needed to offer only 10 percent, whereas
the Official List required companies to offer at least 25 percent of shares to
the public.[34]

The LSE, pursuing its goals, thus gave the USM a protectionist feeder form.
The USM's low quoting and disclosure requirements assured that smaller
companies could easily list and postponed the selection of high-quality companies. The goal of creating a market that would attract investors took a
backseat, as the best-performing USM companies could easily and inexpen-
sively move up to the Official List. Instead, the USM itself served as a selection mechanism to channel the best companies to the official market.

Another Feeder Market

In its first five years, the USM was a vibrant market in unlisted company
shares. Financial service providers and investors eagerly participated, as they

expected a stream of new revenues from the entrance of smaller companies into the market.[35] From the LSE's vantage point, however, the USM had fallen short of expectations.

In the early years, the USM did meet the LSE's goal of providing a flow of high-quality companies. In the first five years of trading, 34 of 422 USM companies transferred to the Official List. Of these, 26 were among the best-performing USM companies, and of the very best-performing companies (those reporting profit growth rates of more than 50 percent per year), 12.4 percent transferred to the Official List.[36] The trend continued as the USM began to sputter in the late 1980s. Thus in creating its smaller-company market as a midway point to a full listing, the LSE was able to preserve the preeminence of the Official List. The USM facilitated equity financing for smaller firms without fostering competition, as in the United States, where the NYSE failed to lure the Nasdaq's most successful companies, like Microsoft.

Nevertheless, the USM did not stamp out all residual activity on the OTC market. By the mid-1980s, approximately twenty-two dealers traded in the shares of some 210 OTC companies, and the LSE again interpreted the simmering of OTC activity as a competitive threat and responded with a second new market.[37] Emerging from the Big Bang liberalization and regulatory reform (discussed in Chapter 5), the exchange sought to take advantage of its continued de facto monopoly while it lasted by thwarting even the most minute indications of competition. In January of 1987, nine months before an international market crash, the LSE opened the Third Market, in yet another attempt to prevent the emergence of a Nasdaq next door. The form, again based on the feeder model, encompassed even lower barriers to listing than the USM. Companies needed only one year of audited accounts (and this could be waived for some start-ups), and sponsors belonging to the exchange, not the LSE's quotations department, vetted firms seeking quotation. The Third Market essentially offered an over-the-counter market with one added protection for investors. Member firms enjoyed exclusive trading in Third Market shares, but investors gained guaranteed compensation in the case of member failure.[38]

The Third Market managed to attract only ninety-two companies, many of which eventually transferred to the USM. Even this small number managed to sap some of the activity from the OTC market, and the effects of the 1986 Financial Services Act took care of the rest. Under the act, OTC dealers had to meet capital adequacy and registration standards, which reduced their incentives to risk their own capital in the thinly traded smaller-companies market. When the LSE officially closed the Third Market in 1990, three years after it opened, the OTC market had been much reduced, and the LSE had gone a long way toward meeting its protectionist goal.

In sum, from the late 1970s until the late 1980s, the LSE dominated market-making processes in the British smaller-company sector. Government agencies were hesitant and lacked the expertise to interfere in the minutia of creating financial markets. The traditional industry lobbies had little influence, and British venture capitalists, as an identifiable group of actors with concrete goals, did not exist in any meaningful political sense. They would take the lead in the 1993–1994 domestic debates over smaller-company markets, but before then they had still not yet entered the political arena.

Stock Market Experimentation in France

The Second Marché, introduced with great fanfare as one of President François Mitterrand's 1983 U-turn financial reforms, was the third smaller-company stock market experiment in France since 1973. Like its two predecessors, as well as Britain's USM, the Second Marché emerged from a primarily domestic creation process, and the story of its origins can be told with scant reference to Brussels or international developments. The national financial systems and the financing problems facing smaller companies differed profoundly on the two shores of the English Channel. Not surprisingly, the politics behind the new markets and their ultimate forms varied too. The absence in France of a cartel of brokers relatively autonomous from government distinguished the French from the British process. The French stock exchanges, in fact, had hardly any influence at all. Rather, a technocratic elite, enabled by a state-dominated financial system, initiated proposals for new markets and saw them implemented.

Financial Decision-Making in France

Creating new markets is a challenge in any financial system. The credit-based French arrangements of the 1970s and much of the 1980s, characterized by state-administered pricing, provided a particularly unfriendly setting for experimentation in market-based solutions to financial problems. This historical context had two main implications. First, creating a market was not, in and of itself, likely to yield the intended outcomes of improved financing mechanisms for the smaller-company sector. Promulgations to the contrary, the new markets of the 1980s were not a success.[39]

Second, only state civil servants, empowered by a financial system that largely insulated them from parliament and societal groups, could have carried out such a bold and idealistic policy endeavor. As other scholars have noted, France's capital markets and underdeveloped securities industry, despite Valéry Giscard d'Estaing's efforts to promote them, remained on the margins of national finance throughout the 1970s and much of the 1980s.[40] The French cartel of securities brokers, which nominally controlled seven stock exchanges, lacked the autonomy, resources, and legitimacy of its British counterpart. The brokers' executive organization was essentially a policy tool of the Ministry of Finance and the securities regulator, the Commission des Opérations de Bourse (COB). Furthermore, the authority to make listing rules, as well as the discretion to judge compliance, belonged not to the brokers but to the COB. Like the rest of the French financial system of the period, power was ultimately concentrated in the Ministry of Finance, which controlled the COB and the brokers through formal and informal means and enjoyed a position relatively insulated from the pressures of politicians and interest groups.[41]

Given these relations among the players and the relative unimportance of the securities industry to the economy, the process that led to the Second Marché's creation was necessarily top-down, insular, and incremental. Initiated by the Planning Commission at the end of the 1960s, this process began in earnest through a series of government-commissioned studies authored by committees of the financial elite. Between 1972 and 1983, the Ministry of Finance selected three proposals for new stock markets and had them implemented by the COB. In this way, the creation of the 1983 market and its two predecessors remained the domain of the elites, outside of the arena of public debate.

Ironically, the policy experiment in smaller-company markets sprouted largely from the same seed as the dirigiste policies aimed to forge giant national champions in strategic industrial and high-technology sectors. Both trace their roots to a large degree to the Treaty of Rome in 1959 and the drive to make French firms, protected behind tariffs, competitive under the new European Economic Community trading regime. The European challenge prompted French planners to shift emphasis from output maximization to individual firm competitiveness, a pattern reflected in the change of priorities between the Fourth Plan (1962–1965) and the Fifth Plan (1965–1970).[42] While the national champions dominated French industrial policy in the 1970s and early 1980s, they were not the only outcome of this new attention to firm competitiveness. A concern about SMEs and a specific recommendation in the Sixth Plan (1970–1975) to investigate ways to breathe life into the moribund over-the-counter market set off the process that eventually led to two market experiments in the 1970s and the Second Marché in 1983.[43]

The interest in SMEs among the financial establishment also had roots in postwar political and social bargains. In pursuit of the twin goals of economic modernization and social stability, French governments tried to balance resources between favored strategic firms and sectors on the one hand and groups, such as family farmers, who stood to lose from economic rationalization on the other. Among the most affected were SMEs in traditional industries. Creating new markets specifically designed to increase the availability of financing for some of these firms was among the multiple post-1968 policies and programs aimed, at least in part, to appease well-organized smaller-company groups, ultimately with an eye to maintaining social order. That many of the country's medium-sized suppliers sold to provincial markets explains why policy discussions about creating the Second Marché and its predecessors were inseparable from broader debates about political and economic decentralization and the role of provincial financial centers.[44]

The range of available ideas about the causes of and solutions to the mounting economic crises also shaped the motivations of technocratic elites. The specific notion that a healthy smaller-company sector was an essential ingredient for economic renewal in France (and that an ailing one required a remedy), for instance, reflected academic currency. Some political economists, sensing a historic economic juncture in the early 1970s, had begun to doubt the ability of large firms, designed to take advantage of economies of scale, to produce the levels of economic growth and technological innovation that had sustained a steady increase in living standards for three decades. These political economists entertained a future of highly specialized, horizontally organized firms, as opposed to the postwar hierarchical structures predicated on mass production and economies of scale. They envisioned a future of smaller, nimble firms producing for niche markets. For example, for the Regulation School (École de la Régulation), a leading French intellectual source of these ideas, the nation's economic troubles represented the breakdown of a postwar configuration. The combination of Fordist modes of production and attendant social relations had run its course, and at least part of the remedy lay in smaller companies, better able to benefit from and develop new technologies and to compete in an increasingly international economy.[45]

The French planning elite had begun to absorb these ideas, connecting the fate of smaller companies (and therefore the resolutions of their problems) with future competitiveness, innovation, and job creation. By the middle of the 1970s, the political discourse the planners used depicted the health of SMEs, especially high-technology firms, as a strategic issue of critical public policy concern. As a source of future employment, technological innovation, and economic growth, the well-being of smaller companies came to represent a vital element of France's economic rejuvenation and international position. As Jonah Levy and others have noted, the ideas culminated first in the "small-is-beautiful rhetoric" of the rightist government of Raymond Barre and in the prioritization of smaller companies in the 1976–1981 plan. These ideas resurfaced in the 1980s under the guise of the "associational liberalism" project of the leftist government of Michel Rocard.[46]

The Challenge of Financing Smaller Companies

Given this institutional, political, and ideational backdrop, it is not surprising that some French technocrats attributed the decade's economic troubles to dirigisme's neglect of the smaller-company sector. When the economic and currency crises of the 1970s exposed the shortcomings of dirigisme, these policymakers inside the Ministry of Finance and the Planning Commission already had at their disposal an interpretation of the problem and an alternative set of solutions: both featured the smaller-company sector.

Certainly, these firms suffered during the 1970s. The financial balance sheet of French smaller companies had experienced a gradual deterioration throughout the decade. As revenues and profits waned, French smaller companies grew increasingly reliant on borrowing, especially on short-term credit at unfavorable rates.[47] In 1967 short-term loans comprised 40.2 percent of liabilities in French companies with less than 500 employees. By 1976, the same statistic had reached 50.9 percent.[48]

Apart from the few favored by the national champion policies, however, all sectors suffered, and the statistics do not support the notion that dirigisme neglected the smaller company over others. Nor did the relative difficulty that smaller firms faced in acquiring financing necessarily presuppose market failure. In times of economic crisis, as banks become more risk averse, they tend to raise interest rates disproportionately for smaller firms because of their vulnerability to bankruptcy. Nevertheless, in the France of the 1970s, with smaller companies viewed as a strategic sector, the policy elite began to blame a dirigiste financial system biased against these enterprises.

The state-dominated national financial system of the 1970s, characterized by the *encadrement du crédit* and a banking system concentrated in a few semipublic and private firms, enabled the Trésor to favor a select group of national champions.[49] Despite the Barre government's smaller-company rhetoric, its policies intensified a pattern in which the lion's share of financial resources flowed to a select number of giant strategic firms.[50] So as economic problems mounted, it became increasingly plausible to interpret the support of national champions as a zero-sum game, with smaller companies the losing party. Not only were the large benefiting at the expense of the small, it seemed, but also the concentration of leading big banks in Paris was contributing to the dearth of credit and equity financing at the provincial and local levels. In 1979, for instance, the government-commissioned Mayoux Report interpreted the financing problems of smaller firms as intimately tied to the centralization of banking in Paris and, consequently, recommended a major decentralization program that included the dismantling of *encadrement du crédit*.[51]

The Mayoux Report, like other policy documents of the times, maintained that smaller companies could take advantage of far fewer financing options, especially when compared with the national champions. Next to an unending list of government investment funds, programs, and tax incentives, the argument today seems perplexing. There simply was no shortage of official efforts aimed at supplying financial resources to smaller companies. Reflecting the highly centralized financial system in France, most of these programs offered capital to smaller enterprises through fiscal incentives or government-controlled allocation mechanisms. As part of a general campaign to support smaller companies, the Giscard-Barre government, for example, adopted a series of fiscal measures between 1977 and 1979 to improve the companies' profitability.[52] These provisions were accompanied by a substantial increase in the government-subsidized lending and investment activity of regional development corporations *(les sociétés de développement régional)*. The 1970s, moreover, saw a proliferation of local, provincial, and national investment funds *(les instituts de participation)*, many targeted specifically at smaller enterprises. The funds were primarily national government initiatives, often emanating from the *institut de développement industriel* (IDI), and included such experiments as Sofinnova, a "venture capital" firm created in 1972 for investing in innovative smaller French companies.[53] The authors of the Mayoux Report were able to list eleven government measures introduced between 1977 and 1979 that were designed specifically to improve the availability of equity financing for smaller companies, from tax incentives to the introduction of new types of ownership shares.[54]

Despite seemingly abundant sources of financing, policymakers could still claim a relative deprivation of opportunities for smaller companies. The reasons were complex. First and foremost, SMEs and the other passed-over economic sectors could not as readily benefit as larger companies could from a constant and guaranteed flow of credit, and the statistics show that the bulk of resources, despite the rightist government's rhetoric, continued to flow to the national champions.[55] Second, investors and lenders did not always have incentives to tie their money up in illiquid, nonquoted companies. In the France of the 1970s, investors and lenders had to compare the benefits of participating in government programs for smaller companies against often more-enticing options that reflected alternative government goals and the general bias of the financial system.

Finally, the owners of smaller companies, like their counterparts in the United Kingdom, often avoided the financing options that did exist.[56] Whether this pattern revealed the storied fear of losing control of the family enterprise, or a tax system biased against equity financing, the owners of SMEs usually chose independence over letting outside financiers purchase shares of their companies.[57] The team of financial elites who authored the Mayoux Report echoed a widely held perception in associating perverse incentives that undermined the smaller-company sector to the underdevelopment of provincial financial centers, the concentration of finance in Paris, and the neglect of SMEs under dirigisme.

The turn toward smaller companies therefore reflected not only the absorption of academic ideas into elite policy circles but also a reaction to an underperforming package of dirigiste policies and a financial system that enabled it. If policies and arrangements that damaged the prospects of smaller companies failed to revive the French economy, then its converse, the promotion of the sector, seemed a pragmatic alternative.

The Bourse Problem

Beginning with their preparations for the Sixth Plan (1970–1975), French technocrats identified an endless stream of smaller-company financing problems and remedies, including what ultimately became the refrain of the Second Marché's planners: the markets supplied by the seven French stock exchanges catered exclusively to large, established firms. The requirements for an exchange listing, according to the logic, prevented small and medium-sized companies from raising capital through an initial public offering and dampened the potential aftermarket for their shares. These rules eliminated cheap and abundant financing through direct access to national savings, leaving only less attractive intermediated financing from government programs and public and private banks. The partial exception was the uninviting *marché hors cote,* the French OTC market that had all but dried up by the early 1970s.

Interpreting the forms of stock markets as a problem reflected in part a cross-border trend, as we saw above in the UK cases. By the mid-1970s, ideas very similar to Hartmut Schmidt's had already permeated smaller-company policy discourse across Europe. Yet despite the possible international influences, the French smaller-company bourse problem had primarily native origins. Between 1961 and 1974, the French government had introduced a number of reforms that reduced smaller markets' access to stock markets. Designed to modernize the securities industry, the reforms had the effect of centralizing equity market activity in Paris, where barriers to quoting were too high for even medium-sized companies.

Two measures in particular hurt the six provincial stock exchanges (Bordeaux, Lille, Lyon, Marseille, Nancy, and Nantes) and, by extension, smaller companies that depended on financial services of these exchanges. Both measures belonged to the 1960s government attempt to encourage investment in stocks and bonds, a project that, despite short interruptions, continued into the twenty-first century.[58] First, in 1961, the government sought to improve price efficiency by centralizing trading of any one stock on a single stock exchange (ending the tradition of trading the same stock on more than one exchange) and introducing a central post-trade quotation system in Paris *(l'unicité de cotation).*[59] The mechanism, based on a commission-splitting arrangement, sent orders and revenues to Parisian brokers, a trend that further diminished the working risk capital of provincial brokers and, as a consequence, the liquidity of provincial bourses.[60] Second, in 1968, the newly created COB launched a campaign to purge the exchanges of infrequently traded and non-dividend-bearing stocks.[61] Between 1968 and 1978, the stocks of 353 companies quoted on provincial exchanges were delisted. During the same period, only 12 new ones were introduced.[62]

In undermining the activity on provincial stock exchanges, these measures also hurt the financing prospects of small and medium-sized companies. Listing on the Paris exchange required the flotation of a larger number of shares than on the provincial exchanges, imposing a significant barrier for the owners of smaller companies primarily concerned about control.

A Technical Solution

Officials inside the Ministry of Finance and the COB sought to redress the bourse problem with a bourse solution. Giving smaller companies easier access to national savings through a properly designed market, they reasoned, would provide a financing option formerly reserved for established large companies. The first effort came in 1973, at the tail end of the Georges Pompidou presidency. The idea to revive the OTC market was first broached in the Sixth Plan as part of a general modernization of the French exchanges and was subsequently picked up in 1971 in a COB study on stock markets. The Ministry of Finance then asked the COB to devise a specific plan. Finally, in July 1973, by introducing new rules that changed the way French brokers traded OTC shares, the COB began a thirty-year experimentation process in smaller-company markets.[63]

The new rules extended market making *(la contrepartie technique)*, introduced earlier in the trading of officially listed shares, to the OTC market. Previously, French brokers, acting strictly as agents for their clients, had earned their trading revenue from fixed commissions for matching buy and sell orders of company shares *(la procédure ordinaire)*. The new market-making system allowed brokers to risk their own capital but obliged them to quote a designated stock and to buy and sell it on demand at their quoted price.[64] The introduction of *contrepartie technique,* at least in theory, added a dealer element to the existing auction trading system.

The contrast between French and British experimentation in their respective OTC markets shows the differing motivations of the actors who spearheaded the processes of change. In the United Kingdom, the over-the-counter market existed largely outside the purview of the powerful official cartel of brokers, under the LSE umbrella. Efforts to stimulate OTC trading began in the early 1970s at the instigation of private financial companies operating outside the exchange. Even though the Thatcher government indicated it would support these initiatives as a means of pursuing enterprise policies, the London exchange was able to use its relative autonomy from government and its prominent historical position in the financial system to preempt the campaign and shape change toward the LSE's own goals.

In France, the process followed a different path. Unlike the member-owners of the powerful LSE, French brokers were government officials *(les officiers ministériels)* appointed by the Ministry of Finance. Since 1968, brokerages could merge with each other, but thick firewalls separating banking from trading firms had promised brokerages' continued low capital base and helped to perpetuate their marginal role in the allocation of financial resources. The government further enfeebled the securities brokers, who maintained an official cartel over trading, by consolidating them into a single national association *(Compagnie nationale des agents de change)*. Although they elected their own eight-member executive body *(La Chambre syndicale)* and its chairman *(le syndic)*, the Ministry of Finance appointed the general secretary, who oversaw the secretariat consisting of approximately 500 employees.

In addition, when the government created the COB in 1967, it vested in the new securities regulator, not in the brokers organization, the authority to decide the listing rules (that is, the listing authority) and the companies that would comply with them. Though the COB was modeled loosely on the U.S. Securities and Exchange Commission and allegedly given a degree of autonomy from the government, the Ministry of Finance in fact kept a tight leash on the COB, especially in its first decades, and used the new securities regulator as a means for controlling the brokers and modernizing the stock exchanges and the securities industry.[65]

The COB's motivations in introducing market making on the *marché hors cote* thus primarily reflected government goals of meeting the financing needs of smaller companies, and the COB's ability to carry out the policy stemmed from a financial system dominated by the state. The British notion of "off-exchange" trading had no real significance in France, as over-the-counter flows had to go through a member of the official cartel of brokers as readily as trading activity on the official list. So unlike their counterparts in the United Kingdom, the French brokers stood to benefit from government efforts to stimulate the *marché hors cote*. Even if they had had the wherewithal to oppose government efforts, which they did not, the French *agents de change* had nothing to lose in government efforts to introduce market making.

The COB's 1973 experiment was part of the incremental effort since the 1960s to reform the financial system by bolstering the stock and bond markets—a policy of which the COB's own creation was a part. But French policymakers also borrowed from the 1971 reorganization of the U.S. OTC market, for decades an active dealers' market based on market making. French officials hoped that the market-making trading system would encourage investment in the infrequently traded companies of the French OTC market, as it appeared to be doing in the United States; end the stream of OTC-company expulsions; lower costs; and improve the availability of equity financing for smaller companies.[66]

The market-making experiment, however, failed to take hold and, as a consequence, failed to enliven the French OTC market. International and domestic economic conditions were not conducive to equity markets. But the main culprit behind the experiment's failure lay in a financial system characterized by incentives that encouraged risk-averse behavior. France was still infertile terrain for the risky business of market making. The *marché hors cote* reform came fifteen years before the "little big bang" would crack open the brokers cartel in 1988.[67] The high capital reserve requirements of the times ensured that few brokers could accept the risks of market making. And those who did soon abandoned the enterprise, as low levels of investor participation and burdensome regulations on bookkeeping left little scope for compensating the enormous risks of holding illiquid shares of companies that did not provide high levels of information.[68]

The uncertain quality of companies whose shares traded on the *marché hors cote* posed an additional problem. OTC companies did not have to comply with the COB's stringent (but infrequently observed) admission requirements.[69] In fact, apart from meeting the relatively low reporting standards for public companies, the OTC companies had few other requirements, were practically unregulated, and, as a result, attracted little investor interest. More important, these companies were among the least likely to support a market-making system that depended on the availability of large numbers of shares. The owners of OTC companies—largely the founding families—tended to use the market as a mechanism for occasional trading to solve succession and working capital problems, while ensuring they retained control.

If there is a broader lesson, it is that a mechanism for enhancing liquidity cannot work in the absence of interested buyers and sellers, unless market makers are somehow compensated for the provision of the public good. France in the early 1970s provided neither incentive for investors to trade OTC shares nor subsidization for market makers. Low barriers to quoting and low informational standards created a perception of a market of poor-quality companies, so market makers were not willing to supply liquidity for long. The risks of getting stuck with the shares of low-quality companies were simply too high.

Another Market Experiment

The COB created its second experiment in smaller-company markets, the Compartiment Spécial, in November 1977, more than a year after Raymond Barre, a conservative economist, became prime minister but still before the 1978 *loi Monory* (named after Finance Minister René Monory) blew new life into the French securities markets.[70] In doing so, the French national securities regulator adopted one of the key recommendations of the de Vabres Report, an investigation into how to reverse the decline of the six provincial exchanges. The COB had commissioned the report the previous year in response to the recommendations of the Seventh Plan (1975–1981), which saw support for smaller companies as a priority.[71] The origins of the Compartiment Spécial, like those of its predecessor, thus lie primarily in the policy currents of the times, which identified solutions to the dirigisme's shortcomings in the decentralization of French finance, in the promotion of regional financial centers, and in support of SMEs.[72]

The COB intended the Compartiment Spécial to be an exclusive segment midway between the OTC and the official list on all seven French stock exchanges and to provide companies historically too small for the main market with a timetable and expedited route to official listing. To gain access to this "fast track" process, candidate companies had to agree to meet the requirements of an official listing, including the much higher disclosure standards and thresholds of minimum percentages of circulating shares, within a three-year period. The Compartiment Spécial thus shared the key attribute of the feeder model. With the 1973 failure to revive the *marché hors cote* fresh in their minds, COB officials resorted to another strategy to give smaller companies the desired access to capital markets. They chose to leave behind the lemons and segment off the best companies— a design that actively ensured the *marché hors cote* would suffer from an adverse selection bias.[73] The strongest firms from the OTC market were expected to populate the Compartiment Spécial and three years later move upward to the official list.

The Compartiment Spécial's origins, form, and failure deviated from other

European feeder markets in ways that underscore the import of national financial systems, the particular actors who dominate them, and their motivations. The COB and Ministry of Finance officials treated the Compartiment Spécial as another technical and incremental effort in response to an earlier failure to improve smaller-company access to the capital market. Because of the government's clear control over the cartel of French brokers, the Ministry of Finance, unlike ministries in the United Kingdom, did not have to cope with an empowered stock exchange that could oppose and reshape policy initiatives. The absence of significant opposition meant that the Compartiment Spécial, like its predecessor, was much more a reflection of public policy goals. The centralization of decision making also meant that a separate market that might compete with the official market never entered the discussion. The old cartel of brokers would trade on the new Compartiment Spécial, which would ultimately help their businesses by sending young companies to the official list.

The Compartiment Spécial also failed. Its inability to foster the desired market dynamics was again rooted in the absence of willing buyers, sellers, and intermediaries, a symptom of the broader state-dominated financial system. Economic conditions between 1977 and 1983 did not help matters. Until the new tax incentives from the 1978 *loi Monory* kicked in, in fact, French households had continued to shift their savings into safer investments.[74] But the incentives did not extend to shares traded in the OTC market or the Compartiment Spécial.

Nor did companies show much interest in using the Compartiment Spécial as a stepping-stone to an official listing or to cheaper and more abundant financing. One reason was the enormous gap to be bridged in the three-year transition period. OTC companies typically offered a tiny percentage of their shares to the public, and Compartiment Spécial companies had to offer only 10 percent initially. Within three years, however, they had to meet the COB's requirement that officially listed companies float a minimum of 25 percent of the shares. The distance between the informational standards was equally wide. The OTC market served a purpose as an occasional trading mechanism that allowed owners to maintain control, and companies quoted on it did not necessarily want an official listing even if it promised easier financing on cheaper terms. The Compartiment Spécial failed to address these and other deeper and more complex obstacles to listing, including incentives that encouraged debt over equity financing.[75]

Mitterrand's U-turn and a Stock Market's Creation

In response to the failure of the Compartiment Spécial, the government, this time leftist under Mitterrand, created a third experiment in French smaller-company markets, the Second Marché, in February 1983. Like the two previous market experiments, the Second Marché was the immediate outcome of a government-sponsored report. The Dautresme Report, commissioned four months after Mitterrand's May 1981 victory and written as the economy fell deeply into crisis, gave a sweeping overview of the French savings and investment system. Recognizing the failure of the Compartiment Spécial in solving the bourse problem, Dautresme's committee offered a blueprint for a replacement smaller-company market, which it called *le marché cote*.[76] Five months after the report's April 1982 release, the Ministry of Finance, under Jacques Delors, approved the proposal for a new market, named the Second Marché. In January 1983 the COB announced plans for trading to begin on February 1.[77]

The French Socialist government created the Second Marché six months after the second devaluation under Mitterrand. Political economists have explicitly pointed to it as an example of the first wave of postdirigiste policies.[78] While Mitterrand's other economic policies may have departed decisively from earlier arrangements, the Second Marché represents continuity. Just as the previous rightist government continued to speak the language of markets while pursuing dirigiste policies, the new leftist government, despite an intensification of the state-led industrial policy, had not abandoned all traces of its predecessor's agenda.[79] Given Mitterrand's lack of interest in technical economic issues of this kind, the minister of finance and other top economic policymakers enjoyed a degree of autonomy to make incremental reforms, even before the policy switch.[80] The change of governments, for example, did not slow the COB's ongoing effort to modernize the stock exchanges.[81] Incremental changes to the smaller-company market, like those that turned the Compartiment Spécial into the Second Marché, were exactly the type of financial reform the Ministry of Finance could effect, via the COB, even during the early months of Mitterrand's presidency.

By the time of Mitterrand's 1982 decision to keep France in the European Monetary System (EMS), Delors' policymaking team had already put a socialist stamp on the bourse solution, as well as a number of other financial reform proposals similar to those of the previous market-oriented rightist government. The Dautresme Report—commissioned by the new socialist government's finance and budget ministers (Delors and Laurent Fabius) and released before the devaluation—provided political cover for Delors and the technocrats of the Ministry of Finance, who believed the preceding government had delayed necessary market-based financial reforms.[82] At least in terms of political rhetoric, then, Delors could claim he was not merely dusting off a Giscard-Barre–era market-embracing proposal.

Most important, here, the members of the Dautresme committee's working group on smaller companies, and later the Ministry of Finance and COB officials, saw in the Second Marché a domestic solution to a domestic problem.[83] The new market reflected an incremental and technical policy, designed to reverse the failures of the Compartiment Spécial. In this sense, the government promoted a market-based solution, not in contradiction or as a replacement to its overall socialist program, but rather as a way to compensate for the limitations of dirigiste policies.[84] In presenting the idea for a new market, the working group discussed at length how it would redress the shortcomings of its predecessor. Three stand out. The old rules prevented brokers from using a liquidity mechanism *(la contrepartie en avance)* that was in operation on the main market. The old rules also prohibited large institutional investors from owning shares. And the three-year period of transition to the official market proved too short for many companies.[85]

The Second Marché's Form

In deliberating over form, members of the Dautresme committee considered three alternative models.[86] The first, the U.S. Nasdaq model, reflected international best practice. In the eyes of multinational financial firms, especially the large institutional investors and their broker-dealer agents, the U.S. market already by 1982 represented the most successful form known. The second was Britain's USM model, a feeder market, which two years after its opening appeared an unabashed success. The failed French Compartiment Spécial, also a feeder market, was the third.

The USM and Compartiment Spécial shared the same underlying feeder principle: lowering disclosure standards and barriers to quoting was supposed to allow smaller companies easier access to capital markets and eventually, at least for the most successful firms, to move upward to the official national list. Despite their similarities, the two feeders had clear differences. By lowering standards quantitatively to ease company access to capital markets, the creators of the USM and Compartiment Spécial had not changed the quality of the standards, which remained firmly within distinct national traditions. Copying the USM model would have meant convergence with British standards, an impractical and radical change. Variation among the national feeder markets across Europe was very large, mirroring the vast differences in postwar financial systems. To give a sense of the distinctive bundle of national rules and traditions embedded in these markets, the Dautresme committee identified nine separate domestic laws and regulations governing behavior on the Compartiment Spécial. These rules ranged from those defining what stocks institutional investors could hold to those determining how share ownership should be registered to those governing the type of shares company owners were allowed to issue to ensure continued control.[87]

Considering these complexities, the Dautresme committee members and ultimately the Ministry of Finance understandably chose a slight modification of the Compartiment Spécial for the Second Marché. The creators of the 1983 market intended it, like all feeders, to serve as a staging ground for the nation's future corporate giants. The best companies would be selected out and graduated to the official market after first residing on the Second Marché. Informational standards and barriers to quoting were lower than on the official market (see Tables 2.1 and 2.2, pages 24, 26). The new French market required company owners to place only 10 percent of their shares in external hands, compared with 25 percent for the official market, and in certain cases smaller companies could issue preferential nonvoting shares.[88] To gain a listing, companies did not need a special audit of accounts, which was required by the COB and represented an intensive interrogation few smaller companies were willing to undergo. They merely needed to meet the much lower disclosure standards specified in national securities acts. Instead of the expensive procedure of issuing a listing prospectus, moreover, Second Marché companies only had to circulate an announcement in the official gazette.

Continuities with the Compartiment Spécial were unmistakable. The Second Marché companies had to use French accounting standards and reporting norms.[89] By making the new market part of the official exchange, its creators extended to the quoted stocks the same *loi Monory* tax benefits given five years earlier to investors of officially listed shares. This feature was a direct response to the problem, as interpreted by Dautresme's committee, that investors lacked incentives for holding Compartiment Spécial shares. The committee members recommended and the COB adopted new relations between the issuing company and a broker to help ensure liquidity. The proposal came in reaction to the Compartiment Spécial's failure to attract high volumes of trading. The contracts were to guarantee liquidity within rules that preclude U.S.-style market making. The creators of the Second Marché also adopted a modified version of the Compartiment Spécial's three-year program. The old market had required companies to graduate upward within three years, a rule that meant companies also had to comply with the tougher standards within the same time frame. Finding the requirement too burdensome, the Dautresme committee modified the program so that after three years a company would have alternatives: graduate, remain on the Second Marché, or move downward to the *marché hors cote*.[90]

Finally, the Second Marché's form, like the Compartiment Spécial's, reflected French policy debates that saw the financing problems facing smaller companies and the decline of provincial stock exchanges as integrally related. When the COB introduced the Compartiment Spécial, it simultaneously determined, based on location, the exchange on which a company would list.[91] The Second Marché inherited the same geographic divisions. In the United States, in contrast, geography ceased to be an issue with the advent of Nasdaq's electronic quotation system, which enabled equal access regardless of location, whereas in the United Kingdom the debate had ended with the 1973 closure of the British regional exchanges and centralization of trading in London.

In sum, the Second Marché's form was an effort to improve its predecessor incrementally. Like the decision to create a new market, its form resulted from a highly centralized, top-down, and domestic political process. The bourse solution and the specific plans for the Second Marché had emerged from domestic debates about French economic problems and embodied one branch of proposed remedies for the financing problems facing French smaller firms. In the first months of the Mitterrand presidency, a government-commissioned committee developed the plan for the new market. As in the British example, French financiers whose activities might qualify only under a loose definition of venture capitalism had no political voice and no place in the financial policymaking establishment.

The timing of implementation coincided with Mitterrand's historic U-turn. In this respect, the external constraints that prompted Mitterrand's policy about-face probably triggered the implementation of the new market proposal as well. By April of 1982, however, still before the second devaluation and the EMS decision, the Ministry of Finance was already in the process of creating the Second Marché. Even without the major shift in economic policy, the Socialist government would likely have carried through with its implementation, albeit with less fanfare and irony, and perhaps not as rapidly.

Thus the French market-creation processes that gave rise to new smaller company stock markets in the 1980s were very much like the British. Problems perceived by domestic actors prompted the creation of new markets, and existing national financial arrangements strongly conditioned the direction and extent of change, yielding new feeder markets with national flavors. The competitive and ideational effects of Nasdaq's success were beginning to seep into domestic discussions but were not more than background factors. Finally to return to the book's main argument, the impact from regional developments was marginal at best. The early and modest EEC intergovernmental agreements to coordinate company listing rules had only a small indirect effect on domestic market-making processes. The absence of European-level lobbies and debate, moreover, gave interested Brussels bureaucrats few if any opportunities for effecting change. In short, the efforts by European Commission officials to improve financing possibilities for smaller companies via supranational solutions, outlined in the previous chapter, had no detectable effect on market-creating processes at the domestic level.

CHAPTER 5

Capital Mobility, Politics, and New Financial Interests, 1992–1994

A year can make all the difference. Between April 1994 and June 1995, national exchanges in Europe abruptly became market innovators, and this chapter focuses on the months before the turnaround. It addresses head-on the argument that capital mobility, as opposed to EU developments, provides a better explanation for the outbreak of the competitive mimicry and the organizational forms of the resultant new stock markets. According to this line of reasoning, as levels of capital mobility rise, financial intermediaries, like venture capitalists, who manage investment portfolios develop preferences for more-efficient national arrangements and win battles with immobile local officials and stock exchanges. This proposition, as Chapter 2 discussed, rests on the notion that mobility gives venture capitalists, quoted companies, and other market participants alternatives to national financial centers, drawing exchanges into cross-border competition and pressuring them to adopt models considered best suited for retaining customers.

Two types of evidence demonstrate the insufficiency of cross-border capital mobility as an explanation for the creation of venture capital preferences and their enhanced influence in altering domestic financial arrangements. First, by 1993 levels of capital mobility had already enabled cross-border financial activity in Europe for at least five years in a number of sectors, including the trading of large-company shares. If higher levels of capital mobility were responsible for the strengthened position of venture capitalists, the creation of the new stock markets—or at least competition in the smaller company sector among Europe's exchanges—would likely have occurred earlier.

Second, country-level evidence ties the origins of U.S.-style venture capitalism to the creation of the feeder markets, offering a vivid example of how public policy plays a major role in spawning new economic interests. To be sure, cross-border capital mobility was a necessary condition for the emergence of venture capital in Europe. Yet the creation of the USM and the Second Marché, both political responses to the problems facing smaller companies, gave rise to new expectations among private-sector financiers about the prospects for venture capitalism in Europe. These embryonic interests coalesced when the feeders did not recover from the 1987 international market crash, leaving the new financiers with a common "exits" problem: lots of investments in young companies but no stock markets through which to sell them for profit. As the tale of policy battles in the United Kingdom and France attest, as recently as 1994 Europe's venture capitalists were politically and organizationally weak, failing in contests against exchanges, regulators, and ministries. Despite relatively high levels of capital mobility and a new awareness of common problems, venture capitalists overcame their political liabilities only in the aftermath of the Brussels intervention, as Chapter 6 shows.

The Timing of Change

Chapter 2 spelled out the 1994–1995 turning point in the market-creation pattern. Having made decisions regarding their failing feeder markets only months before, the national exchanges announced plans to launch new stock markets that would better meet the needs of venture capitalists. The timing of this apparently new venture capitalist influence did not follow a discernable increase in capital mobility.

By 1992 speculative financial flows were already sufficient to wreak havoc on the European Rate Mechanism (ERM) of the European Monetary System (EMS), forcing devaluations of several currencies, leading to the British pound's eventual removal, and jeopardizing plans for a single currency.[1] Yet as early as the mid-1980s, securities trading and capital easily crossed national frontiers in the region. Perhaps the best example is that of the London-based dealers who stole trading activity away from the Paris, Frankfurt, and other European exchanges. Cross-border turnover statistics are notoriously difficult to gauge in Europe during the late 1980s and early 1990s, because exchanges used different methods for calculating turnover, and the activity of London-based dealers shifted on and off the exchanges (where trades were recorded), depending on national and EC rules, which were very much in flux.[2] These statistical problems notwithstanding, the early success of the London Stock Exchange's SEAQ International quotation system, which formalized and encouraged existing activity, paints a clear picture of a vibrant London-based dealer market in continental stock trading. Thus since at least the 1986 Big Bang, when the London exchange launched this first salvo into what remains a highly competitive market, capital mobility had reached adequate levels for European securities dealers to create markets across borders.

An examination of quantitative measures of capital mobility leads to similar conclusions. Openness indicators, focusing on government restrictions on inward and outward financial flows, reflect some of the underlying costs of moving capital across borders.[3] The timeline in Figure 5.1 demonstrates that many European countries had lifted capital restrictions more than a decade before the mid-1990s rash of market innovation. The United Kingdom, Germany, and the Netherlands made their last major liberalizations in 1979, 1981, and 1983, respectively, and have since remained among the world's most financially open countries. Other European governments liberalized later, following their EC commitments. Italy made its last major liberalization in 1988, and France in 1989. While France kept minor restrictions until

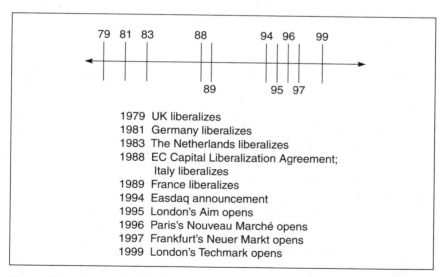

Figure 5.1. Capital mobility and the timing of the new stock markets.

1998, Italy fully opened in 1993. Another indicator of capital mobility, actual flows of financial assets, yields a similar story.[4]

If increased mobility strengthens the hand of the owners and managers of financial assets, venture capitalists should have done better in their conflicts against immobile stock exchanges during the late 1980s and certainly in the early and 1990s. Instead, as the next sections of this chapter show, British and French venture capitalists and their allies made little headway in battles against immobile national exchanges through 1994.

Creating Venture Capitalism in the United Kingdom

In the United Kingdom, before the creation of the USM, American-style venture capitalists—financial intermediaries investing in high-growth companies at early stages of development—had not emerged in significant numbers. The only identifiable venture capital industry was what Americans called private equity—the use of capital for management buy-outs, buy-ins, and mergers. There were no industry organizations, no industry standards and statistics, and no political voice.[5]

British venture capitalists entered the political and economic arena as an identifiable industry when the USM was created in 1980. Private equity firms had not participated in the discussions about the USM's creation in the late 1970s. They were not focused on start-up companies at that time and had no pressing agenda for the USM's form. Once the feeder market showed promise, however, especially in the relatively high valuations of its early days, private equity firms began to think of the USM as a potential Nasdaq of Britain—a mechanism through which they could sell successful companies, including young ones, to investors.

As Chapter 1 discussed, a U.S.-style venture capitalist firm attracts capital from asset managers and wealthy individuals, invests it in risky young companies, and makes profits for the firm and its investors by selling those companies for more than the firm paid. The range of exit mechanisms includes sales either to larger companies in the same industry (trade sale) or to other financiers. Because of the potential to get a better price, however, venture capitalists generally prefer to sell shares to the public through a listing on a stock market.

With new expectations of profits through risky investment in small, high-growth enterprises, some British private equity firms dove headlong into the risky world of American-style venture capitalism. The new venture capital activity thus grew largely out of expectations forged through the USM's introduction.[6] British private equity firms began to solicit capital from pension funds, insurance companies, and other institutional investors for their newly created venture capital funds.

Britain's experiment in venture capitalism would not have mattered much had the USM's creation not coincided with the 1979 abolition of capital controls in the United Kingdom. In the 1980s, as American and Japanese institutional investors raced into London, relatively large sums of international risk capital began to enter Europe for the first time in the postwar era. As part of their asset-allocation strategies, the portfolio managers of these savings pools designated a portion of their capital to high-risk and high-rewards investments. They saw in the new regional economies another Silicon Valley to supply entrepreneurial companies, especially around Cambridge.[7] According to the British Venture Capital Association (BVCA), created the previous year, by 1984 venture capital firms had invested 38 million pounds in early stage and start-up companies, from a near-zero base. By 1989 their investments had reached 215 million pounds. Thus at the very same time that British venture capitalists began soliciting risk capital, asset managers were searching for opportunities in Europe to invest in the shares of risky young companies, as they had been doing since the late 1970s in the United States.[8]

Venture capitalists were not the only ones with an interest in smaller-company stock markets. A second group of financial companies had developed a specialization in providing services to USM companies, especially in assisting them to enter the new market. Rather than the merchant banks of the Issuing Houses Association, who had traditionally provided services to enterprises entering the Official List, most of the smaller-company service providers were brokerage and accounting firms, including both members and nonmembers of the LSE. In the first five years of the USM, only seven of the top twenty sponsors of new issues were traditional issuing houses.[9] The business of these conservative merchant banks rested on bringing high-quality companies to the Official List. The issuing houses feared that the potential for poor postquotation performance and bankruptcies among the risky USM companies would in the long run damage the issuing houses' own reputations. Their reluctance to sponsor USM companies also corresponded to a recovery of the new issues market for the Official List. Together, these two factors opened the door to other financial firms willing to develop a specialization in smaller firms. In addition to public-offering specialists, the emerging sector included niche-market making, public relations, law, accountancy, stock brokering, merchant banking, and investment management firms.

Between 1980 and 1985 the new smaller-company service providers earned large sums from fees attached to newly quoted companies. Revenues from USM activity amounted to 40 percent of the overall fee incomes from equity issuing, for example, and the newly specialized firms were well positioned to provide the USM companies with future services.[10] However, in 1985 the USM activity began to decline, and by the end of the 1980s, the feeder market proved a disaster for participants. Unlike the Official List, the USM showed no signs of recovering from the 1987 international stock market crash or the 1989–1991 recession.

An End to a Decade-long Experiment

The decline of the once-successful 1980 feeder market and the Third Market's utter failure and 1990 closure (see Chapter 4) prompted a rethinking at the LSE of its role in providing a financing platform for smaller companies and set the stage for shutting down the USM. The absence of a competitive threat from the OTC market removed the pressure to provide a separate market for smaller companies, and LSE members offered three arguments for why the exchange should retreat from its experiment in smaller company markets.

The first argument was the same one raised in opposition to the creation of the USM. Only in the early 1990s the promulgators of this argument could point to two failed smaller-company markets as evidence. They contended that the lesson from the USM's post-1985 decline, its inability to recover after the 1987 international stock market crash, and the Third Market's disastrous experience was that markets with low levels of regulation would eventually fail to attract investors and damage the LSE's credibility as the overseer of orderly and fair markets.[11]

The second argument reflected the need for the LSE to behave more like a private company with a bottom line in facing the revolutionary changes beginning to take place in global finance. By the early 1990s, the exchange faced a revenue squeeze as it entered a new competition in the large-company sector. This meant a renewed focus on providing trading, listing, and informational services aimed at large companies, the LSE's primary source of revenues. The strategy not only met the needs of the LSE as an organization in transformation but also suited the big international financial houses that dominated the board of directors and that cared little about smaller-company equity finance in the United Kingdom. For these influential LSE members, there was little rationale for providing financing services to smaller firms.[12]

The final argument maintained that the USM duplicated the role of the Official List and thus represented unnecessary and potentially damaging fragmentation. There had always been some overlap between the Official List and the USM.[13] But LSE members began to point out these redundancies with the implementation of the European Economic Community's Admissions Directive (79/279/EEC)—evidence that during these years European integration was beginning to affect domestic market-making processes, albeit on the edges. The directive mandated that officially listed companies in Europe needed only a three-year trading record. In implementing the rule, the LSE had reduced its Official List requirement from five to three years. Even though it had lowered the USM's requirements from three to two years in 1990, many believed the new one-year gap gave companies the incentive to list directly on the Official List and bypass the USM altogether.

Then in 1992, the LSE indicated it would make provisions to ease official listing to qualified young companies, with track records or not, that were developing and commercializing new technologies. This change in the LSE's rulebook (Chapter 20) came in response to potential foreign competition from the Nasdaq itself. UK biotechnology and other companies had begun to raise capital by listing on the U.S. market, and the LSE acted to stop this trend in its tracks. LSE officials were whispering that the Official List would become Britain's Nasdaq, a line of thinking that would later seem naive.[14] In making these changes, the LSE simultaneously undermined any remaining incentives for young companies to list on the USM. "Now, in response to European directives," argued an LSE official in a public address, "entry to the Official List is available on essentially identical terms to those of the USM. It is often said that you cannot have too much of a good thing, but to have two, almost identical, markets in one exchange is going too far."[15]

An LSE with different constraints and objectives might have considered a range of alternatives short of the USM's closure. Its survey of USM participants, completed in May 1992, yielded a broad range of solutions for the market's problems.[16] The two extreme solutions were either to do nothing and wait for the USM to recover with the economy or to close it. But those surveyed also proposed a number of intermediate measures to change the rules and regulations of the USM and make it more attractive to participants. The ultimate creation of AIM, described in Chapter 6, and the public debates about its form shows the merits of these in-between options, albeit in retrospect. Although the LSE in 1992, under the leadership of chairman Andrew Hugh Smith and chief executive Peter Rawlins, had alternatives, it decided that the Official List would be the only market in town.

When the LSE announced its intention to close the USM in 1993, the exchange had the legal authority to determine which markets it would supply and what their forms would be. In January, the LSE circulated a consultative document, in which the exchange made public the decision to stop new USM listings on June 30, 1993, and trading activity on December 31, 1995. The LSE offered existing USM companies a simplified process of entry to the Official List and a dedicated index covering smaller companies on the Official List, beginning in January 1993. The document, announcing a short three-month consultation period and a proposed schedule to begin in six months "read more like a White Paper rather than a truly consultative document," wrote a USM company official.[17] Without competition over the trading of smaller-company shares at home, the LSE had decided to shore up its large-company business in the face of an increasingly contested international environment.

New Interests Battling Old

The venture capitalists and other services firms reliant on the USM believed any serious strategy for improving the financing problems of smaller companies and reviving the industry surrounding them would feature a separate market. Both groups doubted the LSE's commitment to smaller quoted firms and believed a single British market for all enterprises would spell the continued decline of the smaller-company sector and its profits. These financial firms formed the core of a coalition opposing the LSE's plan and organized under the aegis of CISCO (City Group for Smaller Companies), a smaller-company interest group created only a few weeks before the LSE's announcement.[18] By the early 1990s, the LSE no longer served as a trade association representing and lobbying on behalf of its members. The exchange instead supported the emergence of new specialized interest groups—including Proshare and the Association of Private Client Investment Managers and Stock Brokers (APCIMS)—to replace its former advocacy role. But the LSE fostered no organized forum giving voice to firms specializing in smaller-company finance. CISCO's creators, concerned by the general decline in their sector and the absence of a body promoting their specific needs, intended to fill this gap. The USM's planned closure gave the new pressure group its first challenge.

Despite a well-organized lobby campaign that made judicious use of the financial press, CISCO on its own was no match for the LSE. In some respects, the exchange was already a shadow of its pre–Big Bang self. In 1993, it was in the beginning stages of a long process of unbundling. In addition to supplying equity markets, the LSE umbrella had handled the government gilt market for the Bank of England; provided settlement, clearing, and information services; supervised its members and trading on its markets; and served as the industry association and lobby for its members. By 1993, the LSE had shed most of these roles and was undergoing a difficult transition from an official market authority, a protected organization performing official public services, to a largely private organization competing in an international market of trading services, with a significantly smaller official role. The LSE was stumbling badly, and the heads of chief executives were rolling. The exchange lost market share in the trading of European continental stocks and faced huge expenses from its investments in a new trading technology and a badly botched settlement system. Nevertheless, seven years after the 1986 Big Bang, the LSE still retained its two official functions, as well as informal advantages that, combined, empowered it to stave off domestic objections, like CISCO's, to LSE control over the supply and form of domestic markets.

As a registered investment exchange (RIE), the LSE continued to operate, regulate (as the first tier in a two-tier regulatory regime), manage, and set the rules and regulations for a market in company shares (provided the rules and regulations met national and EU minimums). The Thatcher government designed the RIE status in the 1986 Financial Services Act primarily to end the LSE's national monopoly over the quoting and trading of company shares. In practice, however, creating new markets from scratch is an enormous challenge, and those in the United Kingdom who managed to acquire the RIE status in the early 1990s faced formidable barriers to competing effectively with the LSE. Its de facto monopoly played no small part.[19] As most financial intermediaries in the equities sector (including the international houses who had bought into the LSE after the Big Bang) drew revenues via LSE channels, the exchange had leverage to influence and, if need be, coerce. Indeed in the early 1990s, few LSE members were willing to oppose the exchange publicly.

The LSE's second function, as the competent listing authority for the United

Kingdom, further perpetuated its dominant position in the British financial system.[20] The EEC Admissions and Listing Particulars Directives (80/390/EEC) required each member state to have such an authority to assure that companies acquiring the listed status meet the minimum requirements.[21] Most European governments delegated this role to national regulatory bodies. France, for instance, made the COB, not the Société des Bourses Françaises (SBF), the competent authority. The British Treasury, however, delegated power to the LSE, exemplifying the tenacity of traditional British financial arrangements that separate government and finance. Thus all companies aiming to attain listed status, regardless of the markets in which they would quote and trade their shares, had first to pass through the LSE. The dual functions of supplying a market and regulating the listing process created conflicts of interest by which new competing markets would have to direct applicant companies to the LSE for approval.

Despite the LSE's advantages, the CISCO coalition did manage, through an intense lobbying and media strategy, to win the first round in what turned out to be a two-year contest. In April 1993, four months after the LSE publicized its plan to shut down the USM, CISCO released a counterproposal that received support from the Treasury, CBI, SIB (Securities and Investment Board), DTI, Bank of England, BVCA, and the financial press. By 1993, the financial problems of smaller companies had once again become a highly political issue in the United Kingdom. Just before CISCO released its proposal, the CBI had made recommendations to improve the financing mechanisms for these firms, recommendations that included a USM replacement market. Meanwhile the Bank of England, concerned about a breakdown in lending relations between clearing banks and their small-company clients, was in the process of initiating its series of annual reports, *Finance for Small Firms*.[22] Because of the outpouring of official support for CISCO's platform, the LSE wanted to appear willing to compromise. It gave the USM a "stay of execution" and announced the creation of the Smaller Companies Working Party, which included many of CISCO's leaders.[23]

Rather than fight to keep the USM alive, CISCO focused its counterproposal on the continued demand for a separate market for smaller companies, a finding the LSE had chosen to ignore from its own study on the USM.[24] CISCO aimed to draw the LSE into a debate structured around its members' concerns, not just those of the LSE's board, which was dominated by giant international securities firms with little interest in smaller companies.

The CISCO proposal did more than pressure the LSE to postpone the

USM's closure; it also revealed how particular organizational forms of stock markets favor the interests of some actors more than others. In contrast to the process that had led to the creation of the USM in 1980, in 1993 the LSE was no longer the sole actor to make a connection between particular goals and a particular market form. The example of the U.S. Nasdaq helped bring about this realization. Although different actors elicited different lessons from the Nasdaq experience in the United States, everyone recognized that its rules and regulations, unlike those of the NYSE, especially benefited financial intermediaries with expertise in entrepreneurial finance, venture capitalism, and young enterprises. In 1993, while still in the process of developing beliefs about and preferences for the form of new markets, CISCO's venture capitalists and their allies were well aware that the USM's feeder design embodied the LSE's largely protectionist goals much more than it did their own.

At the heart of CISCO's proposal was a detailed blueprint for restructuring the LSE's markets into three segments, reflecting internal divisions.[25] The first segment, the International Equity Market, would list the top 350 shares and look and be managed like the Official List. The second segment, the National Market, would meet the needs of the smaller-company services providers and their client firms by housing the less frequently traded remaining 1,800 stocks of the Official List as well as USM shares. With lower barriers to listing and lower informational requirements, CISCO envisioned the National Market as mimicking the USM's feeder model. The CISCO members backing this segment wanted a new market that looked like the old USM, only with more support from the LSE. They cared more about a constant flow of new company quotations (and thus a constant flow of revenues) than particular types of firms coming to the market. Their proposal was thus the lightly regulated, "cheap and easy" National Market. The profile of National Market companies, like that of the USM, would resemble the LSE's broad range of enterprises in different economic sectors rather than primarily the high-technology companies that were the targets of the U.S. Nasdaq.[26] And like USM firms, the new feeder's companies would use a quotation for a number of different reasons. Some firms, for example, would use it as an inexpensive stepping-stone to the top segment, or as a convenient mechanism for placing a small portion of equity in public hands, without the expenses and rigorous prevetting processes of an official listing. Others would use the National Market, as they had the USM, to solve financing and succession problems, without the costs and disclosure requirements of an official listing and without ceding as much control to other shareholders.[27]

The key innovation in the CISCO proposal was the third segment, the Enterprise Market, proposed as an "exits" market for venture capitalists. With high information requirements that included quarterly reports—a U.S. standard not even required on the Official List—CISCO wanted the Enterprise Market to be a British Nasdaq copy, designed to attract institutional investors to a carefully selected pool of high-risk, high-technology venture-backed companies.[28]

The fall of the USM came as an enormous blow to British venture capitalists, who by the late 1980s had portfolios filled with high-risk investments but no market for selling them. They had piled up these investments, in part because of the new availability of Japanese and American capital looking for higher returns but primarily because of, they believed, the availability of an exit mechanism.[29] Although the statistics from this period are not entirely reliable, they do capture the gap between investment and divestments. One prominent venture capitalist estimated that in 1992 European venture capitalists (the majority British) held ECU 20.4 billion, or 53 percent, of accumulated investments in over 10,000 small and medium-sized companies, whereas divestments at cost in 1992 totaled ECU 2.3 billion. Only a fraction of these divestments were public offerings through a stock market.[30] According to EVCA's 1992 yearbook, all European IPOs, including those of larger companies, amounted to ECU 410 million in 1992.[31]

The USM experience clarified at least one point: not all markets were the same. Different designs did not embed the same expectations in all investors, intermediaries, and quoting companies and did reflect the goals of different market participants. In 1980, when private equity firms began to shift toward venture capitalism, one organizational form seemed as good as another. The USM's failure sharpened the ability of participants to discern forms that promised to create beneficial incentives and expectations that might further their goals.

In 1993, as in the 1980s, British venture capitalists wanted to achieve the same profit levels of their U.S. counterparts. They knew Nasdaq's presence played a key role in fostering those returns, and most believed that, like the U.S. exemplar, any new market would have to attract institutional investors. Otherwise, British venture capitalists feared the market would not have the liquidity and high valuations needed to recoup investments at an acceptable profit rate, given the levels of risk. The proposed Enterprise Market reflected this belief by copying the Nasdaq form in two ways. First, CISCO's venture capitalists emphasized the need for high informational standards, including quarterly reports. By distinguishing between high barriers to quoting (for example, minimum capitalization, several years of operations, etc.) and high informational standards (see Chapter 2), the British venture capitalists were proposing something very different from the 1980s feeder markets like the USM. The problem with the feeder market, they believed, was that few investors would risk their capital in a company for which they had little information. The proposed Enterprise Market would keep the barriers to quoting low but require very high informational standards.

Second, the venture capitalists foresaw the Enterprise Market having an independent board and operating as an independent commercial entity. They now recognized the built-in adverse selection bias of the USM.[32] Serving its own goals, the LSE had designed the USM so that the best companies would graduate to the Official List. This gave investors, especially institutional ones, incentive to wait for the weeding out process to occur rather than investing in USM shares early on. A clearer separation from the Official List, a distinct identity, and more autonomous management and control, the venture capitalists hoped, would stop the outflow of successful companies. So long as smaller-company shares contributed only a minor portion of revenues to the LSE and its members, CISCO argued, the exchange would not give smaller-company markets the necessary support.

In the spring of 1993, CISCO still emphasized its preference for creating the Enterprise Market and the National Market as autonomous entities under the LSE umbrella. When the LSE agreed to create the Smaller Companies Working Party, CISCO officially declared it would suspend talks with other possible market suppliers. CISCO's proposed markets were to benefit from the LSE's infrastructure and expertise but to leave control over rules and regulations, promotional strategies, and other policies to new independent bodies. As Chapter 6 will demonstrate, some of CISCO's members, most notably venture capitalist Ronald Cohen, chairman of Apax Partners and Company, remained open to alternatives, suspecting that the LSE was the wrong actor to supply the market they wanted.

Venture Capitalists' Failure to Influence the LSE

By the end of 1993, it became clear that CISCO's April victory against the LSE would not translate directly into the markets CISCO wanted. Even though the LSE never released the Smaller Companies Working Party's final report, its conclusions were well known. All but one member of the Working Party voted to create a new market very similar to CISCO's original Enterprise Market proposal. In October 1993, when the LSE first appeared to be delaying publication, the results were leaked to the *Independent* newspaper.[33] But even in June of 1993 at an EVCA conference in Brussels, Ronald Cohen, a member of the Working Party and the driving force behind CISCO's Enterprise Market proposal, presented his ideas for an "EASDAQ-UK," which would be based on the same eight points recommended by the Working Party.

In an unabashed attempt to divert attention from a subject that made its leadership uncomfortable, the LSE made smaller companies the theme of its annual conference in November and did not mention the conclusions of the Working Party. Then in December 1993, the LSE board adopted two measures that together revealed its intention to maintain only one market for all types of companies, including venture-backed entrepreneurial ones. If there was going to be a Nasdaq in Britain, the LSE was determined it would be the Official List. To this effect, first it introduced Chapter 20 to its Yellow Book of listing rules, making it easier for technology enterprises, primarily scientific research–based companies, to list without the normally required three-year record. Second, claiming insufficient evidence of demand for a USM replacement, the LSE announced it would not circulate the conclusions of the Working Party until further research, commissioned by MORI Research, was completed in March 1994. Perhaps because of the Nasdaq example, the LSE did not embrace the Working Party's recommendations for a market with a distinct identity, a market to be managed and controlled independently, even if it would fall loosely under the exchange umbrella.[34]

By commissioning another study, the LSE carried out a strategy of attrition against CISCO. British financial arrangements, even seven years after the Big Bang, still greatly favored the LSE, which continued to enjoy relative autonomy from the government and industry. As an RIE with a de facto monopoly over share trading and as the official British listing authority, the LSE had resources that no other British actor, including the government, possessed to supply a new market. The exchange executives understood that the government would not intervene and that the neophyte CISCO coalition did not have the political clout or economic muscle to create a new market on its own.

Indeed government backing for the CISCO proposal never moved beyond moral support. The Treasury, under chancellor of the exchequer Norman

Lamont, for example, adopted the fictional position that the 1980s financial changes had created an industry that was open to new entrants and that no longer favored the LSE.[35] In correspondence and conversations with CISCO's leadership, government officials emphasized the absence of legal barriers to competitive exchanges and ignored the enormous difficulty the coalition would face in setting up a market from scratch. In characteristic British regulatory style, the government indicated a preference for an outcome decided by market actors themselves.[36]

On April 26, 1994, the LSE formalized what most had already expected. The exchange rejected the Smaller Companies Working Party recommendations and by extension the CISCO proposal for the Enterprise Market. In its place, the LSE offered a seven-point plan of half measures that satisfied neither wing of the CISCO coalition. Instead of the proposed Enterprise Market or National Market, the LSE announced it would transform Rule 535(2) into a distinct market with a "suitable" level of regulation. As Chapter 4 discussed, Rule 535(2), formerly 163(2), was a facility that allowed LSE members to trade unregulated shares not quoted on its markets. Rather than an exits market for venture capitalists, the proposal seemed more a protectionist initiative aimed at an August 1993 joint venture between Reuters and Jenkins and Company, to provide information and research on unregulated companies trading under Rule 535(2). The LSE's plan also included an index for venture-backed companies, a measure falling short of a separate Nasdaq of Britain, and the creation of a smaller-companies advocacy group apparently designed to usurp CISCO's role.[37]

Despite the December 1993 blow, the CISCO leadership did not cease its high-profile campaign to get the markets it wanted. On March 16, 2004, for example, only one month before the LSE's April announcement, CISCO, led by new chief executive Katie Morris, held a well-attended conference on the Enterprise Market. Representatives of the Bank of England, the City, and the LSE gave presentations and listened to the keynote address by a DTI official. But CISCO's smaller-service providers were less willing than the venture capitalists and some investment bankers to criticize the LSE and more willing to accept Chapter 20 as a genuine attempt to attract entrepreneurial companies and transform the Official List into an exit for venture capitalists. Many of these firms were members of the LSE and relied on it for their revenues. The stock exchange, apparently sensing these divisions and remaining unfazed by widespread opposition, pressed forward with its plans to accommodate all but the least traded companies on the Official List.[38]

In April 1994 the LSE's position in the British financial system enabled it to dismantle the USM almost as easily as it had supplied it fourteen years earlier. Despite a significant rise in cross-border financial flows from 1980 levels, venture capitalists could not parlay their mobility into influence. As demonstrated in the next chapter, however, the LSE's autonomy and resilience to venture capital's influence precipitously declined only a few months later—not because levels of capital mobility spiked, but because the ripples from a European Commission–backed initiative reached British shores.

Fostering Venture Capitalism in France

In France, the origins of American-style venture capitalism and the "exits problem" followed a similar history, on a much smaller scale. Before the Second Marché's creation in 1983, venture capitalism of this kind hardly existed and certainly had no industry identity, organization, or political voice. The apparent success of the first years of the Second Marché began to foster new expectations about possible profits from investing in risky young firms.

In its first three years, the Second Marché's role did not mirror the Nasdaq's as a financial conduit for entrepreneurial high-tech firms. The listed companies tended to reflect "old," not "new," economic sectors.[39] But many market participants were getting what they wanted. The owners of smaller French companies used the market to resolve inheritance and succession problems, gain publicity, provide liquidity for their shares, and even raise new capital. Having opened to trading in 1982, Jacques Delors' showcase second-tier market could by 1986 boast 180 listed companies. French brokers, the *agents de change* who still comprised an official cartel, and other financial intermediaries were also benefiting. In addition to the flow of new initial public offerings, trading activity levels on the Second Marché, measured in trading volume, were in 1986 approaching those of the main French market and were about equal to volumes on London's USM. Investors too had grounds for celebration. By the end of 1986, the Second Marché's price index outperformed the Cotation Assistée en Continue (CAC, the French equivalent of the Dow Jones Industrial Average index), and studies suggested that the new market had attracted some of the most profitable smaller companies in France.[40]

French observers were not alone in deeming the Second Marché a success. In July 1987, Joseph R. Hardiman, the president of NASD (National

Association of Securities Dealers), made a highly publicized visit to the French financial community.[41] At the time, the NASD owned and managed the Nasdaq Stock Market, then sixteen years old and the world's third largest equity market. Hardiman's presence in Paris fanned the high expectations of the Second Marché. While his intent was to lure French companies and their financial advisors into Nasdaq's planned European venture, the effect was to convince local financiers that entrepreneurial finance had arrived in France.[42]

By the end of 1986, cross-border trading of company shares appeared more feasible in western Europe than in the past. This seemed to be so because of increased capital mobility following the 1985 European Commission's White Paper on capital liberalization. The Chirac cohabitation government (1986–1988) had begun to lift many capital controls in 1986 and vowed to liberalize the rest within a few years, a promise fulfilled, as noted earlier in this chapter, by 1981. Equally important, the LSE's SEAQ International electronic dealers network had significantly increased its share of continental trading.[43] In 1987, Nasdaq had gained official recognition in London as a registered overseas investment exchange (ROIE) and brokered a deal in which SEAQ International would quote Nasdaq companies. With the expectation of a single European market for financial services in the near future, NASD officials saw 1987 as the moment for transforming the U.S. Nasdaq into a cross-Atlantic market for entrepreneurial companies. In 1986, French financial authorities launched Matif (le Marché à Terme International de France), a futures market. By 1987, officials had introduced an electronic trading system and phased out *encadrement du crédit*. With the other dramatic financial reforms following Mitterrand's U-turn, the recent removal of capital controls, and intensified reforms promised by minister of finance Edouard Balladur, the accomplishment of the Second Marché seemed to Nasdaq officials a clear signal that France had turned a corner. French smaller companies were now perceived as potential customers for quotation.

In a 1986 study entitled "Second Marché: Bilan d'un succès," the COB concluded that the Second Marché's first three years had been an unmitigated triumph.[44] The COB and other French observers appraised the performance of the new second-tier market with reference to previous efforts to spur similar equity-based activity in the French smaller-company financial sector. Against the complete failure of the Compartiment Spécial, French observers, not surprisingly, were elated by the early signs of vibrant activity, even if modest by comparison to smaller-company equity finance in the United States.

Formation of a Venture Capitalist Political Agenda

These developments triggered new expectations and an investment spike in risky companies at the earliest stages of their development.[45] The numbers pale compared with similar figures in the United Kingdom and the United States. In the France of the early and mid-1980s, many features of the national financial system still seriously hampered the development of venture capitalism. Unlike the situation in the United Kingdom, where the Thatcher government had abolished all capital controls by 1980, for instance, French venture capitalists could not easily solicit capital from American, British, and Dutch institutional investors and instead had to rely on limited partners from the smaller pools of unrestricted national savings. Even so, a year after the Second Marché opened for trading, French venture capitalists had recognizable common interests and a need for a political organization through which to participate in politics, an organization that was actualized in the 1984 creation of AFIC (Association Française des Investisseurs en Capital), the French venture capital association.[46]

Within three months of Hardiman's 1987 campaign to extend Nasdaq's reach into France, however, the international stock market crash of October 10 revealed several underlying problems that rapidly sobered early hopes for the Second Marché and, more generally, for smaller-company equity finance in France. Investors tend to flee risky investments during rough market conditions, causing price indices of smaller-company shares to be volatile compared with those of larger companies. So it was to be expected that the 1987 crash would affect activity on the Second Marché more than on the main market. But in the months following "Black Monday," investors returned to the main market, not the Second Marché. Just as it had for the other feeder markets in western Europe, the crash marked the decline of the Second Marché.

Measured by a range of standard indicators, activity on the Second Marché essentially dried up. Newly admitted companies, for example, peaked in 1987 at sixty-four and then began a steady decline. In 1988 there were thirty-four. In 1989, thirty-six. In 1990, twenty-two, and by 1991, only eleven new companies joined the Second Marché. The volume of transactions also diminished. After peaking in 1987 at 64.4 billion francs, the volume leveled off to around 50 billion francs in 1989 and 1990 and then plummeted to 27.2 million francs in 1991. The prices of the Second Marché shares reflected these indicators of low investor demand. The index of the Second Marché stocks trailed those of companies listed on the main French market, a trend clearly warning investors that they would not likely receive commensurate reward for the higher risks involved in buying the shares of smaller companies.[47]

Like the USM in London, France's feeder market started to fail at a moment when financiers had begun to make investment decisions that hinged on its existence. Venture capital investment in early stage companies, according to EVCA's statistics, had risen from to 206 million and 254 million French francs in 1986 and 1987 to 768 million in 1988. When it became clear several years after the 1987 crash that the Second Marché would not recover and thus would not provide an exit, French venture capitalists, like their counterparts throughout Europe, owned portfolios filled with high-risk companies but had nowhere to sell them.[48] Their initial reaction was to stop investing, a pattern identifiable in EVCA's statistics, which show early stage venture capital dropped to 212 million French francs in 1991. By early 1993, venture capitalists believed they were facing a crisis. Without a robust market, they could not expect to reach profit levels that would compensate for the chances they were taking. Risk taking in France, in sum, did not pay, and the exits problem had become the number one issue of AFIC.[49]

Official Response to Failure

In hindsight, the statistics from 1988–1990 seem like clear signs that the incentives embedded in the Second Marché's form were undermining its success and that early expectations of a vibrant French sector for equity-based smaller-company finance were ungrounded. But it took the French financial policymaking elite until 1992 to return seriously to the issue of the smaller-company market. In 1988, 1989, and 1990, officials inside the COB, the bourse, and the Trésor interpreted the Second Marché's decline as a temporary and typical pattern of financial markets. COB officials were not, of course, oblivious to the Second Marché's problems and indeed cracked down by increasing informational standards and improving enforcement.[50] But several years passed before they discerned a more serious problem.

Perhaps the main reason for the delayed government response to the Second Marché's decline was the increasing importance of a new public policy goal: the transformation of Paris into Europe's financial center. The new priority had the unintended consequence of subordinating the aim of improving equity finance options for smaller companies. One of Balladur's responses to the LSE's bid to make SEAQ International the Continent's stock market was to give the French exchange's board a broad degree of discretion over the markets it would supply. In the late 1980s and early 1990s, a competitive and profitable stock exchange meant the ability to attract listing and trading of larger-company shares to its proprietary systems. With the abolition of fixed commissions, executives of the French exchange (still at the time, the Société des Bourses Françaises, or SBF) understandably concentrated on the services for larger-company shares, where they made the bulk of revenues.[51] So by encouraging the now privately owned SBF to become a more competitive exchange, technocrats inside the Trésor and the COB had inadvertently demoted their commitment to improving smaller-company access to equity financing.

The subordination of one public policy goal to another did not last long. Officials inside state financial agencies still believed the bourse solution was an appropriate response to the financing problems of smaller companies and critically important to resolving what had become an unemployment crisis. By 1992, public authorities could not but compare the stagnancy of the French job market with the hyperperforming American one. And many of those jobs across the Atlantic appeared to be coming from young entrepreneurial firms, financed via the Nasdaq Stock Market.

The American example was not the only factor responsible for the timing of the Second Marché's reform. As in 1983, a combination of domestic and international factors finally prompted French officials to conduct an April 1992 study and to carry out the recommended reforms. First, the Second Marché was approaching its tenth anniversary, giving the securities authorities the excuse to issue a long-overdue review. Second, by 1992 the Second Marché's failure was increasingly affecting a broad swathe of actors—smaller companies, investors, financial intermediaries, and venture capitalists—and could no longer be easily ignored, even if it meant the imposition of public goals onto the newly privatized SBF. A final factor that prompted the COB's study had international roots. In 1992, the Nasdaq Stock Market was once again trying to establish a European beachhead.[52] In January, it announced the opening of the London-based Nasdaq International. While the project ultimately failed to generate interest, in early 1992 the French government officials and financial elite had not forgotten Nasdaq's earlier attempt to push into Paris and lure away French companies and their financial advisors. The possibility of U.S. competition over the listing of French smaller companies—especially the entrepreneurial type that populated the Nasdaq—helped focus attention to the Second Marché's dismal performance.

Revamping of the Second Marché

The initiative to assess the performance of the Second Marché came from state officials inside the COB and the Trésor, not from the increasingly independent stock exchange, in response to its failed feeder market. And the reforms bore the stamp of the official French financial policymaking elite. Once prompted into action, technocrats inside the COB, the Trésor, and the SBF maintained control over the process, ensuring an outcome consistent with their goals: incremental reforms and the preservation of the feeder form. Thus not only did COB officials launch the process, but they also pursued and accomplished an agenda that reflected the aims of the French technocrats, not those of international or other domestic actors.

The particularities of the French financial system determined the options available to COB officials in the reform process. The COB and the SBF never seriously entertained ideas promoted by venture capitalists, who were not part of the decision making. The alternative preferred and pursued in the United Kingdom and elsewhere in Europe—closing the failed feeder market—was also never considered in France, where COB and Trésor officials had a stake in keeping the moribund market alive. Dismantling what was once a centerpiece of the Mitterrand-Delors' financial reforms would have come too close to an admission of failure. In early 1992, how thoroughly the government would reform the overall financial system was still an open question. So once again the goals of promoting Paris as a financial center conflicted with policies aimed to improve the financing options for smaller companies. Closing the Second Marché and admitting failure in the "marketization" of French finance was not a politically appealing option for functionaries and politicians in need of continued support to carry through with the long-term reform project. Instead, COB officials, refusing to accept what all the participants knew and the statistics documented, finessed the study to judge the Second Marché a success.

COB officials accomplished this slight of hand by comparing the French market with the other dying European markets. Indeed the Second Marché, partly because of the public support it had already received, did not look quite so dismal next to its counterparts. The finishing stroke was a deliberate use of case-selection bias. COB officials eliminated Nasdaq from their study: Nasdaq and the Second Marché were not the same types of markets, the report conveniently and tautologically argued, because including the fantastically successful U.S. financial institution would have distorted the study.[53]

The COB could not, of course, declare the Second Marché in perfect condition. But COB officials managed to skirt the core problems—the feeder form, the adverse selection bias, and the lackluster support from exchange members—and instead identified a few marginal areas for improvement. The SBF created a working group with the COB in June 1992 and, after consultations with the broader financial community, issued a report in February 1993, "Le Second Marché: Rapport du groupe de travail." It offered a set of recommendations, some later implemented, amounting to window dressing. The most significant change was perhaps the introduction of a mechanism for enhancing liquidity.[54] But in the end, the newly reformed Second Marché looked remarkably like the original. The required informational standards and barriers to quoting hardly differed. The Second Marché remained the poor cousin of the main market, where the best young companies were still expected to migrate. Like the original, the reformed feeder market was not likely to attract investors, who lacked information to assess company risk and had incentives to wait and find out which companies would advance to the big board.

Venture Capitalists and Market Forms

Given the marginal importance of their contributions to French finance, the exclusion of venture capitalists from the Second Marché reform process in 1992–1993 was only normal, however troubled their industry.[55] COB and SBF officials were largely unaware of the venture capitalists' problems and goals. The COB's director general, Pierre Fleuriot, for example, used the occasion of the Second Marché's tenth anniversary in June 1993 to advertise the Second Marché's recent reform package. Seemingly oblivious to what would appeal to venture capitalists, he emphasized the Second Marché as a market for household savers, not professionals. He also proudly highlighted the Second Marché's role as a feeder to the primary market, a staging ground where companies could adjust to public scrutiny.[56]

French venture capitalists were financial outsiders and were politically weak. They had little voice in official circles and almost no influence. An incipient venture capitalist agenda did not find its way into the Second Marché reforms because the COB and the SBF knew next to nothing about the venture capital industry and felt little pressure to change.[57]

In the early 1990s, French venture capitalists tended to develop preferences different from those of their European cohorts.[58] Operating in a much less-developed capital markets–service industry, French venture capitalists believed from the start that only a market with a pan-European scope would attract sufficient numbers of investors and companies.[59] In London, leading venture capitalists first sought to create a British Nasdaq and only later, after a year of failed efforts and much persuasion, supported the Commission-backed pan-European project, which is discussed in the next chapter. Reflecting a more centralized domestic system, the French financiers were also much more inclined to work with their stock exchange and within official channels than were British venture capitalists. There was an unmistakable fluidity between public and private funds in French venture capitalism. The government had been involved in venture capital programs, at least in name, since the late 1970s.[60] In 1992 Part'Com, a branch of the quasi-government Groupe Caisse des Dépôts was one of the largest, if not the largest, venture capitalist firms in France.[61] It is not surprising, then, that AFIC, the French venture capitalist association, eventually lobbied for the SBF, an umbrella of French financial officialdom, to supply the infrastructure for a pan-European Nasdaq.[62]

French preferences over market form took shape only in the decade after the creation of the Second Marché and followed a slow, gradual process. The few existing venture capitalist firms lacked experience with equity markets and did not necessarily discriminate among (or think much about) the various possible market designs. They had expected the Second Marché to function in France as the Nasdaq functioned in the United States—as a mechanism through which venture capitalists could sell their shares in high-risk companies to the public. French venture capitalist firms simply lacked experience and knowledge that would have helped them identify forms well suited to their needs. Despite different inclinations from their British cohorts, not all French venture capitalists arrived at the same conclusions. Some believed that even a pan-European Nasdaq would never succeed in an increasingly international economy. Rather than create yet another market, they advocated the extension of the original Nasdaq into Europe, while others preferred more SBF support for the existing feeder.[63]

A Failed Venture Capitalist Campaign

In February 1993, the same month that the COB and the SBF released the second report on the Second Marché, Denis Mortier, a leading French venture capitalist and president of AFIC, attended an EVCA-sponsored seminar in Venice on smaller-company markets and other "exits." Mortier heard complaints from other European venture capitalists similar to those he and his French colleagues had recently voiced about the Second Marché reform process: processes of reforming Europe's feeder markets did not take into consideration the needs of venture capitalist business models. These financiers were telling themselves that Europe was an uninviting place for their business, and the official policymaking processes, centered on national stock exchanges, gave them little reason to expect improvement. Everywhere they looked, they saw efforts either to reform the failed feeder markets or to close them down without offering satisfactory replacements. Europe's venture capitalists, as a rule, had little if any influence.[64]

The EVCA seminar also exposed Mortier to a set of possible solutions to the exits problem being discussed across Europe. One of these, a pan-European Nasdaq alternative especially promoted by Jos Peeters, became the starting point for a process that within two years would give birth to a second French smaller-company market, this one designed to meet some of the needs of venture capitalists. But, as the next chapter illustrates, until the Commission's backing of Easdaq, Mortier and AFIC's bottom-up campaign did not influence the financial elite in government and at the Paris exchange.

Within two months of the publication of the Second Marché reform package, Denis Mortier and AFIC launched their lobbying effort to create an alternative market, a pan-European Nasdaq. Mortier used his positions as director general of Financière Saint-Dominique and executive of AFIC to orchestrate a public relations campaign through which he attempted to introduce politicians, public officials, and the insider financial firms who owned the stock exchange to an alternate set of arguments about smaller-company markets.[65]

He began with familiar French political themes. Economic growth, technological innovation, and future jobs lay largely in the health of French entrepreneurial companies, especially those developing and commercializing high-technology products. Compared with the international competition, he argued, the French financial system had fallen short in providing these sorts of companies with the capital they needed. Part of the reason was the underdeveloped venture capital industry. Taking chances simply did not reap reward in France, and the main reason was that there was no stock market serving as a venture capitalist exit.

The Second Marché model, Mortier maintained, had died and could not be resuscitated. Emphatic on this point, he maintained that France's financial services industry was too small to sustain its own market for dynamic young companies. Tinkering with liquidity contracts would not breathe life into the Second Marché. And even if the government were to introduce pension funds—a big if—he doubted France could supply enough capital for an entrepreneurial market. Investors need financial information about high-risk companies, he maintained, and a pure French market could not provide the scale necessary for the desired level of analyst specialization. Fanning the worst fears of financial insiders and politicians, Mortier predicted an outflow of French high-tech companies and a brain drain to the United States and Britain. Either the Nasdaq would become the source of financing for French high-tech companies, or London would step into the European gap and assume the role.

Mortier's solution was a pan-European Nasdaq, supported by the French authorities and the Paris bourse but carried out and managed by private firms. A Europe-wide market for high-tech companies, he argued, would not only contribute to the competitiveness of French companies and economy and the prosperity of the French venture capitalist industry. Becoming the lead player in the pan-European scheme, was, in Mortier's eyes, a shrewd strategy for Paris, the financial center, to catch up with its Anglo-Saxon rival. With the just-passed European Community's ISD coming into effect in three short years, London stood to become Europe's center of financial activity.[66] Paris, in contrast, looked hopelessly behind. Mortier envisioned the pan-European market as part of a French developmental strategy to offset the predominance of the City by making Paris the motor and using Europe's scale.

Despite the broad acceptance of Mortier's logic, the venture capitalists had little to show for their efforts in the first year and a half of the campaign. The best they could boast was to have convinced an executive of the SBF to attend EVCA's meetings. While it is true that Mortier had also caught the ear of the minister of enterprise and development, Alain Madelin, and other politicians, this achievement mattered little in terms of making changes in financial markets.[67] In the early 1990s, in the realm of financial institutions, the empowered and relevant government agency remained the Ministry of Finance and especially the Trésor. Officials there still stood at the peak of a policymaking network that included the COB and the SBF and continued to implement the Second Marché reforms, without regard to the agenda of Mortier, AFIC, and other supporters of their ideas.

Mortier's efforts had other effects too. Officials at the COB and the SBF had become aware of what venture capitalists wanted, and felt the need to respond to the initiative to create a pan-European market with a counter–public relations campaign of their own. For example, in May 1994 the COB published a study claiming that the new liquidity contracts, the centerpiece of the Second Marché reforms, had reinvigorated the old feeder market. Before long a barrage of articles applauded its revitalization.[68] In addition, the newly reorganized brokers association—no longer an official cartel and now the organization with the most to lose from a pan-European market—came out strongly against pan-European schemes. Alain Ferri, president of L'Association Française des Sociétés de Bourse (AFSB), countered Mortier's logic. He argued in favor of the feeder model (which would ensure that trading activity remained in the hands of his membership) but compromised in one area. He advocated the addition of a European element to the Second Marché.[69]

In sum, the 1989 lifting of most restrictions on cross-border capital flows in France did not enhance the position of venture capitalists. The Second Marché's 1992 reform and the inability of venture capitalists to influence it resembled the domestic institutional-change processes that had led to the creation of the feeder market in 1983 and to that of its 1977 predecessor, the Compartiment Spécial. Differences existed, of course. The 1992 process was top-down and state-led, like its predecessors. But it did not emanate from quite so high a level. The blueprints for the Compartiment Spécial and the Second Marché came directly from reports rooted in official state planning and commissioned by ministers. By contrast, a COB study, probably prompted by the Trésor and occupying a lower public profile, was the immediate source of the Second Marché's reforms. Also, the Second Marché reform process was notably less centralized than that of its predecessors. The COB included the reorganized stock exchange to a much greater extent than it had previously. No longer a cartel of brokers, the SBF was technically a private organization and, in its follow-up report, began to act like a private corporation sensitive to customers.

In comparison to the United Kingdom, where market-reform processes sometimes became highly contentious public debates, the 1992 reform process in France remained conspicuously centralized. Absent from the French reform process were venture capitalists, who remained outside the official channels of financial policymaking and whose newly forming preferences over market design did not influence the resulting reforms of the Second Marché. The French financial arrangements contrasted with the British financial system along this dimension. In 1992, the same year as the COB study, it was the member-owned LSE—not the new British securities regulator, SIB—that initiated the process leading to the closure of London's feeder market. At least in terms of choosing the markets it would supply, the LSE had by 1992 gained even more autonomy and independence from the British government than in the previous decade. The LSE carried out policies based on internal assessments about how best to survive and prosper in the newly competitive environment for European listings and trading. The British government played no direct part. The comparison of France to the United Kingdom illuminates how financial policymaking in the Europe of 1993 and 1994 had not changed significantly from that of the nationally distinct processes of the 1980s.

Thus by zeroing in on the months just before the exchanges began to accommodate the venture capitalist agenda, this chapter has provided strong evidence of capital mobility's insufficiency as an explanation for the rash of regional competition over smaller-company stock markets. Despite levels adequate for cross-border financial activity, venture capitalists were unable to achieve their goals in battles with national stock exchanges. Only in the aftermath of a Brussels intervention, as the next chapter shows, were these financial outsiders able to overcome their political liabilities and marginal positions within national financial systems and alter the course of European smaller-company arrangements.

CHAPTER 6

A Brussels Intervention and Europe's New Stock Markets, 1994–2007

The ability of venture capitalists to shape outcomes shifted rapidly in 1994 with the Easdaq proposal for a pan-European Nasdaq copy. A faction of EVCA proposed the new stock market, carried out the formidable day-to-day challenges of getting it off the ground, and managed it after its launch. Yet from a perspective attentive to the political nature of market formation, European Commission civil servants were the actors most responsible for Easdaq's creation, the new uncertainties that the national exchanges confronted, and the subsequent rise in venture capital influence. It was fifteen years of unobtrusive Brussels initiatives culminating in a direct intervention that largely accounted for Easdaq and the unintended battle over national new markets that it ignited.

This chapter documents the Commission's intervention and its impact, showing that both stemmed from a new supranational political arena for contesting smaller-company financing arrangements. First, it examines why Brussels officials supported Easdaq but none of the four previous proposals for pan-European stock markets that crossed their desks in 1985 and 1989. Partly due to their own previous actions, which Chapter 3 described and Figure 1.2 (page 17) illustrated, a well-organized and active venture capitalist interest group and a permissive environment gave the civil servants reason to believe an intervention would be effective. This self-made political landscape, traceable to the 1970s and 1980s, thus presented itself in 1994 as an opportunity.

The pages that follow show why a seemingly modest intervention had the unanticipated consequence of unleashing cross-border competition and prompting the creation of multiple national stock markets. The transformed EU political context and the efforts of Brussels civil servants and others to take advantage of it were the main causes. The promotion of competing ideas about appropriate markets and liberal interpretations of new EC laws—two strategies used to circumvent internal and external opposition to Easdaq—spawned uncertainties and changed perceptions about the viability of alternatives to protected national financial industries, kindling reactions from the London, Paris, Frankfurt, and other European and American exchanges.

Old Initiatives, New Conditions

The belief that a pan-European stock market would promote venture capitalism, solve financing problems of smaller companies and improve the Continent's international competitiveness continued to percolate inside the European Commission in the early 1990s. Especially inside DG13 (Innovation), DG18 (Financial Operations), and DG23 (Enterprise Policy/SMEs)—including a few of the same individuals involved in 1989—officials remained eager to see a pan-European stock market created, despite sometimes intense opposition from inside and outside the bureaucracy.[1] On four previous occasions, as Chapter 3 outlined, they had stepped back from direct interventions that would have helped launch markets based on similar proposals. At the end of the day, these prointervention officials were either blocked or unpersuaded that they could overcome opposition from stock exchanges, governments, and other DGs.

The estimations of Brussels officials changed in 1994. Three conditions, put in place mostly by colleagues in previous years, gave them confidence that an intervention would have far-reaching consequences. First, Brussels officials thought the May 1993 passage of the Investment Services Directive (ISD, Council Directive 93/22/EEC) might create new possibilities for a pan-European market. They interpreted the measure liberally and deliberately fanned uncertainties about its effects.[2] The directive's long-awaited passage extended the principle of mutual recognition, a form of shared sovereignty, to investment services entities, including stock exchanges.[3] On the surface, an exchange regulated in one EU country could, by 1996, operate in another via electronic networks and computer terminals.[4] In combination with the 1989 Prospectus Directive (Council Directive 89/298/EEC),[5] it was conceivable that the ISD would facilitate a pan-European market and cross-border competition for trading and listing services and diminish the ability of national authorities to control (or block) listing procedures and share trading in four ways: (1) financial intermediaries licensed in one EU country would only need to notify local authorities before operating in another; (2) stock exchanges regulated in one member state could put trading screens and have members in another; (3) a company's prospectus approved in one member state would not need approval in another before selling equity to local citizens; and (4) EU stock markets would function as if they shared a single application, rule book, and market authority so that investors would not need to worry about a company getting onto the market through a regulatory back door.[6]

Yet reaching agreement about investment services proved more difficult than doing so about banking, insurance, capital liberalization, and other financial areas targeted for integration in the late 1980s. After four years of tough negotiations, Europe's governments produced only a watered-down agreement. Ambiguous passages and escape clauses handed a victory to continental exchanges and other interests seeking to repel London's attack on their trading businesses and to slow the pace of change to allow for modernization.[7] Commission officials, like everyone else, doubted the directive would meet its purported aims. Article 15.5 was a main source of ambiguity. After seemingly extending a cross-border passport to European exchanges, it gave national authorities the right to freeze out new entrants. "This Article," the text reads, "shall not affect the Member States' right to authorize or prohibit the creation of new markets within their territories."[8] Only in 2004, eleven years later, were financial elites ready to revisit these sensitive issues and clarify the rules of cross-border competition, when they replaced the ISD with the 2004 Markets in Financial Instruments Directive (MiFID, EP and Council Directive 2004/39/EC).

The importance of the ISD, however, does not lie only or primarily in the content of the actual text or in the precise intentions of the member governments. There was no mention of a pan-European stock market, let alone the Nasdaq form, and the text did not give Brussels discretion for implementing the directive, as the European Commission had originally proposed.[9] Rather its salience, like that of so many pieces of legislation in the EU and elsewhere, stems largely from the opportunities it offered policy entrepreneurs with preexisting agendas.[10] Created to manage processes of change, the ISD opened the door to challengers of the status quo. No one, especially not officials at the exchanges, knew what the implications of a European "passport" in the financial services would mean. Commission officials, in a deliberate attempt to push the envelope and test the limits of the new legislation, took advantage of these unknowns by backing Easdaq and arguing that the new EC legislation would permit it to compete in all member countries.[11] "Until now it has been difficult to contemplate the creation of a true pan-European stock market," states a 1995 Commission publication. "With the coming into force of certain Community legislation, most importantly the Directive on Investment Services in the Securities Field on 1st January 1996, the opportunities will improve markedly."[12] The ISD thus gave Brussels civil servants a rationale in 1994 to intervene directly in support of Easdaq. In 1985 and 1989, Commission officials knew that even if a pan-European Nasdaq got off the ground, the exchanges had a range of protectionist tools for bringing about its failure by sheltering national cartels of brokers from competition and thwarting participation on an upstart market. In 1994, officials deliberately fanned uncertainties about the possibility of creating an alternative to established national markets and the effectiveness of old strategies for undermining it.

Second, the presence in 1994 of a compelling political argument that featured the Nasdaq form as a solution to Europe's economic problems fostered a new climate of possibility.[13] This new framing, promoted by Brussels officials and their EVCA allies, was an important factor behind the decision to intervene and also explains the emphasis on the U.S. market form. Structural unemployment, at the center of European politics by the early 1990s, had opened the door for an expanded range of policy ideas.[14] Reflecting preferences for supranational solutions, the civil servants commissioned studies that drew attention to the failure of national markets and the feasibility of pan-European ones.[15] As they learned from the past, however, the logic of European, as opposed to domestic, markets was unlikely on its own to silence financial interests vested in domestic arrangements. What made their message difficult to oppose in the early 1990s was the international celebrity status of the Nasdaq Stock Market, then twenty years old. Pointing to its role in creating American jobs, the officials implied that a similar market would solve the unemployment problem in Europe, just as it had in the United States.[16] The 1985 and 1989 market proposals also included copying parts of the Nasdaq. But stressing the American form at a moment when unemployment was reaching crisis levels had new appeal, especially because of the implication that such a market would resolve the unemployment problem without making painful political decisions about labor markets or social welfare systems. Commission officials, as much as any other European political actors, promoted this political discourse, which linked jobs, venture capitalism, and the Nasdaq form, and did so to make it more difficult for the exchanges and their governments to maintain public stances against a pan-European market.

Contrasting Commission officials' intervention in Easdaq to their refusal to support 1980s proposals for pan-European stock markets illuminates the import of the Nasdaq framing to the 1994 decision. The officials believed an appropriate political argument would help them overcome resistance to the pan-European market idea. In 1985, when Jacques Delors endorsed a proposal for a pan-European market, their effort to use the ECU to attract interest in the project failed to resonate with potential participants.[17] Then, as in 1989, Brussels decided not to intervene, in part for lack of a gripping political discourse to ensure that finance ministries and exchanges would have a difficult time countering an intervention publicly. Commission officials in 1989 tried to sell the pan-European market idea as a solution to the hollowing out of local financial centers. But again, this framing had little appeal.[18] In 1994, officials found more-persuasive language in the linkage between unemployment, venture capitalism, and the Nasdaq design. One of Easdaq's ardent Commission supporters, Daniël Janssens of DG13, said, "Of all the choices, Easdaq had the fewest number of opponents. That it was a Nasdaq copy gave it legitimacy. It worked in the U.S. and still does. That's why the Commission went with Easdaq."[19]

Some Brussels bureaucrats and venture capitalists believed deeply in the merits of the Nasdaq principle: that quoted companies be required to reveal high levels of information about their operations and finances. One newcomer to the prointervention camp, Paul Goldschmidt, for example, had come to the European Commission after spending more than two decades at Goldman Sachs.[20] He feared that the venture capitalists wanted to create another "cheap" feeder market that would allow them to unwind their investments in risky companies easily and would not be in the long-term public interest.[21] Jos Peeters, the Belgian venture capitalist behind the Easdaq proposal, possessed almost missionary zeal for the Nasdaq design. Nevertheless, as the rest of this chapter demonstrates, the officials from DG13 and DG23, who used their units' budgets to support (albeit indirectly) Peeters' proposal, were pragmatists who borrowed the Nasdaq's appeal whenever useful.

An Interest Group and an Entrepreneurial Individual

Above all, by 1994, ten years after Brussels civil servants catalyzed venture capitalists, there was an interest group, EVCA, eager to lead and take advantage of any backing the Commission was willing to give. The bureaucrats happily hid behind it to launch Easdaq.

The 1994 proposal for a pan-European Nasdaq copy surfaced in EVCA's European Capital Markets Working Group, headed by Peeters. He and his group represented the faction among EVCA's members who believed the only solution to the exits crisis, despite the conflicts it might foster with traditional national financial insiders, was a Europe-wide Nasdaq-like market independent of national stock exchanges. EVCA had been deeply divided about how to address the urgent problem.[22] Commission officials used their resources, close interactions, and encouragement to tip the balance toward Peeters and his idea of a Nasdaq for Europe.

The EVCA board and its top executive favored the conservative path of working within the financial establishment. The survival of any new market, they submitted, would depend on liquidity from the participation of intermediaries, who were unlikely to jeopardize relations with the stock exchanges: certain to draw strong opposition from the exchanges, an independent market was doomed to fail.[23] Despite these misgivings, EVCA's board chose Peeters, who had publicly called for an autonomous market, to head the working group. Two reasons likely account for the decision. The first was simply a miscalculation: the board thought it had enough checks on Peeters to control his activities. The second was a desire to appeal to EVCA's supporters inside the European Commission. In the early 1990s, the venture capitalists were intimately tied to some of the same units inside the European Commission that had originally assisted in EVCA's creation. In 1993, for example, 26 percent of the organization's budget came from Commission funds, and in 1994 they were projected to supply 45 percent.[24] In addition, one DG13 official served as a member on EVCA's Exits Committee. At a meeting between the Commission and EVCA in October 1993, an annual event to share agendas and perspectives, the venture capitalists pleaded with the Brussels civil servants to help them solve the exits crisis.[25] Commission officials had already made known their continued preference for pan-European markets, in June of the same year, having encouraged the Council of Ministers (Industry Council) to sponsor an investigation into the feasibility of supporting the creation of a European-level capital market for entrepreneurial companies.[26] According to reports from participants of the meeting, Goldschmidt and other Commission officials pushed for a new market based on high regulatory standards. Rather than a "quick fix," he insisted that any new market require listed companies to meet tough standards like the Nasdaq's. While other officials at the meeting had their own reasons for favoring the Nasdaq form, the venture capitalists left with a clear understanding of the type of proposal Brussels officials would be willing to support.

The EVCA board's selection of Peeters was most likely a response to these Commission preferences.[27] Wanting to ensure that the Brussels civil servants would fulfill their promise to pay for half the planned working group, which was charged with raising the public profile of the exits problem and organizing a lobbying campaign, the board members went out of their way to pick a chair who appealed to Commission functionaries.[28] Peeters was an obvious choice.

The Intervention

The Commission's intervention came in three stages. Reflecting the heightened importance of SMEs in European political debates, DG23, under Heinrich von Moltke, was now in the lead, though DG13, EVCA's original sponsor, continued its strong support. The intervention primarily involved funds from two separate spending programs.[29] In the first stage, the Commission civil servants paid for outside contractors to conduct two preliminary studies investigating both the failure of the 1980s feeder markets and the demand for a pan-European replacement.[30] In the second, they provided half the funding (ECU 87,000), as agreed, for the expenses of Peeters' working group. These early funds gave Peeters a degree of autonomy from EVCA, emboldening him to press forward with what had become a radical and innovative Easdaq initiative. The funding from the Commission, according to a former EVCA executive, "was a way for Peeters' working group to get around the conservative board."[31]

On April 18, 1994, twenty-six leaders from the financial services industry attended Peeters' first official meeting of the working group in Brussels. The list of attendees displayed his attempt to attract a mix of private- and public-sector actors to commit themselves to creating a pan-European Nasdaq. The participants, from nine European countries and the United States, included representatives of banks, institutional investors, three directorates general of the European Commission, a national securities regulator, brokerage firms, a consulting company, CISCO, and venture capitalists. Most important to the history of Europe's 1990s new markets, the list also included envoys from four national stock exchanges, including representatives from the Paris and London exchanges and from Deutsche Bank, the largest shareholder in the Deutsche Boerse AG, Germany's newly centralized stock exchange based in Frankfurt.[32]

In this first meeting, Peeters attempted to steer the participants toward his vision of a pan-European market for smaller companies. Consciously attempting to generate support and mask over potential conflicts, he kept discussions and conclusions general. In a carefully crafted summary circulated to participants a few days later, he drew five main conclusions: (1) Europe had a sufficient supply of young growth companies and a sufficient demand among investors for shares; (2) European financial services firms lacked expertise in entrepreneurial finance but could potentially make money supplying the services to a new dedicated market; (3) the optimal market for these companies would be pan-European in structure; (4) the development of a new market would require a determined initiative; and (5) the European Commission would support the initiative if it were pan-European.[33] Peeters followed the summary with a call to join the next phase of his working group, the development of a detailed blueprint of the future market.[34]

With the important exception of a few forward-looking individuals, the presence of national exchange officials at the meetings did not indicate a genuine interest in backing Peeters' agenda.[35] Support and cooperation were essentially off the table from the beginning. Either the exchange leaders did not believe there actually was a financing problem to which Peeters offered a solution, or they considered existing measures sufficient to redress it. As Chapter 5 detailed, the financial establishments in London and Paris had recently deliberated, devised, and implemented policies concerning smaller-company markets. At the newly centralized Frankfurt exchange, smaller-company markets ranked low on the list of priorities as the Deutsche Boerse entered a period of complete restructuring of its organization, technology, and markets. Executives of Germany's largest banks told Easdaq's promoters that national small- and medium-size firms did not face financing problems and that German investors were not interested in high-risk, smaller-company shares.[36]

There was little in Peeters' ideas that appealed to the exchanges. Easdaq would be a Nasdaq copy. This meant the new market would cater to high-growth young companies, rely heavily on market makers and financial analysts, and, most important, aim to attract institutional investors by requiring quoted companies to meet extremely high informational standards. For the most part, the firms who owned and controlled the national stock exchanges tended not to make their revenues from this financial sector. They did not generally possess expertise in market making and in analysis of high-growth entrepreneurial companies, and they feared that U.S. firms with such skills would benefit most from any new market based on these activities. For the exchanges, the Nasdaq form presented a conflict to their interests and seemed an invitation for American financiers to dominate.

It was also clear in April 1994 that Peeters envisioned Easdaq, like Nasdaq, to be the permanent home of high-growth companies. Its best companies would not eventually graduate to the main lists in London, Paris, and Frankfurt. Unlike the 1980s feeders, Easdaq would have an independent identity, thus raising the twin issues of control and competition. The national exchanges were especially anxious to ensure that trading continued to pass through their channels. Trading flows were not only a primary source of revenues for the exchanges. Without trading flows, member firms would see the benefit from exchange membership greatly reduced.[37]

Peeters obviously wanted the participation of national bourses. The French and British exchanges had recently invested heavily in state-of-the-art electronic trading systems, and Frankfurt was in the process of developing its own. Controlling trade flows through cutting-edge systems had become an integral part of competing in the contest over the future financial center of Europe. Peeters saw that Easdaq would have to meet the new technological standards and using the trading and clearing infrastructures of one of the exchanges rather than building a new one from scratch would save money, time, and effort. Yet it was hard to imagine why or how a national exchange would offer its proprietary trading system without also taking control. Peeters was proposing a pan-European market, by definition not controlled by any of the established exchanges. Why would a national exchange provide infrastructure but cede control to another body?

The exchanges had long opposed and had become adept at burying plans for pan-European markets. As previous chapters showed, Easdaq's proposed characteristics were not particularly new (see Table 1.1, page 4). In 1985 and 1989, the national exchanges, working through the Federation of European Securities Exchanges (FESE) and DG15 of the Commission, blocked plans for pan-European markets very much like the one Peeters was advancing, and individual exchanges had undermined homegrown initiatives. In light of this history and the fundamental challenge Easdaq posed, it is not surprising that the exchanges, despite the awareness of several exchange executives that Europe needed regional markets, could never figure out how to cooperate with Easdaq.

By June 1994, with the momentum for the initiative growing because of widespread press coverage, Peeters and the Commission officials recognized that Easdaq needed its own organizational structure, as well as more start-up funding.[38] The situation grew desperate by November, when the Paris bourse withdrew its initial promise of support. The French change of mind left Easdaq's promoters on their own, facing opposition from every major national stock exchange. From the perspective of at least some of EVCA's leadership, Peeters was out of control, having taken the Easdaq project well beyond his mandate. A conflict on such a scale seemed to be pushing EVCA in directions that would undermine the organization's long-term interests.

Freeing himself from the confines of EVCA's conservatives by creating a separate organization clearly appealed to Peeters. From his vantage, however, the French departure created a critical problem of a different nature. It signaled an urgent need to find alternative sources of financing. Even before its sudden and unexpected withdrawal, Peeters had not intended the French bourse to be Easdaq's primary source of financing. He, Ronald Cohen, and Peeters' other early allies sought to ensure independence through a broadly dispersed ownership structure. They had, however, been counting on the Paris exchange to be one of several owners, and most important, they believed its support would indicate to potential outside investors that the Easdaq initiative might very well succeed. Without French involvement, moreover, the need for additional funds had suddenly increased.[39] Peeters had expected to use the Paris bourse's quotation, trading, and settlement systems. Creating systems from scratch would require an entourage of outside experts and add to Easdaq's mounting expenses.

Then in November 1994, the Easdaq initiative faced a crisis. Peeters, Cohen, and the others knew there was a very high probability that Easdaq would never open for trading. Failures litter the history of smaller-company market proposals in Europe, and Easdaq's owners understood why. Creating a new market is an incredibly difficult feat under any conditions. Venture capitalists, as politically weak financial outsiders attempting to give life to a form that every major national stock exchange opposed, had taken on a doubly audacious task. Table 1.1 lists five proposals for pan-European markets modeled on the Nasdaq form.[40] In every case, venture capitalists and other financial outsiders initiated the proposal, and in every case, until Peeters' 1994 Easdaq initiative opened for trading in 1996, national financial insiders succeeded in preventing its creation.

In the winter of 1994–1995, the factors that had undermined the creation of the earlier pan-European market proposals were in place and in the process of bringing the Easdaq initiative down as well. Easdaq's venture capitalists, like their predecessors, could not create a market on their own. In the medium term, they would need to attract the support of at least some European financial insiders. But every indication suggested that the early signs of insider support had turned into vehement opposition. On the front lines, both the London and Paris exchanges had made known the imminent creation of their own competing markets, which are discussed later in this chapter, and Paris had launched a cartel-like initiative, called Euro.NM, through which the Continental stock exchanges would seek to shut out the upstart Easdaq and prevent the London new market from dominating. The Frankfurt exchange, while it contemplated the French initiative, was actively pressuring German banks not to participate in the venture capitalist scheme.[41] Ending any lingering doubt as to who had been opposing the Easdaq initiative, the exchanges openly attacked the pan-European proposal in July 1995 in Milan at a Fédération International des Bourses de Valeurs (FIBV) conference.[42] Given the predominant role of the exchanges in the national financial services industries, few investment banks and market-maker firms were willing to invest in Easdaq. Even the Nasdaq Stock Market, which had given early support, lost interest once the potential for Easdaq's failure became palpable.

Moreover, behind the scenes, the exchanges had succeeded, through heavy lobbying of their government protectors and agents within the Commission, to stop some of the most overt displays of support for Easdaq. A Commission official scheduled to speak at the November 1994 Easdaq conference in London pulled out at the last minute.[43] But despite heavy pressure, especially from the French Trésor via commissioner and former prime minister Edith Cresson, and "intensive discussion" within the Commission and member governments, the Brussels officials from DG23 and DG13 commenced the third stage of their intervention, pointing to strong support from national government authorities in charge of industrial policy, especially from authorities in Germany.[44] "We heard about the protests of national stock exchanges but we never received any written complaint," wrote one of the civil servants involved.[45]

This was Easdaq's critical hour and the reason Peeters' proposal initially survived the wall of opposition where earlier ones had perished. Receiving strong backing from consecutive commissioners charged with enterprise policy, the Commission civil servants stepped in to fill the mounting financing gap.[46] Given their druthers, of course, Peeters and his supporters would have preferred not to enlist the Brussels bureaucracy. In their eyes and those of European financiers more generally—just as in the halls of Europe's treasuries and ministries of finance—the European Commission was not a legitimate actor in the realm of finance. This attitude stemmed in part from prior interactions. When Commission officials sought to catalyze national stock exchange integration in the late 1970s, member governments, on behalf of national financial industries, made it clear that these efforts were inappropriate and unwelcome.[47] The precedent could be seen in the negotiations for the ISD, when the Commission did not play a large role and was not given discretion over its implementation. But the attitude also had roots in a widespread set of beliefs among financiers, who consider political actors and especially bureaucratic ones to be major obstructions to efficient markets. For Easdaq's venture capitalists, a Commission connection was likely embarrassing, as they feared potential investors and other financiers would conclude that the Easdaq initiative would not need Commission subsidies if it had an economic rationale.

The Commission's third round of financial contributions, again shared between DG23 and DG13, amounted to about ECU 500,000 ($600,000) between May 1995 and October 1996.[48] Even during these months, when Commissioners and governments sought to stop the support from Brussels, officials at a relatively low level of the bureaucracy used shrewd political skills to sustain the flow of subsidies. The contracts for and actual delivery of funds occurred both before and after the 1994–1995 change in Commission presidents (from Jacques Delors to Jacques Santer) and Commissioners overseeing Moltke (from Raniero Vanni d'Archirafi to Christos Papoutsis). DG13 committed ECU 200,000 on December 22, 1994, even though the contract does not appear to have been signed until April 10, 1995, and reads May 24, 1995. In the text, the contract gives a completion date of December 20, 1994, suggesting that an expense incurred during the Delors presidency occurred in time to beat the December 31, 1994, expiration date of the SPRINT (Strategic Programme for Innovation and Technology Transfer) funds' one-year extension.[49] DG23's contract for ECU 308,110 began in September 1995 and appears to be backdated to July 1, 1995.

In providing these funds, the Brussels civil servants faced a problem. The

Commission could not subsidize private corporations. Yet Easdaq, an early instance of what has subsequently become a trend for market owners, was a private venture. This explains why Easdaq's promoters established two organizations instead of one: Easdaq, the private for-profit corporation that would own and run the market, and EASD (European Association of Securities Dealers), which, because of its not-for-profit status, would receive funds from the European Commission.[50] Commission officials and Easdaq's venture capitalists tried to obscure EASD's political purpose by choosing a name that financiers would associate with the NASD, the self-regulatory organization created in the 1930s by the U.S. Congress, which at the time owned and regulated the Nasdaq Stock Market. The EASD-Easdaq relationship was entirely different. Aside from a temporary political device for transmitting Commission subsidies to support Easdaq in 1995 and 1996, EASD's reason for existing and its relationship to Easdaq developed over the course of several years. But EASD never had an official regulatory role. Under the ISD, a national securities regulator would have to recognize and regulate Easdaq in order to gain status as an official market mutually recognized in every EU member state. That responsibility ultimately rested on the Belgian Banking and Finance Commission, but only after it became clear that the list of willing national regulators was shrinking in tandem with the rise of national exchange opposition to Easdaq.[51]

The Commission officials from DG23 and DG13 knew as well as the venture capitalists that Easdaq could only survive in the medium and long term with the support of Europe's banks and other financial service providers. From the Brussels perspective, officials were witnessing a real-time instance of market failure.[52] How otherwise, Commission officials reasoned, could one explain the reluctance of private-market actors to participate in what was obviously an economically sound idea—providing new financial markets for young companies in need of capital? "We came to the conclusion that the logical answer to this problem [of undercapitalized SMEs] was the creation of a true European capital market for SMEs, which could play the role in Europe currently played by Nasdaq in the USA, a market focused on young companies with high growth potential, especially in high-tech areas," argued Moltke. "But a public institution such as the Commission," he continued, "has neither the competence nor the expertise nor the funds to create such a market itself. So the strategy adopted by the Commission was to try to stimulate the interest of capital market participants in such a project."[53]

In the world of finance, perception can mean everything. This is why

Easdaq's promoters attempted to borrow Nasdaq's legitimacy by making the EASD-Easdaq relationship seem parallel to NASD-Nasdaq.[54] "From 1994–96, it was all mirrors. We had to convince [financial] players to get involved or miss out," said a former EASD official who had also worked for Peeters' working group.[55]

The importance of perception also explains why the Commission's subsidies mattered so much. On the one hand, they were important to Easdaq's operations. Outside the inner circle of original investors, the Commission was Easdaq's only backer, and its subsidies, first through EVCA, then through EASD, helped keep the market experiment afloat at a precarious moment.[56] Even Peeters, who understandably interprets his own role as somewhat more substantial and that of Brussels as somewhat less than the depiction here, concedes that there was always good support within the Commission. "The little drops of money were a great help," he said.[57] On the other hand, the amounts were small in terms of what would be needed after the 1994 and 1995 financial crunch ended, when the enterprise would have to move beyond the ragtag Easdaq operation. It was imperative to attract additional financial backing as well as market participants. In this sense, support from the EU, widely covered in the press, added significantly to the perception that Easdaq might survive and pose competition to incumbent markets.

In influencing the selection of Peeters and subsidizing his working group and then the Easdaq initiative, the European Commission helped venture capitalists overcome fragmented ideas about the design of new markets. Its backing ensured that the future competition would be over markets with a Nasdaq organizational form and a European scope, even if the results sometimes turned out to be more rhetorical than substantive. As the next section illustrates, Easdaq's existence was short-lived, but its effects quickly spread, sparking cross-border competition over who would supply Europe's future Nasdaq and prompting the creation of AIM, Techmark, the Nouveau Marché, the Neuer Markt, and the other European new markets.

New Stock Markets in Europe

The specter of new European competition revealed itself at the very moment the LSE flexed its muscles to control change processes in domestic equity markets. News of the Easdaq initiative hit London only months after the exchange's victory in the yearlong domestic contest over the closure of the USM (discussed in Chapter 5). Staving off CISCO's campaign, it turns out, represented only a temporary success in the LSE's efforts to undermine outsider challenges to its autonomy in dealing with smaller-company stock markets. Suddenly venture capitalists had a new weapon that enhanced their influence: they could threaten to leave London for a new EU market, and no one could be sure whether they were bluffing. The London exchange was merely the first to react to this Brussels-induced competition by creating a new stock market of its own. The Paris bourse and the other continental exchanges followed in rapid succession.

A Credible Threat of Exit

The LSE's December 1993 announcement to close the USM marked a shift in the minds of those CISCO members who wanted a British Nasdaq. Increasingly, they doubted whether the LSE was the right actor to create the market they desired and began privately and through CISCO to explore alternative partners. One British venture capitalist, Ronald Cohen, chairman of Apax Partners and Company, had been hedging his bets for several months. The driving force behind CISCO's proposed Enterprise Market (see Chapter 5), Cohen had been one of the organization's creators and chairmen and a member of the LSE's Smaller Companies Working Party. Since the LSE first announced its plan to close the USM in January 1993, Cohen had personally lobbied British government and Brussels officials and LSE leaders. He had commissioned lawyers and consultants to advise him on the legality of obtaining independent RIE (registered investment exchange) status and had a proposal of his own for a British Nasdaq, named Easdaq-UK, independent of but similar to CISCO's Enterprise Market. Most important, Cohen had corresponded throughout the summer of 1993 with Nasdaq officials and believed he had gained their support for a Nasdaq-like market in Britain.[58]

By February 1994, several CISCO leaders—including its chairman, Andrew Beeson; two executive committee members, Brian Winterflood and Graham Cole; and its chief executive, Katie Morris—were in conversation with Peeters and participating in the earliest deliberations of EVCA's Capital Markets Working Group. But the critical tie between CISCO's efforts and the ongoing Easdaq-creation process occurred at the March 16 CISCO conference, when Peeters persuaded Cohen to join forces.

Cohen had from the start envisioned a European dimension first to CISCO's Enterprise Market and then to his own proposal for Easdaq-UK.

But unlike Peeters, he was promoting a federated model that had every European country's own Nasdaq-like market linking into a European network.[59] At this point, he still hoped that the LSE would support his efforts and had raised the subject with Michael Lawrence, the LSE's new chief executive. Yet Peeters convinced Cohen that the LSE would never create a British Nasdaq, that Chapter 20 was a disingenuous gesture, and that CISCO's members with strong LSE ties would in the end reject a market outside the LSE. Peeters persuaded Cohen that a pan-European market would better attract a critical mass of companies; prevent national authorities, including stock exchanges, from putting up protectionist obstacles; be feasible under the new ISD; and ensure early and critical support from the European Commission.[60] Peeters and Cohen also agreed at the CISCO conference to call the pan-European Market Easdaq, instead of Peeters' original name, EEMEC (European Electronic Market for Entrepreneurial Companies), and to use Nasdaq's small-company admission requirements.

Thus by the time the LSE discarded the recommendations of the Smaller Companies Working Party in April 1994, the CISCO leadership was backing Peeters' proposal for a pan-European market. At this stage, the Easdaq project appeared to have the participation of British venture capitalists and investment bankers and the Nasdaq (thanks to Cohen's efforts), as well as European venture capitalists, the European Commission, and the Paris bourse.

So long as the debates over markets were strictly contained within national borders, the LSE never doubted its ability to resist CISCO's efforts. This calculation changed dramatically, however, with the departure of Cohen and the potential exodus of other British venture capitalists and financiers. Venture capital support of Easdaq represented a tactical shift from working within the British financial system to abandoning it for a still-unrealized European financial system that might one day be more hospitable. At least since the lifting of capital controls in the late 1970s, British venture capitalists could technically exit, as the slow trickle of UK companies raising capital on U.S. markets exemplified. But this alone was not sufficient to prompt the LSE into action.

Contrary to arguments that emphasize the causal role of mobile capital (see Chapters 2 and 5), the ability to exit became a credible threat to immobile national interests only when combined with an alternative institutional foundation. Until 1994, only the United States offered risk capital a friendly financial system, even though its distance from Europe greatly reduced the threat it posed. One of the main reasons the LSE introduced Chapter 20, in fact, was to quell the potential exodus of British high-tech firms and their venture capitalist investors to the Nasdaq. In other financial sectors, such as large-company equity and derivatives markets, continental financial centers had developed regulations and markets that pressured the LSE and London International Financial Futures and Options Exchange (LIFFE) to adapt. Until 1994, however, venture capitalists had nowhere in Europe to go.

In June 1994, when the financial press reported Easdaq's success in attracting support, the LSE began to sense the European environment was changing. Suddenly Easdaq seemed a real danger to the exchange's control over the supply and creation of smaller-company markets, by appearing to provide British venture capitalists with an attractive European foundation on which to lodge. Not only did the Easdaq project appear to have the backing of the European Commission, the SBF, and Nasdaq, but with the ISD came the possibility, much trumpeted by Brussels civil servants, that the new market would be rooted in EU regulation.[61]

A New Market, Then Another

Less than three months later, on September 7, 1994, the LSE abruptly changed course by circulating a proposal that led directly to the creation of the Alternative Investment Market in June of 1995. Without the challenge of potential European competition from Easdaq, it is unlikely the LSE would have created AIM or any other new market for smaller-company shares. In April 1994, the LSE appeared to have won its domestic battle with CISCO. Five months afterward, the Easdaq proposal reopened the issue, providing the first indication that the LSE was losing control over the change process.

The LSE's reaction to the perceived Easdaq threat had three dimensions. First, the LSE opted to create a rival market rather than cooperate with Easdaq. Unlike the French bourse, which at first tried to control the Easdaq project through a strategy of cooperation, the LSE was dead set from the start on undermining potential support for Easdaq and thereby making sure it never got off the ground. In fact Ronald Cohen, still convinced in September 1994 that the LSE was the obvious supplier for a European Nasdaq, offered the LSE leadership in Easdaq.[62] But the LSE's Michael Lawrence refused the offer and maintained the view that the LSE itself would become the Nasdaq of Europe. In 1994 the LSE was by far the largest and most important stock exchange in Europe, and its Official List combined with SEAQ

International was the world's third-leading market. These were the days before Eurex's LIFFE coup, before the French and German counterattacks brought SEAQ International to its knees, and long before the NYSE purchased Euronext.[63] The LSE's executives and board members simply could not imagine a joint venture initiated by outsiders. They apparently did not see why, if there was going to be a Nasdaq of Europe, Easdaq needed to assume that role.

Second, the LSE decided to use its formidable resources to act immediately rather than wait to see whether Easdaq would amount to real competition. Once the LSE decided to create a new market, it was able to take advantage of its prominent position in the British financial system, especially its RIE status, to carry out a preemptive strategy—of quickly putting together a market that would steal Easdaq's thunder before it became operational. The LSE was able to act swiftly in creating AIM, much more swiftly than Easdaq's promoters, who had to raise funds; to find a national regulator willing to oversee the first pan-European market under the ISD; to put together electronic information, execution, and settlement systems; and to attract a critical mass of users. The LSE already had in place the legal authority, the technical infrastructure, the regulatory apparatus, and the resources for promoting a new market. AIM would have the status of a "regulated market," supervised and operated by the LSE, which was an RIE under the British Financial Services Act of 1986. Trading and settlement would take place through the exchange's existing systems and be accessible from terminals already on LSE members' desks.

Finally, the LSE adopted a native organizational form for AIM, rather than the Nasdaq form, which Easdaq's promoters were copying. The LSE at this point had two goals. On the one hand, reflecting its intent to retain the effective monopoly over British trading and listings, the exchange sought to ensure that all companies appropriate for public quotation would ultimately end up on the Official List. On the other hand, it now aimed to ensure that Easdaq would not become competition in the trading services of the smaller-company sector. To preempt the Easdaq challenge, the LSE decided to accommodate at least some of the items on CISCO's agenda.

The LSE had not wanted to create a new market. Nevertheless when it came to choosing the organizational form, the LSE managed to split the CISCO coalition and attain much of its objectives. AIM's design met a key CISCO demand. The new market was separate from the Official List and had an independent management team.[64] In contrast to the Nasdaq design, which required companies to meet rigorous reporting and disclosure requirements, the new market instead relied heavily on advisors whose concern for their own reputations was to send signals to investors about the quality of listed companies (see Tables 2.1 and 2.2, pages 24, 26). At the same time, the LSE left it unclear during the planning stages whether AIM's selection process for separating out the best companies would take place before or after a company entered the market. In this sense, AIM shared many of the attributes of the easy-access feeder markets of the 1980s. Compared with the Official List and even with the USM, AIM had lower barriers to quoting, lower informational requirements, and an inexpensive quotation process. In the early days, it was still an open question whether AIM would truly be independent or whether its best companies would eventually graduate to the Official List. The LSE knew such a market would not satisfy everyone in the CISCO coalition but hoped to appease some of CISCO's members—at least enough to split the CISCO coalition and reduce British support for the Easdaq challenge.

In two respects, the LSE's approach succeeded. Of CISCO's proposals for new markets (discussed in Chapter 5), AIM came closer to the National Market than to the Enterprise Market. CISCO's smaller-company service providers had promoted the National Market as a means to reopen the flow of smaller companies seeking quotations. Many of these firms belonged to the LSE, earned much of their revenues through LSE channels, and would have been reluctant to oppose the exchange by supporting the Easdaq project. AIM intentionally went a long way in meeting their demands and consequently put CISCO in an awkward position. The LSE was supplying one of the markets CISCO had sought. Even though CISCO's leadership was especially concerned about the absence of a market for entrepreneurial companies, one that would draw institutional investors, CISCO could not adopt a completely adversarial position without losing some of its members and diminishing its emerging role as the voice for smaller UK companies. Thus CISCO, while continuing to promote Easdaq and other markets to fill the remaining "gaps," also had to support and promote AIM.

The LSE strategy also succeeded in a second sense. AIM attracted many British and international companies that might have otherwise listed on Easdaq. One of Easdaq's shortcomings, despite a design that catered to institutional investors, was its inability to attract a sufficient number of companies. The reason underscores the political realities of national financial services industries. Financial advisors, as opposed to an objective set of efficiency criteria, exert the primary influence on a company's decisions about seeking a public quotation or not and about selecting a market. Chosen largely on the basis of personal contacts, these advisors belong to a historically protected national financial community embedded in organizations like stock exchanges. Despite significant financial liberalization, British smaller-company service providers still had incentives in the early 1990s to take firms to market through traditional channels. In principle, British companies might have lined up to join Easdaq. In practice, they usually opted for AIM. Together with the French and German exchanges, which also created new markets in part for the same reasons, the LSE succeeded in undermining support for Easdaq and slowing the flow of new issues.

Despite Easdaq's failure, the exchanges were unable to reverse its impact on expectations and cross-border competition in smaller-company finance. Ironically, in making AIM, the LSE hastened the arrival of new rivals. AIM's creation influenced the decisions of the French and German exchanges to launch the Nouveau Marché and the Neuer Markt, respectively, and both countries' exchanges, despite a veneer of cooperation, aspired for their respective markets to become the Nasdaq of Europe.

In this sense, the LSE's strategy seemed at the time to have backfired in a critical way. In reacting first, the British exchange also countered the Easdaq challenge least effectively. In attempting to thwart a potential competitor through immediate action, the exchange committed itself to a form before it was possible to grasp the full impact of the Easdaq initiative. At the time, the exchange did not know that Easdaq's creation would also drag the French and German exchanges into the ring. More to the point, the LSE could not have anticipated the particular contours of the new European competition: a race to become Europe's Nasdaq by mimicking the U.S. market's rules. At the moment of AIM's creation, Easdaq's form was still at the cusp of becoming a new focal point.

It is also ironic, in light of AIM's relative success since 2001, that in its first five years, the European exchange with the most distinguished history in supplying equity markets was playing catch-up with its continental rivals and Easdaq. First in August 1997, under criticism for creating an insufficiently regulated market that was (contrary to marketing campaigns) dissimilar to Nasdaq, the LSE raised AIM's regulatory standards, primarily by enhancing the role of nominated sponsors and increasing the transparency of insider activity and the powers of the exchange to sanction noncomplying companies.[65] AIM had succeeded in attracting 300 companies and had a gross capitalization of 5 billion pounds. It was obviously meeting the needs of some market participants. But others—especially institutional investors, who mattered the most—seemed to have new, much higher aspirations about what they could expect in European smaller-company markets. They claimed to want high-quality, high-growth high-tech companies circulating a large number of shares and providing U.S. levels of information: in short, a European Nasdaq. AIM's companies, in contrast to those on the newly created Neuer Markt and Easdaq, spanned an eclectic range of industries, were allegedly too small for professional asset managers, had experienced a number of public scandals, and provided relatively low levels of information. Even though the LSE never intended AIM to be a Nasdaq copy—indeed the Official List was supposed to double as Europe's Nasdaq—the LSE felt forced to make AIM seem more like the other new markets. But the LSE found itself behind the eight ball, and its improved regulatory standards appeared to be too little, too late.

When the Deutsche Boerse's Neuer Markt catapulted ahead of its rivals in the number of quoted companies in 1999, the LSE all but declared AIM a failure. Neither the Official List nor AIM seemed to meet the new expectations of investors for a Nasdaq-like market. As London and Frankfurt were negotiating over the future of Europe's stock exchanges, it was becoming apparent that the Deutsche Boerse could use the Neuer Markt to its advantage.[66] The LSE simply could not fulfill its goal to become the stock exchange for Europe without supplying a Nasdaq copy of its own. Thus in November 1999, it created Techmark, a segment of the Official List reserved for high-growth technology companies. But unlike other officially listed companies, Techmark's firms had to meet higher informational standards, including quarterly reports, the hallmark of the Nasdaq form (see Table 2.2, page 26). The LSE encouraged already listed technology companies to join Techmark, a strategy that gave the new market 244 companies in its first year.

In 1994, the LSE sought to frustrate potential competition from the Brussels-backed Easdaq in the same way that it had undermined domestic competition in the 1980s and early 1990s: by making use of its dominant position in the British financial system and creating new national markets to redirect trading activities to its own channels. The failure of this traditional strategy captures the intrusion of Brussels-sparked European competition into domestic affairs and the relative loss of discretion over the market-creation processes. The old tactic's apparent weakness was that it was developed at a time when national financial systems, especially smaller-company sectors, were largely cut off from foreign competition for listing companies, investors, and financial intermediaries. In the mid-1990s, however, the LSE was unable to parlay its traditional position into an effective plan for stamping out competition from Europe—at least that was the perception inside the exchange. Believing it faced a new environment, the LSE recalculated and created new markets, one of which was a Nasdaq copy, designed to compete with the Neuer Markt, Frankfurt's answer to Easdaq.

Competitive Responses from the Continent

The origins of Paris' Nouveau Marché, its timing, and its organizational form were, like those of AIM and Techmark, rooted in a European-level interdependent process, whereby stock exchanges suddenly made decisions in response largely to what their counterparts were doing. Easdaq-spawned competition, traceable to Brussels bureaucrats, was the underlying cause.

Understanding the seeds of the French new market also helps elucidate the about-face in Frankfurt, where the stock exchange created the Neuer Markt in 1997. As recently as the summer of 1995, Deutsche Boerse's majority stockholders, the traditionally powerful universal banks, held firmly to their position that Germany had no need for markets based on U.S. forms. But the Frankfurt exchange, like its Paris counterpart, came under a new set of constraints, and suddenly the preexisting ambition to become Europe's premier stock exchange required a new element: a Nasdaq lookalike. By 1996, the Deutsche Boerse had announced its intention to create its own national Nasdaq copy, the Neuer Markt, which opened for trading in March 1997 and adopted the French proposal for a European network of national new markets. In supplying their own market for smaller companies, Frankfurt's exchange officials sought to ensure Easdaq's failure and to diminish the risk that Paris or London might become the center of a new European financial sector for dynamic young firms. Thus a competitive process, begun with the Easdaq initiative, led not only to the creation of AIM, Techmark, and the Nouveau Marché but also to the Neuer Markt and other new markets listed in Table 1.1 (page 4).

French Venture Capitalists Gain Influence

Until June 1994, financial policymakers in France defended the Second Marché reforms with only a campaign of words. As Chapter 5 showed, they made no modifications to please venture capitalists and betrayed no signs of doing so. The financial establishment had the power to ignore the arguments and demands of venture capitalists, who remained on the margins of official French finance.

But the same set of events that strengthened the hand of British venture capitalists in June 1994 also empowered their French colleagues. The widely publicized Easdaq initiative and the outpouring of interest at a Paris meeting of Peeters' working group convinced financial authorities in France, as it had in the United Kingdom, that the Commission-backed pan-European market would indeed get off the ground. Critically important was the perception that Peeters and the other venture capitalists promoting Easdaq had strong support not only from the European Commission but also from some of Europe's exchanges as well as the American Nasdaq itself.

The response from Parisian financial authorities came in two stages. The executives of the exchange (still SBF at this point) reacted first when they turned their noncommittal participation into a definite promise to support the Easdaq project. With the Easdaq celebration taking place in their city, the executives of the French bourse felt obliged to respond immediately to two new developments: the potential for competition in what had formerly been the nationally protected sector of smaller company finance, and the emergence of new expectations among market participants that the pan-European Nasdaq form was best practice and a new focal point.

The SBF executives could have done nothing and accepted the possibility that another national exchange would support Easdaq, provide its infrastructure, and ultimately become the center of trading for continental shares in young, entrepreneurial companies. Or they could have become Easdaq's prime supporter themselves, extend the existing SBF trading system to the new sector, and eventually use the pan-European market as one way to challenge London's preeminence.

Eager to promote Paris as Europe's future financial center, SBF president Jean-François Théodore did not equivocate in giving his exchange's support for Easdaq. For Théodore, as for the executive in charge of smaller-company issues, Dominique Leblanc, being a financial hub meant fostering a vibrant venture capital industry and supplying a Nasdaq copy among the array of capital markets. The Europe-wide form seemed a good way for France to take advantage of the newly passed ISD and leapfrog into first place in a budding sector. Taking advantage of the fanfare surrounding Easdaq at the

Paris meeting, Théodore announced to the financial press on June 17 that the SBF would support Easdaq—but would not seek to control it. After the June meeting, the Paris exchange became one of three organizations to contribute $30,000 to the Easdaq project.[67] Théodore apparently imagined a market that would operate through the Paris-based electronic trading system and otherwise be tailored to meet the preferences of AFIC's and EVCA's venture capitalists—by being pan-European in scope, with a form based on the Nasdaq and, notably, with a management and an organization independent of Europe's national stock exchanges.[68] He also apparently thought he had the authority to commit the exchange in such a way.

The second stage of response from the Parisian financial policymakers became public only five months later, when the SBF abruptly withdrew its support of Easdaq, just two weeks before the November 1994 conference in London. Peeters' working group had spent much of the interim months hiring consultants to prepare a detailed plan for the proposed market's actualization and operation.[69] Taking Théodore at his word, the working group members believed France had solved one of their main problems. In the early 1990s, putting together an electronic information, trading, and settlement system posed a significant hurdle inherent in creating a financial market. New systems were expensive and time consuming and raised difficult issues regarding compatibility. Grafting Easdaq onto the SBF systems would have resolved all of these challenges in a single swoop. The purpose of Peeters' November conference in London was to win firm commitments of support from European investment banks and other financial firms. A key selling point in the plan Peeters and his EVCA colleagues had intended to distribute highlighted the future role of SBF systems.

The plan, "Easdaq: A Conceptual Paper," however, never circulated through Europe's financial community.[70] Three weeks prior to the conference, the SBF informed Peeters that France would be conducting its own study before the exchange could commit to Easdaq, tried to delay the London meeting, and explicitly forbid him from using the SBF name in promotional literature.[71]

Why did the SBF withdraw its support of Easdaq? In large part, the answer lies in the late-1980s reforms to the French financial system. An important element in the deliberate expansion of markets in France was the stock exchange's modernization. The stock market reform laws of January 1988, among other measures, ended the cartel of brokers by changing their status (from state officials to companies), permitted domestic and foreign financial firms more easily to forge partnerships with and purchase the former cartel members, and expanded the number of financial firms with access to the exchange.[72] One result of the 1988 reforms was that the SBF executives did not always see eye to eye with the board of directors.[73]

The point should not be exaggerated. The executives and owners belonged to the same small circle of financial elites, and they shared ambitions to turn Paris into an international financial center. But while the executives had the luxury to promote a long-term program to transform the bourse into an internationally competitive exchange, the owners had the obligation to promote the prospects for their own particular firms. Neither denied the need for a Nasdaq-like market. The Easdaq initiative, in this sense, had created a new set of expectations around the U.S. model. The June 1994 Easdaq announcement had set off a process that was quickly gaining momentum and increasingly narrowing choices. On September 22, for example, Business Objects, a splashy French software company, became the first French company to list on Nasdaq. In having refused to accept the listing on the SBF, the Paris exchange demonstrated its inability to provide financing for high-technology, entrepreneurial companies with short track records. The ease with which Business Objects was able to find an alternative to the SBF came as a shock to the exchange and other financial authorities and intensified the conviction that Paris had to supply a Nasdaq-like market of its own or face a drain of high-tech companies and venture capitalist activity.[74]

Even so, the bourse executives and owners, with different priorities concerning market forms and the issue of control, did not agree on whether to join the Easdaq project. The executives appreciated the efficiencies of a pan-European form. The owners, in contrast, worried about competition from European and American firms, seeing the Europe-wide Nasdaq design as an invitation to foreigners to capture a share of the French financial services industry and give nothing in return.[75] Meanwhile, the owners wanted to join the Easdaq project only if they could control it and thereby ensure that the rules of competition favored their firms' respective expertise. Discussions between Easdaq and the French bourse continued on and off through 1996. President Denis Mortier of the French venture capitalist association, placed in an awkward position with one foot on each side, tried on several occasions to broker a deal. But negotiations always collapsed on the issue of French control. Peeters and Cohen, insisting on a venture capitalist market independent of the national exchanges, refused.

The Nouveau Marché, Euro.NM, the Neuer Markt, NextEurope . . .

In the end, the owners, led by Bruno Roger of the investment bank Lazard Frères et Cie and coordinated through the Trésor, pulled the SBF out of the Easdaq initiative.[76] Still, this action represented more a beginning than an end for market creation in France. Before June 1994, the SBF, the COB and the Trésor had no intention of revisiting the smaller-company market issue, having just completed the Second Marché reforms. They had even launched a publicity campaign celebrating their resounding success and rejecting AFIC's demand for a Paris-supported pan-European Nasdaq copy. But the repercussions from the Easdaq initiative only intensified with the LSE's announcement of AIM. In February 1995, in a "co-decision" with the Trésor, the SBF announced plans to create its own new market, called the Nouveau Marché.[77] At the top of the SBF's concerns was ensuring that French venture capitalists and their client companies remained in France.[78]

Despite the new interest in venture capitalists, change was inevitably slow. Even after the decision to create the Nouveau Marché, the major French investment banks gave it lukewarm support. Instead, it was smaller players (especially Crédit Agricole) looking for new niches, that were the most active players early on. Only when valuations began to soar did the traditional French investment houses step in. The same pattern repeated itself in Frankfurt, where Deutsche Bank stood on the sidelines and DG Bank created a market for itself by providing services tailored to the Neuer Markt.

Originally conceived as an alternative version of Easdaq, the Nouveau Marché was a national Nasdaq copy, tied through carefully managed connections to other Nasdaq copies in Europe. The new market met several of the French venture capitalists' demands. In contrast to the LSE's original response, the SBF veered from the feeder form of the reformed Second Marché, especially in establishing higher informational standards. The required quarterly reports, a U.S. convention, went beyond requirements of any other French market (see Table 2.2, page 26). The authorities genuinely sought to create a French Nasdaq and hoped it would foster the type of activity associated with its American cousin. Within national parameters, they implicitly intended to give French financial services firms a period to develop expertise in entrepreneurial finance—an infant-industry strategy of sorts—and the SBF itself played teacher, a role that the Deutsche Boerse later adopted.[79] Finally, by promoting a European network of national markets, the French authorities accepted Mortier's argument that the French financial services industry alone could not support a market of this kind. Never-theless, domestic financial insiders preferred a European design that would leave control over levels of cross-border competition in the hands of the na-tional exchanges—a cartelization of the new sector.

Thus in November 1994, only five months after the Easdaq proposal hit the press and before the effects of the Second Marché reforms could be rea-sonably assessed, the French financial policymaking elite unexpectedly re-turned to the smaller-company market question. And by February 1995 they had announced the creation of a French Nasdaq copy, the Nouveau Marché. The Brussels-backed initiative prompted financial authorities to launch the new market and narrowed the range of alternative designs that exchanges and others perceived as legitimate. Easdaq, in short, led directly to the Nouveau Marché's Nasdaq-like form and its European scope.

The realization that Peeters' market would in fact take off sparked a process that constrained French financial authorities in new ways, prompt-ing them to innovate, just as it had pressed the authorities across the Chan-nel. The behavior of other European exchanges appeared to be a real threat to the formerly protected smaller-firm financial sector, and powerful French financial insiders sensed that market participants had new expectations about appropriate smaller-company markets. The reformed Second Marché, celebrated only months before, suddenly seemed unable to meet the new challenge. The resulting Nouveau Marché marked a decisive shift away from the protectionist feeder design.

A Reaction from Frankfurt

In the summer of 1995, Leblanc and other SBF executives went on a pro-motional campaign encouraging other European exchanges to create simi-lar new national markets for the Euro.NM network. By June 1995, they had persuaded the Brussels and Amsterdam exchanges. The next month, the SBF raised the idea in Frankfurt with the Deutsche Boerse, which was un-der the leadership of CEO Werner Seifert. At the time of the Easdaq an-nouncement, the Frankfurt exchange had been undergoing a comprehensive reorganization and had launched a proposal to restructure its markets in February 1995, one month after the creation of a federal securities author-ity.[80] Initially, the primary owners of the exchange, the large universal banks, had shown no interest in the pan-European project.[81]

Nevertheless, by 1995, there were signs that Deutsche Boerse executives and owners viewed Easdaq, AIM, and the Nouveau Marché as potential competition. At that point, U.S.-style venture capitalism in Germany hardly existed, and the impetus for change did not stem from a bottom-up lobby campaign of venture capitalists or from their possible exodus, per se.[82] Rather, the concern of the Deutsche Boerse's owners rested in the potential departure of small and medium-sized German high-tech companies, which would seek alternative jurisdictions for their financing needs. In 1995, the exchange circulated a letter to its members, instructing them not to participate in Easdaq until the Frankfurt exchange could determine an appropriate policy; hired McKinsey Consulting to conduct a study on the topic; and then conducted several investigations of its own.[83]

In January 1996, six months after the SBF executives first broached the idea, Deutsche Boerse introduced plans to create a new national market, the Neuer Markt, to be linked to Euro.NM.[84] By this time, Deutsche Boerse executives recognized that Easdaq's exceptionally high informational standards had led to new expectations among market participants, who now demanded U.S.-level standards and enforcement. The executives had watched as the French and British exchanges scrambled to bring the rules and regulations of their new markets in line with Easdaq's. Investors had shown their disappointment with poor enforcement of high informational standards on the Nouveau Marché and low levels of regulation on AIM. Meanwhile, Easdaq was itself having trouble attracting new company listings in the face of competition from national financial communities with historically tight relationships between companies and financiers.

Taking advantage of the Deutsche Boerse's position as a late mover, having seen the mistakes of its rivals, Reto Francioni, the Deutsche Boerse executive behind the Neuer Markt, convinced the exchange to adopt exceptionally high informational standards—equivalent to those on Easdaq and more demanding than any other German market.[85] Companies that wanted to raise capital through the Neuer Markt had to report in English, in accordance with international accounting standards, and to submit quarterly reports (see Table 2.2, page 26). The Frankfurt exchange also borrowed the strengths of the French national model by orchestrating an aggressive promotion policy to attract German companies to the Neuer Markt. And, like the French bourse, the Deutsche Boerse adopted the role of tutor for German banks and financial services companies, which had little expertise in entrepreneurial finance.[86]

The explosive early success of the Neuer Markt exacerbated perceptions that the French bourse had created a watered-down Nasdaq copy at best. Executives at the SBF, unlike their colleagues in Frankfurt, lacked the autonomy from the owners to refuse the listing of their clients and to enforce the new high informational standards. The result was the admittance of some seemingly inappropriate companies—those that were too small for a successful float and were outside high-tech or high-growth sectors—and a general lack of company information. Firm performance was poor, sometimes dismal. In November 1996, the SBF reacted by moving the Nouveau Marché's rules closer to the Nasdaq's.[87]

The Closure of Europe's Nasdaq Look-Alikes

The frenzy of new market formation began during the great bull market of the late twentieth century but continued in its aftermath. At the end of 1999, the height of the boom years, the Nouveau Marché, like the Neuer Markt, did spectacularly well in terms of company numbers and valuation levels. At its peak, the Frankfurt market had 342 listed companies and a market capitalization of 234 billion euros.[88] The comparable figures for the Paris market were 167 listed companies and 26 billion euros.[89] The price collapses that began in 2000 had farther to fall than on other markets around the globe that also experienced a speculative bubble.[90] In the final three ebullient years, the price indices for the top 100 German companies (DAX-100) and Nasdaq companies (NASDAQ-100) rose by 117 percent and 459 percent, respectively, whereas the main price index for the Neuer Market (NEMAX-All-Share) was up 1,636 percent.[91]

When the downturn came, it revealed wide disparities between high informational requirements and the exchange's and regulator's capabilities to enforce them.[92] Of course, similar gaps emerged in the United States, most notoriously in Enron's 2001 bankruptcy, and have occurred throughout the modern history of financial cycles. The Nasdaq-100 index, moreover, had, as of 2007, yet to return to its high of March 2000. Few, however, questioned the U.S. market's ability to survive. Conversely, in Europe, at least on the Continent, several factors combined so that survival became a question immediately after the price fall.[93] Compared with older, more-established markets, even the Neuer Markt lacked a large enough pool of quoted companies to compensate for those marked by malfeasance and insolvency. In this respect, Europe's new markets had bad luck. One of the century's worst speculative market crashes occurred when the new markets were in their infancy. Furthermore, while a general problem across European equity markets, the inadequacies of regulation and enforcement were especially pronounced on the new markets. For example, by September of 2002, Burghof and Hunger counted thirty Neuer Market bankruptcies and forty companies that "suffered from alleged insider trading or counterfeited ad-hoc announcements or . . . applied for insolvency (partly because of fraudulent behavior)."[94] These high numbers suggest that the cross-border competitive forces pressured the exchanges to bring inappropriate companies to market. The numbers also reflect the politically charged atmosphere that followed the price collapse. As noted in Chapter 1, French and German households, not asset managers, were the first investors to purchase shares and remained committed investors. The post-2000 losses, widely spread among average people, no doubt drew disproportionate amounts of press as well as the attention of prosecutors.

By the early twenty-first century, the exchanges found themselves under intensified competitive pressures. After the euro's introduction, as the next chapter shows, EU governments agreed to a comprehensive program to build the political and regulatory foundation for Europe-wide financial markets. The major financial cities and their exchanges were jockeying for future position within the so-called single financial market and therefore continued experimenting with smaller-company equity markets. The competition over the seat of entrepreneurial finance was now part of the overall rivalry for the future center of European finance. Having a robust smaller-company stock market not only had become central to what it meant to be a leading exchange but also represented a critical bargaining chip in the on-again, off-again merger talks among the three main exchanges, the LSE, Euronext, and the Deutsche Boerse. In 2000, for instance, the Neuer Markt was the German exchange's most valuable asset in the proposed merger with the LSE, and the parties had planned a new cross-border market based in Frankfurt, not London.[95]

The Deutsche Boerse, the Bourse de Paris, its new partners, and other exchanges in Europe reacted initially to the scandals and bankruptcies revealed after March 2000 by increasing informational standards and regulations—a last-ditch effort to save their markets' reputations. The Deutsche Boerse and German regulators especially took strong measures in this direction.[96] But their actions appear to have sent the wrong signal and in the end could not save the sullied reputation of the Neuer Markt. The extended downturn, the damage to the new markets' reputations, and the intensified competition for a smaller number of listed companies and investors thus forced more drastic measures.

Easdaq, the original new market and the wellspring of the others, was the first to fall. The Nasdaq bought it in March 2001 (changing its name to Nasdaq Europe) but ultimately closed it in November 2003, failing to extend success in the United States to Europe.[97] Euronext (the new entity combining the Paris, Amsterdam, Brussels, and Lisbon exchanges) reacted next. In 2002, it announced the opening of NextEconomy, with even more stringent informational standards than those of the new markets in Paris, Brussels, and Amsterdam.[98] In 2003, the Frankfurt exchange followed suit by revamping its market structures, closing the Neuer Markt, and moving its best companies to Prime Market, a new segment that brought the rules for raising capital even closer to the Nasdaq's. With its extremely high information standards, Prime Market continued to make stock market financing available to young companies, though not on an exclusive market.

A Third Round of Market Formation

The latest round of competitive copying in European smaller-company finance comes in the wake of the surprising success of AIM. Observers initially considered this market a laggard compared with the others, noting its companies' small capitalization, its mix of high-tech and traditional companies, and, most important, its relatively lax rules and regulations. Unlike Easdaq and the Neuer Markt, which imposed Nasdaq-like informational requirements to attract institutional investors, AIM relied on local financial intermediaries to back listed firms and thereby put their reputations at stake. The design purportedly sends signals to investors about the quality of unknown companies, without heavy and costly regulations. By changing the legal status of AIM and its listed companies, moreover, the LSE sidestepped new rigorous informational and other regulatory rules subsequently adopted for companies listed on most EU markets—essentially placing AIM "offshore," at least from an EU perspective, though market participants must obviously comply with UK law and rules imposed by the LSE.[99] In changing the legal status of AIM, the LSE further distinguished it from those markets based on the Nasdaq design. The exchange also prompted others to follow suit. Indeed, Euronext's and the Deutsche Boerse's latest new markets, Alternext and Entry Standard, respectively, replicate key aspects of the AIM form, including the circumvention of EU regulation.[100]

While its low-regulatory design is reminiscent of the feeder model, AIM differs significantly in that it is not a staging area for young companies to mature before graduating to the main market and thus does not appear to suffer from the same type of adverse selection bias that plagued the 1980 feeder markets. Expecting companies to remain on AIM, investors do not have incentives to stand on the sidelines until they identify which companies are headed for the main market. Perhaps more important than the details of its form, AIM operates in a competitive environment that did not exist in the 1980s. Until the Easdaq-sparked competition, the LSE had, like the other exchanges, more or less neglected its smaller-company markets. While certainly some rules are better than others, AIM's early success lies in part from its inheritance (from the USM) of a large number of companies from industries outside the trendy high-tech sectors. At first a source of derision, this liability turned into an asset for weathering the post-2000 bear market. Subsequent accidents of history, including the U.S. Sarbanes-Oxley Act, have contributed to AIM's rising appeal to international companies and asset managers, a subject to which the Conclusion returns. The market's continued success in attracting local and international companies, investors, and intermediaries, moreover, lies as much in the strong backing it gets from the LSE and London's financial services industry (who are concerned about their position in the future EU and global financial system) as in the selection of an optimal organizational design.

In fact, since its creation, AIM has come under constant pressure to lift regulatory standards. Complaints first came from investors and intermediaries, who temporarily saw Easdaq, the Neuer Markt, and the Nasdaq form as best practice. In later years, attacks against AIM's relatively light regulation derived from a seemingly orchestrated U.S.-based public relations campaign designed to deter the flow from New York to London of U.S. and foreign companies seeking capital, intermediaries, and investors.[101] At various times, the LSE made adjustments. In addition to those already noted in previous sections of this chapter, the exchange published rules (based on what it considered best practice) governing nomads and mandated AIM companies to use International Financial Reporting Standards (IFRS) or one of four generally accepted national accounting principles.[102] These actions implicitly acknowledged that some of AIM's critics, despite questionable motives, had reason on their side. Strong support from the LSE or not, the AIM model exposes investors to higher risks and makes the market's reputation vulnerable to scandals and insolvencies. In the 2007 rule changes, the

London Stock Exchange and the City attempted to avoid the pitfalls of light regulation (that is, a scandal-ridden market and a regulatory race to the bottom with foreign rivals) while benefiting from giving a broad range of firms access to capital markets and offering choices to risk-acceptant investors. That AIM's form was still very much in flux suggests that the LSE has yet to reach an acceptable balance. AIM may in fact be following a path similar to the development of the U.S. OTC market, which first developed a threshold of companies, intermediaries, and investors and only later acquired a more rigorous regulatory apparatus. Even after a political process led to a new electronic quotation system (known first as the NASDAQ, or National Association of Securities Dealers Automated Quotation System, and then just the Nasdaq Stock Market) to improve investor protections, market authorities continued to adopt more-rigorous rules to ensure quoted companies did not leave for the NYSE.[103]

Notwithstanding the uncertainties surrounding the sources of AIM's success, the LSE's European rivals seem to be repeating history. Just as cross-border competition led to the mimicry of the Nasdaq form, competitive forces prompted Euronext and the Deutsche Boerse to follow the new leader even before they knew for certain why AIM was ahead. It will be interesting to monitor the evolution of smaller-company stock markets in the aftermath of the 2007 merger between Euronext and the NYSE, one of the outspoken critics of AIM's light regulation and now an owner of Alternext, an AIM look-alike.

Finally, AIM illustrates the paradox of the City's relationship to the EU. Despite constant complaints from London financiers about the unmanageable and irresponsible growth of regulations coming from Brussels, AIM exemplifies how the City benefited from the EU financial transformation. EU developments literally forced a resistant LSE to harness historical advantages. Brussels-spurred competition pressured the London exchange to listen to venture capitalists, create an independent market, and maintain support for it. When U.S. market participants and the Nasdaq itself responded to AIM's success as discussed in Chapter 1, it became apparent that EU competition also enhanced London's position as a premier international financial center.

In sum, this chapter traced a European Commission intervention and its effects on venture capitalist influence and market experimentation back to a new supranational arena. Brussels civil servants, as much as any other actors, were responsible for the arena's emergence. Their actions, carried out over fifteen years, opened new political space for contesting status quo financial arrangements. These civil servants were also the first to take advantage of this space. By granting subsidies to support a pan-European stock market in the mid-1990s, they triggered unanticipated cross-border competition. To regain control over market-creation developments, national exchanges became innovators and in the process redefined what it meant to be a competitive supplier and manager of stock markets at the end of the twentieth century. Nevertheless, the exchanges could not tame the beast of competition. In the aftermath of the 2000 international market reversal, the Brussels-initiated rivalry intensified. As the Nasdaq model fell out of favor, the exchanges launched another round of competitive copying, this time emulating London's AIM.

CHAPTER 7

Taking Stock of the European Union's Financial Transformation

National stock exchanges in Europe created smaller stock-company markets between 1977 and 1993 through processes shaped by domestic politics and financial arrangements. They paid scant attention to developments in Brussels and other European financial centers and all but ignored the increasingly vocal demands of venture capitalists. But in a remarkable turnaround, by 1995 exchanges became market innovators, reacting to EU-backed initiatives, responding to the actions of their European counterparts, and adopting parts of the venture capitalists' agenda. This behavioral shift—expressed in the pattern of adopted market forms from feeders to Nasdaq copies to AIM replicas—reflects the growing impact of the EU polity on European financial arrangements. In the 1980s, membership in the European club mattered little to the stock exchanges. By the mid-1990s, however, it had become critical, pressuring the exchanges not only to innovate but also to reinvent themselves.

Chapters 3 and 6 supplied detailed evidence for why and how the importance of the EU increased. Between the late 1970s and the mid-1990s, legal authority to govern the allocation of capital and regulate competition in financial services industries lay predominantly in the hands of national regulators, legislators and quasi-public authorities like the exchanges. This arrangement reflected the legacy of post–World War II compromises that treated finance as an aspect of national sovereignty. Governments had not agreed to shift a large degree of responsibility for financial governance to the EU level as they had in other areas, like antitrust policies and external trade.

To explain the increased importance of the EU—which enabled Brussels bureaucrats to ignite competition, drove the exchanges into an episode of market copying, and opened corporate capital markets to young firms—I have pointed to the cumulative effects of largely unnoticed bureaucratic steps: the actions of Brussels civil servants are the source of cross-border competition, the adoption of new organizational forms, and the mid-1990s turning point. Comparing early years with later ones illuminated the gradual development of three conditions—political facts—that opened opportunities for European Commission officials and allowed their actions to disrupt the status quo. The confluence of these conditions thus led to the controversial 1994–1996 intervention that drew a competitive and angry backlash from governments and stock exchanges, redirected the allocation of capital toward smaller enterprises, and attracted unprecedented levels of internationally mobile risk capital to Europe. The supranational officials had to accept a Europe-wide competition among national markets instead of their desired pan-European stock market. Yet even by a narrow interpretation, these outcomes, when treated as the effects of a cumulative process, represent extensive Brussels influence.

The purpose of this chapter is to enhance these conclusions by returning to alternative perspectives and exploring the applicability of my argument to other areas of the EU's financial transformation. Chapter 2 described prevalent approaches for understanding institutional convergence. Here, I assess how these perspectives, as explanations for Europe's new stock markets, are either insufficient or complementary to my own. The analysis then returns to the book's primary themes: the EU as an independent cause; the cumulative effects and influence of bureaucratic action; the role of Brussels civil servants and politics in market formation; the indeterminate effects of contingent processes; the endogenous nature of opportunity structures; and the treatment of slow-moving processes as sources of sudden change.

Finally, I consider three subsequent defining moments in the EU's financial transformation: a consensus that emerged in 2000 to move ahead with the FSAP, a sweeping legislative agenda for cross-border regulatory harmonization; the 2002 passage of legislation mandating the convergence of national accounting standards for EU-listed companies; and the 2002 adoption of the Lamfalussy process, procedures that shift financial rule-making (though not implementation and enforcement) from the national to the EU level. As a whole, the three cases help to locate the turn in European smaller-company finance within the broader EU financial transformation. They also serve to strengthen this book's argument: like the evolution of the stock markets, these instances of financial change represent the culmination of slow-moving, incremental, and cumulative processes that bear the imprint of Brussels civil servants.

The Capital Mobility Hypothesis and Other Alternative Views

Europe's stock exchanges engaged in a cross-border contest to lure investment flows and smaller companies seeking financial resources. Such competition could have occurred only under conditions of high levels of capital mobility. Thus a precondition for the competitive copying of market forms was the easy and inexpensive movement of capital across national frontiers. Even so, the empirical chapters of this book underscored the limits of the perspective for explaining Europe's new stock markets.

First, as Chapter 5 showed, there is little correlation between the timing of competition and the changing levels of cross-border capital flows, which were already sufficient in the late 1980s (a decade before the post-Easdaq contest) to spur competition. Second, impersonal economic forces did not drive politics. Bureaucrats inside the European Commission had to push venture capitalists to overcome internal divisions over what type of stock markets to create. The venture capitalists did not, in other words, form coherent preferences as capital mobility explanations predict. These financiers agreed on the need for stock markets but were deeply divided on the issues of scope (whether national, pan-European, or international markets would best serve their businesses) and form (whether the Nasdaq or an alternative was the most efficacious design). Chapter 6 provided evidence of these fractured preferences in the conflicts within EVCA's board, as well as in the industry press and the public writings of leading venture capitalists.[1] A small minority considered a new market unnecessary, because in the age of mobile capital, European companies could list on the U.S. Nasdaq itself. Most European venture capitalists, however, thought this idea would limit stock market financing to a small group of European companies and argued for new, Europe-based markets. Others wanted to avoid confrontation with national financial elites and preferred new domestic markets. The venture capitalists were equally divided over form. The ideal design was obvious for a small group: the one they thought investors demanded—the Nasdaq model with its high informational standards. But others sought national principles for organizing new markets. In the end, the Brussels civil servants shaped the outcome by putting their resources behind the faction of EVCA that preferred pan-Europeanism and the Nasdaq design. The financiers did not receive clear price signals from the international economy, and the political intervention nudged them toward a foreign form that appears, with the benefit of hindsight, to have been poorly designed for Europe.

Third, the ability to exit any particular domestic jurisdiction did not automatically increase the power of the venture capitalists in relation to the stock exchanges. The financiers gained influence only after the Brussels officials had intervened, giving financiers a potential alternative market. The venture capitalists' influence was contingent on the actions of political actors. In slightly different terms, the Brussels-backed market gave venture capitalists a credible threat of exit. Only months before the Easdaq announcement, as we have seen, venture capitalists in the United Kingdom and France had failed to influence the policies of their respective exchanges. This evidence illustrates a broader point. Even for highly mobile actors, threatening to leave will ring hollow if there is nowhere else to go. In some cases, venture capitalists in Europe had technically been able to take their business and capital across borders for over a decade. They managed to influence stock exchange behavior only when there was a viable alternative market on which to list their companies, and this required political action predicated on a more conducive political environment.

Fourth, explanations based on increasing levels of capital mobility presume that changed financial arrangements are more economically efficient, a notoriously elusive concept. It is difficult, however, to maintain that the Nasdaq form is more efficient (however defined) when AIM, at least after the first decade since Easdaq's creation, was the most successful but least Nasdaq-like of Europe's new markets. And as Chapter 6 discussed, the emergence of a second round of competitive mimicry since 2005—this time to emulate AIM's form—suggests that the impulse to follow the temporary leader explains exchange behavior better than efficiency forces stemming from capital mobility do. This study was not designed to determine the best arrangements for ensuring a vibrant smaller-company equity market. The comparison between USM and AIM nevertheless indicates that the independence of the market (that is, the removal of the feeder's adverse selection bias) and strong support from the LSE, in response to Brussels-sparked competition, were more relevant than the relative efficiency of one set of rules governing company access over another.

The London market's relative success is not the only reason to question efficiency arguments. In fact, there is scant evidence to support the claim that Commission officials acted as custodians for venture capitalist firms.

For one, these firms did not speak with a single voice that might have represented best business practice for ensuring industry profits. Moreover, as discussed in Chapters 3 and 6, the Brussels officials who promoted the U.S.-model developed their own strategic reasons for selecting it. They were inundated by formidable arguments that the Nasdaq form could not succeed in Europe, regardless of its record in the United States. Their Commission colleagues with arguably more financial expertise ardently opposed it. These anti-Nasdaq bureaucrats contended that the idea was naive and would not work in the Europe of the early 1990s. Their perspective mirrored the positions of the stock exchanges, many financiers, and securities regulators. The officials argued in public and inside the Commission that Europe lacked the necessary equity culture, high-risk companies, and the legal, fiscal and regulatory systems for U.S.-style entrepreneurial finance.[2] In addition, Commission officials in the early 1990s had good reason to question Nasdaq's performance relative to markets organized by alternative principles. Two years before the launch of Easdaq, a well-publicized academic study, which revealed possible collusion among the Nasdaq's market makers at the expense of investors, led to a multiyear investigation, a billion dollars in penalties, and significant changes to the market's organization and regulation.[3] Supranational public authorities thus did not serve as vessels through which efficiency-minded venture capitalists achieved their goals. Indeed, as Chapter 6 highlighted, the record points the causal arrows in reverse.

Finally, capital mobility explanations expect firms and individuals driven by profit to be the main actors behind economic and financial reform. Jos Peeters, Ronald Cohen, and the other enterprising individual financiers behind the Easdaq project took personal risks, devoted a great deal of time, and created new organizations with their own hands and resources. They understandably see themselves as the creators of Easdaq. By arguing that Brussels bureaucrats were the primary actors behind this and the other new markets, this book does not contend that civil servants were involved in any of the necessary and crucial on-the-ground activities carried out by the financiers. Rather, I maintain that Easdaq and the competition and innovation it fostered were manifestations of an incremental process tied to the development of the EU political system. The multiple Brussels interventions that made Easdaq, the historical event, possible involved not merely financial contributions to support someone else's projects; these interventions also entailed vital steps in the forging of a venture capital industry (including the creation and support of EVCA, and production of a political discourse that identified venture capitalism as a solution to Europe's economic problems) and tested the waters with earlier proposals for pan-European Nasdaq copies. Even the selection of Peeters to head EVCA's European Capital Markets Working Group had the European Commission's imprimatur. Peeters and his team, according to this perspective, were as much a European Commission creation as EVCA. If Brussels officials had not found what they wanted in Peeters, they likely would have found it in someone else.

As Chapter 3 showed, there were several other proposals for similar pan-European markets. Eugene Schulman and Andrew Sundberg put forth an almost identical plan in 1985 and 1989.[4] The Scottish Financial Enterprise also produced a similar 1989 proposal, with EASDAQ as its name. In France, an official committee advanced a 1995 plan for MESEC, a plan that was remarkably close to Peeters' proposal.[5] The important question is why Peeters' Easdaq had major implications for the allocation of capital in Europe, whereas the others became footnotes in history. His answer lies in the particular individuals involved, while the evidence presented in this book points to a Brussels intervention, itself contingent on prior changes in the political landscape.

The Diffusion of Ideas

The empirical chapters of this book showed the insufficiency of perspectives based on the diffusion of ideas. U.S. notions about how best to organize smaller-company stock markets were indisputably disseminated to Europe and indelibly shaped the context of debates, as they have for many aspects of the broader EU financial transformation. Indeed, if ideological hegemony characterized any one economic domain in the early 1990s, it would be the regulation and organization of securities markets.[6]

Nevertheless, the exchanges were not converts to the idea that new markets were needed in the 1990s or that the U.S. design was an appropriate one. The comparison of before-and-after cases from the early 1990s provides the evidence. As the stock exchanges' vociferous opposition and lobbying activity demonstrate, neither the European Commission nor any other actor persuaded the stock exchanges to create Nasdaq copies. In fact, the domestic choices made immediately before the Easdaq intervention (and detailed in Chapter 5) suggest the persistence of distinct national beliefs about how best to organize financial markets; and the adoption of the AIM model since 2005 suggests no particular attachment to the U.S. form. Many policymakers and financiers in Europe of course considered the Nasdaq Stock Market an unmitigated success in the United States. As Chapters 3 and 4 have shown, however, this perception was as prevalent in the mid-1980s, with the rise of such listed companies as Intel, Microsoft, and Apple, as in the booming 1990s, making ideational consensus an unconvincing explanation for the timing of the new markets. The Nasdaq had been in existence since 1971, but there were no copies until the mid-1990s.

While Brussels bureaucrats played the roles of agents of change, moreover, they did not behave as "norm entrepreneurs" committed to specific technical beliefs. When stock exchanges compete, they vie to attract global institutional investors. Because these investors were familiar with the Nasdaq form and perceived it as the most legitimate and efficient way to organize a smaller-company market, Easdaq's near replication of the Nasdaq rule book seemed to set a new standard that its competitors had to meet. This is why cross-border competition became a battle over which new market would become the future Nasdaq of Europe. But the historical record presented in Chapter 6 indicates that perceptions about the appropriateness of the Nasdaq principle were not the primary reason bureaucrats pushed for its adoption.

With the exception of a few officials, most of the Brussels civil servants supporting Easdaq preferred the U.S. form for largely strategic reasons associated with circumventing dissenters from within and outside their bureaucracy. Determined to achieve their goal of a Europe-wide market, the officials wanted an organizational form that would help overcome this opposition. The Nasdaq principle was an obvious choice. Structural unemployment, as a salient political issue, expanded the range of policy ideas considered appropriate remedies. Pointing to the Nasdaq's role in creating American jobs, the officials argued that a similar market would solve the unemployment problem in Europe and implied it would do so without making painful political decisions about labor markets, corporate governance regimes, or social welfare systems. Commission officials spearheaded the promotion of this political discourse—which connected jobs, venture capitalism, and the Nasdaq form—and did so to impede the exchanges and their governments from taking public stances against a pan-European market. Additional evidence of the strategic nature of Brussels officials' choices can be found in their effort to harness Nasdaq's legitimacy by making it seem as though Easdaq was similarly regulated, and in the ease with which they embraced a neutral stance once competition broke out and complaints about Brussels' involvement rolled in.[7]

Thus the content and appropriateness of the Nasdaq form, from the point of view of the Brussels bureaucrats, was secondary to its utility as a tactical tool for overcoming opposition and moving closer to their goal of a pan-European market. Copying the Nasdaq was more about the deepening of the European regionalization project than about the globalizing of ideas.

Domestic Variables, Negotiations among States and the Principal-Agent Perspective

The domestic approach predicts national elites will stabilize and co-opt sudden onslaughts of competition. The evidence from Chapter 6 supports this expectation in some respects. Using established financial relationships to prevent smaller domestic firms from listing on foreign markets, the incumbent exchanges undermined the prospects of the upstart Easdaq. Similarly, the continental exchanges frustrated the LSE's efforts to turn AIM into Europe's answer to Nasdaq, even though the exchanges could not prevent its success with British and non-European foreign companies.[8]

As a set of arguments about conservative patterns of change rather than about innovation, however, the domestic perspective is a more convincing explanation for the 1980s feeder markets than for the new markets of the nineties and early years of the twenty-first century. In fact, the American look-alikes represent an early and enlightening turning point, when national policymakers, accustomed to controlling the direction of financial change, found themselves overtaken by competitive constraints rooted in Europe's supranational layer of governance. In fact, even perspectives that expect British equity markets to succeed and continental ones to fail (because of variance in social and economic arrangements and path dependencies) do not capture the causal story behind Europe's new markets. The LSE created and supported AIM in spite of, not because of, British government-finance relations that worked to preserve the status quo and that had long undermined equity financing mechanisms for smaller companies.

The historical record also offers little evidence in support of the state-to-state negotiations or principal-agent approaches. The new markets did not arise from formal EC legislation or other official or unofficial agreements for promoting cross-border competition in the region. These markets were not the result of top-down and negotiated EU rules, newly delegated powers to the European Commission, or decisions made by supranational judges. Instead, a buildup of incremental actions by Brussels bureaucrats working outside formal political channels, followed by a direct intervention, sparked the cross-border contest of competitive market innovation.

In assessing the relative influence of bureaucrats, we need to keep open the possibility that their actions might reflect subtle influences of legislative authorities, in this case governments working together or independently behind the scenes. This is an important insight of the principal-agent approach.[9] The evidence, however, is clear on this score, eliminating the possibility that national financial authorities (organized in Ecofin) condoned (or expected in their delegation decisions) Brussels civil servants to act as they did. Treasuries and finance ministries backed units within the European Commission that were trying to stop the Easdaq intervention at an early stage.[10] Once the Commission's role became public, in fact, an angry backlash occurred. Ministers of finance supported their respective national exchanges' vehement opposition to the Commission's interference in creating Easdaq and claimed the bureaucracy was an illegitimate actor in the realm of financial institutions. In the United Kingdom, the Treasury maintained its position that private-market actors alone should determine the supply of new markets.[11] In France, the Trésor and the stock exchange rallied together to oppose the Easdaq project and enlisted French commissioner Edith Cresson in the battle.[12]

Some ministers representing their countries in the Industry Council backed Commission actions that might have helped to overcome resistance to domestic market innovation and to solve problems facing smaller companies. Nevertheless, the bureaucrats' role is not consistent with principal-agent analysis. Rather than being mere agents responsive to their principals' preferences, Commission officials had gradually nurtured the support of industry authorities for a pan-European market. More to the point, these national representatives were not the "principals" overseeing the Commission's financial market policies. These representatives had limited powers in this domain, possessed little more leverage over the evolution of financial institutions in the European political arena than they did at home, and were careful to respect the clear division of labor with their colleagues in Ecofin. Arriving when Commission officials had already publicly adopted a neutral position as compared with the competition between Easdaq and the national new markets, the Industry Council's November 1995 statement of support only confirmed its members' weak position.[13]

A close reading of the decisions that gave Brussels civil servants discretion over funds reveals sometimes vague instructions to address the "financial aspects of innovation" and to support the financing of SMEs.[14] One paragraph in an appendix addresses the specific question of stock markets supporting the "appreciation" of such financing mechanisms but omitting a license for direct interventions. It encourages "considering ways and means of facilitating SMEs access to sources of credit and guarantee, including mutual guarantee systems and risk capital; appreciation of the opportunity and feasibility of the development of secondary markets; facilitating SMEs' access to financial instruments provided by the Community, without involving financing of enterprises."[15] To read these guidelines as blueprints for subsidizing stock markets, as Brussels bureaucrats did, is to stretch the authors' intentions and powers.[16]

In the EU of this period, authority in the area of financial markets rested with the heads of treasuries and ministries of finance, who worked, at the European level, through Ecofin. The historical record—both before and after Easdaq's creation—leaves little doubt as to their preferences concerning the Commission and financial markets. Since the late 1970s and early 1980s, when Brussels officials attempted top-down integration of national equity markets, national ministers of finance, reflecting the agendas of their respective exchanges, have objected to Commission involvement.[17]

The reasons national exchanges successfully enlisted their respective finance ministries' support in blocking Commission-backed schemes for pan-European markets lie in the cross-cutting goals of governments. On the one hand, national governments (reflected in the EC Industry Council's concerns) were interested in financial innovation that might benefit smaller firms and their economies. On the other hand, by the late 1980s, these governments were concerned about the fate of their respective financial centers in the future integrated Europe. Government officials sought to promote change, but only to the extent that it supported national exchanges.

Commission officials thus intervened in Easdaq in spite of strong opposition from national financial establishments. Some commissioners backed these career bureaucrats: giving director general Dr. Heinrich von Moltke (the top Easdaq-promoting civil servant) and his staff the green light to carry out actions in support of the new market—while rejecting the complaints of fellow commissioner Cresson and showing very little contrition for doing so.[18] Despite tremendous pressure on Brussels civil servants to couch their interventions in market-driven language, Moltke conveyed the

sentiment of his officials and the commissioners at an Easdaq conference in
June 1996:

> We at the Commission, and particularly in Directorate General 23, the en-
> terprise policy DG which I head, are very happy to see Easdaq being
> launched, because it will fill a very real gap in the financing of European
> Small and Medium-sized Enterprises, or SMEs. It represents one of the
> fruits of the Commission's policy in this area, and I hope you will forgive me
> a small touch of pride when I say that had it not been for the Commission's
> original initiative, we might not all be here today. The proposal would have
> got off the ground, because it satisfies a market need, but much, much later,
> and with greater uncertainty.[19]

Empirical Evidence and This Book's Themes

Even in combination, these alternative views on institutional change are
inadequate for addressing many of the most intriguing questions about European stock market formation. What ignited the competition among exchanges? Why did national elites fail to prevent the process from getting
started, as they had in the past? Why did the competition take on its particular nature—becoming a battle over which exchange could best mimic the
Nasdaq and then the AIM forms? And why did the turning point take place
in the 1990s, not in the 1980s?

This book answers these questions by turning our attention to the EU's
political and economic development, especially the activities of European
Commission bureaucrats. First, the empirical chapters have illustrated how
parts of the EU gradually mutated from mechanisms for facilitating intergovernmental cooperation into supranational arenas that generated independent effects on domestic arrangements.[20] Unassuming measures taken
by civil servants in the 1970s and 1980s accumulated over time to become
causes of institutional change by the mid-1990s. Their earlier actions culminated in new political conditions that enabled officials to act autonomously
from governments and exchanges and made status quo domestic arrangements vulnerable to competitive challenges.

Second, the empirical chapters have highlighted why Brussels civil servants are prime candidates in Europe for challenging national conceptions
of the scope, regulation, and purposes of markets and thereby for setting off
regional market-creation processes. Other studies emphasize the market-

creation tendency of official EU arrangements. They point to the application of legal powers by the European Commission and the ECJ to force governments into removing barriers to cross-border exchange.[21] Here, I stress a built-in yet informal mechanism by which Brussels bureaucrats catalyze market formation through the creation of new entrants and the gradual weakening of protectionist walls.

The evidence from Chapter 3 has demonstrated that an ingrained predisposition for pan-European solutions led Brussels officials to pursue a Europe-wide market to stimulate venture capitalism and put them on collision course with national elites and other European Commission officials. The key to Brussels officials' role as market creators, however, lies in the repertoire of actions available to them. Constrained by relative deficits of legal and material powers and by the mundane realities of bureaucratic politics, Brussels officials, as Chapter 2 has described, sought to create legitimacy for their pet policies and to find ways to circumvent opposition from their colleagues. In the smaller-company–markets story, civil servants forged and subsidized a supportive coalition, framed problems and solutions in ways that resonated broadly, and liberally interpreted new regional legislation. These tactics are classic examples of seemingly unobtrusive incremental actions that, in this case, sparked experimentation with new markets. Finally, by identifying political (as opposed to well-known economic and technological) impetuses of market formation, this study extends research on the sociology of markets. In contrast to recent work on incumbent firms and stabilizing social structures, however, these pages have emphasized specific agents of change, clashing visions, successful framing, and political tensions and have suggested that competing conceptions of markets, endemic in other polities, would also be a source of market formation.[22]

Third, instead of focusing on the European Commission leadership in highly public confrontations at single moments in time, the empirical chapters have directed attention to Brussels civil servants in slow-moving background processes. Doing so has illuminated the endogenous roots of what might otherwise be taken as exogenous opportunity "structures" and impels a broad notion of bureaucratic influence. By reframing an issue over the course of several years in the 1980s and early 1990s, Commission officials were responsible for an enabling condition that, from the vantage point of 1994, might have easily been mistaken for an exogenous event. When civil servants changed the political landscape by playing midwife to and then nurturing EVCA, they made an intervention feasible years later and improved the chances that it would have an impact. The book's focus on long-term incremental actions thus goes hand in hand with a more encompassing conception of bureaucratic influence than those employed in principal-agent and other approaches.

Fourth, the historical chapters have demonstrated why cumulative and contingent processes can lead to unanticipated outcomes and defy facile predictions. For one and a half decades, Brussels civil servants transformed the political environment in which they operated—but not in ways that were conducive only to the pursuit of their own agenda. In fact, once the financial press reported EU support for Easdaq, the Commission officials were at a disadvantage compared with powerful financial interests. National exchanges successfully rerouted the market-creation processes back toward the businesses of domestic financial services companies. Governments and their respective exchanges found it politically difficult to oppose a Nasdaq-like market in Europe but succeeded in achieving a second-best strategy of creating their own U.S.-style markets and, as the next sections in this chapter will show, yanking the new smaller-company policy arena back into the Ecofin-dominated fold. The series of small bureaucratic actions over several years created conditions that opened opportunities not just for the bureaucrats themselves but for a range of actors interested in manipulating the direction of change.

Finally, the empirical chapters have suggested why it is possible to conceive of an incremental process as a cause of abrupt change.[23] The 1994 intervention in support of Easdaq was a public event and easy to verify. It ignited a cross-border rivalry and led to the creation of Europe's new markets. But it was not a cause in a meaningful sense. Its effects were contingent on a more fundamental process. No discrete event could possibly pass as the underlying force of institutional change of such magnitude. As exemplified in the French cases discussed in Chapter 4, to create a stock market from scratch is an enormous undertaking. This book's systematic investigation of previous, less visible Brussels actions has detailed the cumulative causal process behind the formation of new markets. The Easdaq proposal stirred up enough uncertainty to draw the exchanges into an unanticipated competition—precisely because of the previous, albeit less conspicuous, Brussels interventions. The accumulation of these largely hidden actions explains why the Brussels-backed initiative ignited a cross-border rivalry and led to the creation of Europe's new markets, why the exchanges perceived Easdaq but not earlier proposals as a threat, and why it makes sense to label such a process as a cause.

Financial Transformation in the EU

Much changed in European finance after 1994, when the Easdaq plan was introduced. Despite a palpable malaise culminating in the 2005 French and Dutch rejections of a proposed EU constitution, the integration of Europe's societies continued unabated in a number of areas and was especially intense in the regulation of finance. By the turn of the millennium, it was apparent that the creation of new stock markets was a precursor to sweeping domestic financial change in Europe. Rather than deriving from competition uncorked by controversial bureaucratic interventions, the late-1990s changes were imposed top-down from EU political agreement.

In March 2000, EU leaders embarked on a shift to the supranational level in both the content of financial legislation—that is, the harmonization of national rules—and the official procedures for producing, implementing, and enforcing them. This acceleration produced a transformation that was among the most significant developments in global finance of the period. It turned the EU from an arena that produces rules governing financial activity into a more formalized regulator. Comparing the distribution of authority in the EU between the national and supranational levels with the U.S. division between the state and federal levels, European arrangements across financial subsectors lie between the decentralized regulation of the American insurance industry and the complex governance of the U.S. securities and banking industries, governance that places more (sometimes fragmented) authority in Washington than in the states.[24]

This chapter's remaining sections address the extent to which my central themes help explain three major elements of the EU's emerging financial system: the consensus on the Financial Services Action Plan; the passage of an EU law on accounting standards, one of the more important pieces of FSAP legislation; and the composition of the Lamfalussy process.

General Consensus Regarding the FSAP

The EU financial transformation is the product of a conjuncture of multiple and historically specific forces and events. For certain, the euro's advent and the sudden rise in U.S. competitiveness are among the most important.[25] However, as in analyzing Europe's new markets, any explanation that does not take into account a quarter century of incremental actions would be inadequate. While related to the European integration project, these actions were by no means exclusively carried out by Brussels civil servants.

The drive toward a single financial market reached the public arena in May 1999 and March 2000, when the European Commission and the European Council (the EU law-making body comprised of representatives of member governments) respectively proposed and endorsed the Financial Services Action Plan.[26] The FSAP listed more than forty pieces of Europe-wide legislation deemed necessary to integrate national financial services industries and laid out an ambitious timetable for their passage. EU policymakers met their goals by 2005, completing the original plan and even adopting some additional measures. The final list includes laws covering company statutes, money laundering, mutual funds (UCITS), accounting standards, market abuse, occupational pensions, prospectuses, and conglomerates, as well as an overhaul of the Investment Services Directive, which was discussed in Chapter 5.

The consensus among EU policymakers concerning financial transformation that began with the FSAP's endorsement contrasts with the efforts in the late 1980s and early 1990s to create a single financial market in the aftermath of the SEA. The transformation differs both in the number of laws and breadth of issues covered and in the degree to which harmonization and convergence, as opposed to mutual recognition, were used as guiding principles. How much of the general support for regulatory change can be attributed to cumulative effects of previous incremental steps, similar to the kinds of small acts carried out by Brussels bureaucrats in the history of smaller-company stock markets?

The introduction of the euro, itself the culmination of a decades-long process, created new possibilities for financial integration, an area of the EU project put on hold after the 1993 passage of the watered-down ISD. The European Commission under Jacques Santer, especially under internal market commissioner Mario Monti, played the classic role of supranational entrepreneur.[27] Monti's team recognized that the single currency, combined with the American challenge, presented a persuasive rationale for advancing financial integration: the U.S. economy was catapulting ahead of Europe's, and the EU could not reap the full benefits of its major response, the euro and monetary union, until the obstacles to a single financial market were removed.[28] This argument—which resonated with finance ministers, members of the European Parliament, and firms—quickly became a focal point. "No one wanted to be seen to be blocking [financial integration]," in the words of one Brussels official.[29]

The successful framing of the problem and solution did not, however, emerge from scratch in the aftermath of the new currency. As Chapters 3–6 attested, Brussels officials, in particular, had been experimenting with arguments for selling financial integration since the late 1970s. In fact, with the exception of a new euro spin, the language of the FSAP proposal is strikingly similar to slogans about job creation and international competitiveness that were used six months earlier in a Commission document on risk capital and is reminiscent of arguments used in 1994 and 1995 in support of Easdaq.[30] In short, Monti was adding, effectively, to the gradual evolution of frame experimentation.

Member government enthusiasm for financial reform did not emerge merely from a persuasive framing campaign, however. The arrival to the UK Treasury of Gordon Brown in May 1997 reinvigorated financial reform at home and brought new zeal to the sometimes lukewarm British support for EU financial integration.[31] Brown was not the first chancellor of the exchequer to see advantage in a single European market—at least in principle. What set him apart was his discovery in the late 1990s of eager French and German counterparts, who having agreed to the new currency, could not easily counter a legislative program claiming to deliver the euro's benefits. In addition, Brown had allies in the European Parliament, such as Chris Huhne and Theresa Villiers, both of whom could fight effectively for City interests while being part of a surprisingly broad profinancial integration coalition that included social democratic chair of the Committee of Economic and Monetary Affairs, Christa Randzio-Plath.[32]

The general consensus among governments, however, also reflects the particular evolution of regional cooperation in the sector. By the time the Commission submitted the FSAP, preferences of some finance ministries were already in the process of changing. It is difficult to imagine French and German support for the FSAP in 2000, for instance, if the 1993 ISD had not helped to slow down London's growing share of continental equities trading. Provisions and ambiguities in that law, which were described in Chapter 6, gave the continental exchanges time to reorganize and modernize. The expansion of domestic capital markets in the late 1990s—at least partly the consequence of the ISD—imbued both Frankfurt and Paris with a considerable degree of hubris about their prospects for competing with London as the future seat of EU finance. German authorities seemed confident that domestic banks could prosper in a Europeanized regulatory system. The French Trésor, meanwhile, adopted an offensive strategy, believing that the exportation of French-like regulations would support Paris's role as a financial center.[33] In some cases, moreover, governments also were eager to revisit major pieces of EC legislation, such as the ISD, because loopholes, deliberately inserted during negotiations, had resulted in unmanaged competition, similar to the episode that followed Easdaq's creation. Thus the legacy of the ISD and other earlier efforts to cooperate helps to explain why the French and German governments continued to support the reorganization of regulation, even when core pieces of new legislation had a decidedly British flavor.

Financial services firms across subsectors, while not initiators of the reinvigorated financial integration project, were easily persuaded by the Commission's logic.[34] They had watched U.S. financial services companies benefit from a giant home market, develop pan-European businesses, and rise to the top of the financial league tables in Europe. Without enhanced integration, the major U.S. banks were likely to be the biggest beneficiaries of the new currency. Not only did the initiative for renewed financial integration prompt existing business lobbies to develop policy positions, it also prompted the creation of new pan-European political voices. The European Financial Services Round Table, consisting of the leaders of Europe's major banks and insurance companies, formed in 2001 and began to produce research and publish their positions in 2002.[35] Eurofi, representing continental Europe's retail-oriented financial services companies, was launched in 2000 with the stated goal of creating a single capital market in Europe.[36]

Like government preferences, the public policy goals of some financial services companies were also shaped by the evolution of previous efforts to integrate national financial systems. Firm preferences changed as existing EU directives proved deficient in the face of technological innovation. Electronic trading networks and technology facilitating internalization (that is, in-house trading between clients of a single firm), for example, led to new demands for an updated ISD.[37]

In other cases, company agendas can be traced to European Commission bureaucrats carrying out activities similar to what we saw in the politics of smaller-company stock markets. Not all active interest groups emerged in response to the FSAP. Others had been in operation for years, engaging in close relationships with Commission civil servants and sometimes even owing their existence to them. EVCA and FESE are good examples.[38] Similar to the Brussels-EVCA relationship, Commission civil servants had a hand in FESE's origins, provided funding for various initiatives over the years, and generally worked closely with its leadership for decades.[39] In putting together the FSAP, officials relied on FESE to produce recommendations compatible with the officials' own visions. Not only were many of FESE's recommendations adopted, but at times they were indistinguishable from the Commission's.[40] Thus, the central position of Commission civil servants in a network of business lobbies not only facilitated the incorporation of private-sector concerns into proposals and thereby garnered support for the FSAP but also helped to shape what those concerns were.

The European Commission made use of other previously developed political assets to win support for the legislative transformation. For example, Commission leaders parlayed a renewed interest in financial integration within Ecofin into a massive legislative program. Reminiscent of Brussels opportunism following the ISD's passage, this maneuver required political skills and expertise in how the EU polity works. Neither of these political assets was instantaneously produced with the euro but rather developed gradually over time. The impetus for the FSAP came from a modest European Council invitation "to table a framework for action . . . to improve the single market in financial services, in particular examining the effectiveness of implementation of current legislation and identifying weaknesses which may require amending legislation."[41] It is not at all clear that the ministers envisioned their invitation resulting in a regulatory overhaul. Seasoned officials inside DG Market downplayed the ambition of their program, arguing that the passage and implementation of forty-two pieces of legislation would "not require radical surgery."[42] The commission also went to great lengths to appear to be fulfilling a mandate and to make it seem as though the member governments and firms were always in the lead. Brussels officials achieved this, in part through a leadership committee, the Financial Services Policy Group, whose creation they recommended.[43] Mario Monti and his successors, Fritz Bolkestein and Charlie McCreevy, later used this committee's chair to push their agendas.[44]

Finally, Brussels officials tended publicly to depict the specific program of legislation contained in the FSAP as the outcome of intense consultation with vested parties following the June 1998 Cardiff Council.[45] And the civil servants did indeed consult broadly and embedded U.S.-style openness in the new decision-making processes. At the same time, however, the FSAP's program was very much a product of the past, pulling together legislative ideas that had been circulating for decades.[46] As earlier chapters have discussed, a previous relaunch of financial integration began with the Commission's April 1983 "Financial Integration," the main proposals of which made their way into Lord Cockfield's white paper of July 1985, "Completing the Internal Market."[47] In the late 1990s, Commission officials did not simply dust off old proposals that had been sitting in drawers, but more than a fourth of the proposed legislation comprised actual revisions of previous laws.[48] Many original ideas for integrating finance, such as the proposal for a single European stock exchange, changed over three decades, reflecting the perennial state of flux in financial sectors and the many constellations of interests among companies and governments. The substantive focus of legislation, however, was remarkably consistent, revealing the incremental nature of change.

In sum, the cumulative effects of previous cooperation, initiatives, and processes were important causes behind the consensus for financial transformation in the EU. As in the creation of Europe's stock markets, Brussels bureaucrats—though by no means exclusively—propelled the process along. These EU effects are evident in the availability of earlier framing experiments and skilled political actors, the legacy of legislation from the 1980s and 1990s on government and company preferences, the prior creations of interest groups and policy networks, and a decades-old reserve of policy proposals.

The 2002 Accounting Standards Regulation

The broad support for financial transformation did not end with a long list of proposed legislation; it led to the passage of forty-one of the original forty-two FSAP measures by the 2005 agreed deadline as well as others not included in the initial package.[49] The introduction of Regulation (EC) No. 1606/2002 of the EP and the Council—an EU law mandating that publicly traded companies issue their consolidated accounts in accordance with new International Financial Reporting (that is, accounting) Standards, or IFRS—illustrates well how years of incremental change built a foundation for rapid enactment of new legislation in the euro's wake.[50] This example suggests that without decades of a slow-moving process, the FSAP's promoters would have achieved much less.

In July 2002, EU policymakers agreed to the new sweeping accounting law, which directly affected about 7,000 companies and, depending on the decisions of individual member governments regarding unlisted companies, allowed for change in the accounting regime for thousands of other firms.[51] The measure called for a special case of harmonization: standardization.

Hence, the EU went beyond converging national standards to compatible levels, as the U.S. and European standard-setters—the Financial Accounting Standards Board, or FASB, and International Accounting Standards Board, or IASB, respectively—are in the process of doing. EU policymakers instead adopted the same standards produced by an outside private body. They also agreed to coordinate implementation and enforcement through the Committee of European Securities Regulators (CESR).[52] While the regulation delegates the production of accounting standards to IASB, it requires the endorsement of the European Commission, which is mandated to base its decisions on technical and political criteria.

As the contested politics of smaller-company stock markets illustrates, accounting standards are central to capital market regulatory regimes. They specify what information companies must reveal about their internal finances and operations and serve as a means of communication for determining value. In the case of stock markets, accounting standards are part of the disclosure rules that determine access to investors' capital. Until the adoption of IFRS, differences in Europe among accounting standards posed significant barriers to cross-border economic integration and contributed to continued fragmentation along national lines. The politics behind the new law extended the conflict over informational standards, witnessed in the post-Easdaq battle, to large listed companies. The introduction of the law replaced unmanaged competition with formal rules. It also exemplifies how ideas for new EU laws are kept alive and evolve over the years.

The 2002 accounting regulation is an extraordinary measure, in no small part because of the chosen legal instrument. For financial legislation, European member governments and the European Parliament normally use directives, which require national authorities to transpose the measures into national law. Regulations are instead directly applicable, circumventing domestic legislators. Adding to its unusual nature, the 2002 regulation passed in a single reading, despite the European Commission's "dynamic interpretation" that it did not conflict with existing EU accounting legislation.[53] The law's passage represents a distinctive turning away from the previous opposition that large member states had put up against further accounting harmonization. The objective of two previous EU accounting laws—the Fourth (1978) and Seventh (1983) Company Law Directives—was minimal harmonization, and the resulting directives left a wide range of choices for national governments.[54] In fact, by the end of the 1980s, the United Kingdom and Germany had all but abandoned the goal of further regional harmonization.

Even though they had succeeded in imposing a British principle, the "true and fair view," into the EU directives, the UK negotiators found European legislative efforts too constraining and instead collaborated with the International Accounting Standards Committee (IASC) and the United States through the Group of 4+1, to work toward future compatibility among standards based on similar concepts.[55] In Germany resistance to increased disclosure came especially from smaller companies. The regulation's passage became all the more striking in hindsight. Backlashes in France and the United Kingdom raised the question of why the regulation was agreed upon in the first place.[56]

Part of the explanation for accounting standardization lies in the consensus built around financial reform and the opportunities it created for European Commission activism. "Like snow melting," as one Brussels official said, the new currency made the barriers to an integrated regional financial market explicit, and differing accounting standards ranked among the most obvious.[57] From this perspective, the Brussels-fueled sense of urgency resulted in agreement about convergence among European finance ministers, the European Parliament, European Commission officials, and multinational companies. The City, the UK Treasury, and the French Trésor were all strong proponents of standardization, and everyone seemed to agree that convergence of accounting standards would be central to a single financial market. In June 2000, just two months after the approval of the FSAP, the European Commission announced its plan to propose standardization. In February 2001, it rolled out the official proposal, which gained approval from the EP and member state governments the following June.

While this momentum opened the door for a more activist role by Brussels officials, the passage of the law can only be fully grasped by taking into account a series of small political compromises and bureaucratic steps, beginning in the 1970s, that set the groundwork for future convergence.[58] The turning point was the adoption of U.S. GAAP, the U.S. accounting standards, in the early 1990s by some high-profile European multinational firms. This gave Brussels officials the excuse to revisit the issue of accounting standards. The firms, responding to market forces, chose U.S. standards to reduce the cost of raising capital in U.S. financial markets.[59] From the perspective of the European Commission and others in the EU, however, the problem was more political than economic.

EU decision makers considered several options. Beginning in 1995, consensus began to move toward international accounting standards, rather than building directly on existing EU legislation, creating new European standards, or adopting U.S. GAAP. There are several reasons.[60] One concerned the issue of control. The U.S. option was eliminated—despite its appeal and elegance by purely economic rationales—because no one wanted to cede power to the U.S. standard setter, FASB.[61] Some academics downplay the issue of control in the decisions of politicians over accounting standards.[62] Yet in 1995, when the European Commission proposed the strategy, and later, when the EU created the endorsement mechanisms for approving IFRS, European policymakers found IASB attractive largely because they expected to have influence over it. By backing the international body, Europe became its biggest constituent.

European support is what gave IFRS the potential to rival U.S. GAAP and transformed the IASB from a forum for technical discussions into a standard setter whose decisions had wide implications. The importance of the EU to IASB's new role, some policymakers reasoned, ensured European control over the board's proceedings. Although it is a private organization, moreover, many of IASB's trustees are European.[63] Commission officials surmised that a unified position combined with endorsement mechanisms would guarantee influence over, if not domination of, the board. The fact that the U.S. SEC managed to outmaneuver EU officials over IASB's structure reveals a miscalculation on the part of European policymakers but does not change the original reasoning behind their decisions. At least from the perspective of some in the EU, moreover, IASB's structure is still an open debate.[64]

A second reason for the plausibility of adopting IAS was that EU company law already shared with IAS the "true and fair view" principle. Although unintended, the compromise that led to the adoption of the British principle in 1978 and 1983 facilitated convergence to international standards in 2002. A final and related reason was the already close ties between the European Commission and the IASB's predecessor, the IASC. For several years the European Commission civil servants had worked with IASC in a relationship that allowed the two parties to share concepts in developing laws and standards.[65] This tactic on the part of Brussels civil servants and other decision makers promised less painful adjustments in later harmonization efforts.

This brief account of the EU's new accounting standards regulation suggests some parallels with the history of Europe's new stock markets. In particular, just as Brussels bureaucrats had instigated innovation in smaller-company finance, they connected past integrationist efforts to present ones through a series of seemingly innocuous steps that set the stage for abrupt change at a later point in time.

The Lamfalussy Process

The late-1990s shift toward supranational governance of EU finance encompassed more than an increase in the number of laws and a move toward cross-border regulatory harmonization. After 2002 this shift also included new procedures, known as the Lamfalussy process, which altered how laws and rules were made and implemented.[66] Most legislation under the original FSAP followed the old, cumbersome co-decision procedures (established in the 1992 Maastricht Treaty), which involved a European Commission proposal and endorsements by both the European Council and the EP. Negotiating new financial legislation, with all its implications for national sovereignty, was notoriously difficult and, as in the case of the ISD, could drag on for years. Once passed, transposition and implementation by national legislatures and regulators was slow, uneven, and uncoordinated.

In February 2002, EU policymakers adopted the recommendations, almost without revision, of Alexandre Lamfalussy's Committee of Wise Men, an independent group appointed by Ecofin upon a French initiative.[67] The new formal and quintessentially supranational decision-making procedures aimed to expedite the production of EU securities legislation and bolster cross-border coordination mechanisms for transposition, implementation, and enforcement. Early evidence from the first few laws created under the new procedures suggests that the legislative process moved more quickly than in the past and improved the quality and the application of financial regulation.[68] The new procedures distinguished between framework laws, which still require passage through the old system, and detailed regulation, similar to U.S. administrative rules, produced by the European Commission through an elaborate web of expert and regulatory committees (that is, through a modified comitological process, in EU jargon). The procedures also bring together national regulators in bodies like the Paris-based CESR and include U.S.-style public consultation.

As in the previous two cases, nobody wanted to be seen blocking reforms that promised to enhance the prospects of the legislative program and expedite the creation of a single financial market. German finance minister Hans Eichel, for example, agreed to an ambiguous commitment from the European Commission not to override a simple majority (a pledge that appears to have changed little), in order to clear the way for his government's approval of the Lamfalussy process.[69] French finance minister Laurent Fabius' support for financial transformation was so strong that he backed the final report of Lamfalussy's committee, even though it had rejected his proposal for a centralized EU securities supervisor—a European securities and exchange commission.[70]

This near consensus in favor of the procedures was an immediate and intended spillover of the FSAP. The committee explicitly used arguments that procedural reform was necessary to expedite the legislative program and ensure that regulatory structures did not undermine the potential benefits of an integrated financial market. It even borrowed some of the same framing that invokes both the euro and the U.S. challenge: "If [the EU] does not succeed," the Lamfalussy committee's final report argued, "economic growth, employment and prosperity will be lower, and competitive advantage will be lost to those outside the European Union. And the opportunity to complement and strengthen the role of the euro and to deepen European integration will be lost."[71]

Two factors, both intimately associated with the development of the regional polity, are most responsible for the particular form the Lamfalussy process took. First, its adoption was an expression of EU balance-of-power politics and marked a breakthrough in long-standing impasses involving member governments (operating in the Council), the EP, and the European Commission.[72] Ever since the Commission first broached the issue in 1989, governments and the EP had blocked delegating to the Brussels bureaucracy autonomous implementation powers over securities regulation. Governments were unwilling to cede powers to the civil servants in such a highly sensitive area. The EP, for its part, wanted no additional delegations until it gained the same oversight powers as the Council's. These political battles were not about the efficiency of financial arrangements, per se. Rather, finance became one of the forums in which major EU political institutions fought over the distribution of constitutional powers.

Interinstitutional EU political bargains thus account well for the extension of comitology to financial services and, specifically, for the Commission's formal rule-making role and the creation of the European Securities Committee (ESC) as a consultative and oversight body. It also helps to explain the procedures in the Lamfalussy process that distinguish between framework laws and detailed rules that require open consultation. Delegation of powers, if it is to be effective, implies leaving the details to civil servants and technical experts; if it is to be perceived as legitimate, delegation needs mechanisms that give access to the affected parties. Rather than representing global best practice or a functional solution to the problems of regulating financial services in an age of mobile capital, these approaches to EU law-making evolved gradually from the introduction of comitology procedures, made their way into the Commission's 1998 "Financial Services" document, and reflected Brussels' approach to EU governance in general.[73]

The second crucial factor behind the particular form of the Lamfalussy process is that its architects adopted as much from the existing regulatory structures as was possible. By the time Lamfalussy's committee consulted with market participants in 2000 and 2001, financial services firms had had two years to mobilize in response to the FSAP. No doubt the voice of financial participants substantially shaped Ecofin's selection of committee members and directed them toward pragmatic solutions. Indeed, the committee report, perceived as a plausible reform package because its main provisions represented incremental changes, had broad appeal. Most of the reforms were predicated on practical considerations. Rather than opt for ideal regulatory structures like the risky proposal for a European SEC, which would have had to be created from scratch, the committee built organically on what already existed. Arguably, the attraction of the Lamfalussy process was as much rooted in the small steps of the past as in the momentum sparked by the euro and the FSAP.

The creation of two new committees, central to the Lamfalussy reforms in the area of securities regulation, illustrates the point. Both are adaptations of previous ideas or entities. The creation of a regulatory committee, the European Securities Committee, which would monitor the actions of Commission bureaucrats, was a standard element of delegation arrangements. The committee, which includes high-level representatives of national finance ministries, can be traced to prior actions and ideas. As noted, the Commission's 1989 proposal for a directive on investment services recommended the creation of such a committee to oversee implementation.[74] Even though finance ministers rejected the proposal, the Commission kept the idea alive throughout the 1990s. When the ministers finally agreed to a securities committee, the EP, exercising its new powers of co-decision in financial matters, prevented the extension of comitology to securities regulation until the balance-of-power deadlock could be resolved. Thus the ESC met for the first time in 2001, but policymakers created the idea for the new committee over the previous decade.

CESR's creation similarly has roots in earlier EU developments. The European Commission originally proposed the introduction of comitology in the financial sectors without this body composed of national securities regulators.[75] The Lamfalussy committee, concerned less about balance-of-power politics than about feasible ways to improve financial regulatory capacity, stressed the need for a group that could provide technical and regulatory expertise and garner widespread respect among market participants.[76] The committee's recommendation to create CESR by formalizing the existing Forum of European Securities Commissions (FESCO) was thus based mainly on pragmatism. Instead of selecting an ideal model like the French plan for a European agency, which would have required designing an entirely new entity, the committee's recommendations built on what was already in place.[77] This approach—which won broad appeal—ensured that the arguably most important "innovation" of the new Lamfalussy process was in fact an incremental addition to a small and largely unnoticed attempt to coordinate EU securities regulation five years earlier. Given the widespread reluctance to risk the creation of a single regulator for Europe, the Wise Men had no other real alternative. FESCO was already organized, and national securities regulators, responsible for devising and implementing financial rules at home, were the only actors with preexisting expertise, legitimacy, and legal powers.

In sum, in devising the particular form of the Lamfalussy process, decision makers were deeply constrained by interinstitutional EU politics and previous efforts to integrate EU financial regulations. Unlike the first part of this chapter, which weighed my argument for Europe's new stock markets against counterexplanations, this brief analysis of the new rule-making procedures, like those of the FSAP and the new accounting standards regulation, offers a sketch of the causal processes behind some major aspects of the EU's posteuro financial transformation. I examined these cases because of their significance to the EU financial project and interest to the reader rather than for the purposes of systematic analysis. The conclusions nonetheless suggest that a set of forces similar to those identified in the history of Europe's smaller-company stock markets were largely responsible for the sweeping financial reforms at the turn of the millennium. Rather than an end point, Europe's new stock markets are part of the gradual evolution of the EU's regional financial system, which by the end of the 1990s entered a new stage characterized by formal arrangements.

Several of the book's themes highlighted in the second section of this chapter help us to interpret these later episodes of financial change. First, at end of the 1990s, just as in the beginning, the European integration project was a source of change. Existing laws and interpretations of them, previously created bodies and capacities, and ongoing political battles all contributed to outcomes in the posteuro era, as they had a few years earlier. Second, the cumulative effects of seemingly innocuous, incremental actions—many by Brussels civil servants—were as important in the origins of the FSAP, the accounting standards regulation, and the Lamfalussy process as they were in the outbreak of competition over smaller-company stock markets. In the FSAP example, Commission officials drew from business interests and political frames that they had helped to create at an earlier moment in time and from previously developed political skills and legislative proposals. In the accounting standards case, prior political bargains and interactions between the European Commission and the IASC created an opportunity for action many years later. Brussels bureaucrats, moreover, influenced the shape of the Lamfalussy process by being persistent for over a decade in their efforts to win autonomy in the implementation of securities regulation.

Third, all three cases substantiate the deep connections between politics and financial market formation. The ongoing development of the EU polity drove European policymakers toward a single financial market. The most visible example is the balance-of-power bargain expressed in the Lamfalussy process. As in the stock market case, however, an informal mechanism by which Brussels civil servants and others contribute to market formation through the creation of new entrants and through the gradual breakdown of protectionist barriers was also an important factor behind the late-1990s financial transformation. Finally, just as in the aftermath of the Easdaq intervention, the cumulative and contingent process that produced the comprehensive program of new laws, its implementation, and new rule-making and enforcement procedures promised unanticipated outcomes and sudden turns. Perhaps, even more so than in the market innovations that followed the 1994 Brussels intervention, most everyone was struck by the sudden, far-reaching, and fundamental change that gripped European financial regulation in the late 1990s. The single currency was the most important trigger, but it ignited highly flammable material long in the making. The euro's impact was contingent on slow-moving cumulative processes. Just as in the stock market case, the buildup of sometimes unremarkable developments produced conditions that by the late 1990s made EU finance ripe for rapid change.

Conclusion

The fifty-year-old European integration project is transforming the organization of politics and economics inside Europe and beyond.[1] The evolution of smaller-company stock markets is a prime example of a widely overlooked route by which this transformation is taking place. Highlighting the cumulative impact of routine acts by supranational bureaucrats, this book has illuminated and cataloged why and how the EU's ongoing development caused change in European financial arrangements.

Sometimes European Commission officials live up to their paper-pushing image. Indeed, in interviews Easdaq's private-sector owners, board members, and executives complained bitterly about the red tape that obstructed fund transfers from the supranational bureaucracy. At other times, Brussels leaders like Mario Monti, in the case of the FSAP, play the storied role of supranational policy entrepreneurs who seize opportunities as they arise. By taking a twenty-five-year perspective, however, the previous chapters have shown a different side to Europe's supranational bureaucrats. These civil servants are strikingly unheroic figures. They alter political facts on the ground over stretches of time, without necessarily meeting their goals. More than social engineers, they are status quo spoilers with a knack for disrupting existing markets. A weak position within the EU's balance of power, compounded by a fragmented and open organizational structure, drives them to find ways to enhance their legitimacy and circumvent opposition inside and outside the Brussels bureaucracy. The result is seemingly mundane and tepid actions, in concert with other actors and with the intent of diverting attention. For those civil servants advocating a pan-European stock market for smaller companies, their contributions included developing policy ideas through trial and error; assisting private-sector actors to create

Europe-level political organizations and coalitions; experimenting with and promoting political discourses and frames, by commissioning studies and issuing reports; stretching interpretations of laws and rules; and borrowing pieces of foreign models when it suited their purposes. Over the years, these types of activities accumulate without fanfare but change the political landscape nonetheless.

In the case of smaller-company financial arrangements, change came in the form of market creation and experimentation. The Brussels civil servants involved were responsible for policies related to technological innovation and smaller companies, not financial matters. Like most of their European Commission colleagues, they shared a proclivity toward regional solutions to common domestic problems. When these civil servants wandered into the domain of financial market policymaking, they faced opposition at every turn. Their ideas, proposals, and actions clashed with powerful vested interests and government ministries, over the scope, meaning, and regulation of markets. In short, doing their jobs in the name of economic renewal eventually unleashed competition and market innovation.

The history of stock markets contributes to a body of knowledge that challenges images of inflexible European societies unresponsive to the pressures of globalization. For many EU watchers, the role of the region's extra layer of governance and governors in upsetting established market arrangements is indeed a familiar theme and one that frequently features the supranational bureaucracy in Brussels. In the early years of the twenty-first century, highly publicized decisions against international mergers drew attention to the European Commission's legal powers to promote cross-border competition, and many EU experts attribute an inherent bias toward regional markets with "pro-business" regulation to the bureaucracy's official role as the Treaty of Rome's guardian.[2] Europe's new stock markets illustrate another—this time, informal—market-disrupting mechanism built into the European Union's DNA.

In particular, by centering on the role of supranational civil servants, my analysis has shown one way the regional stratum of governance has rendered Europe's financial systems amenable to change. Characterized by powerful interests and symbiotic relations among bankers, regulators, and governments, domestic financial arrangements are notoriously difficult to reform. This is as true in European countries as in other rich democracies. Yet Europeans adjusted to the U.S.-driven globalization of capital and financial services industries much more smoothly than, say, the Japanese, whose financial arrangements had shared characteristics with several European national systems.

This study's conclusions obviously do not bear directly on Japan's costly fifteen-year banking crisis and slow response to a changed international environment. These conclusions are, however, suggestive, in that the relative autonomy of some EU civil servants from financial interests made a difference in reforming Europe's national financial systems. Unlike bureaucrats in many rich countries, officials in Brussels are frequently in a position to create distance from governments and entrenched interests. In finance, this autonomy enabled them to belie hackneyed portrayals of "eurosclerosis." Instead of standing in the way of reform, the actions of these civil servants helped to weaken the foundations on which old arrangements rested and to usher in a period of explosive institutional experimentation.

Europe's New Financing Capabilities

By the end of 2006, it was clear that Europe's leading new market, London's AIM, was competing directly with Nasdaq, attracting international companies and capital, foreign venture capitalists, investment bankers, and others known for their expertise in bringing entrepreneurial firms to the American market.[3] Eleven years since AIM's opening, these were still early days for the London market. Some observers predicted that AIM, because of its relatively low informational requirements, would have its comeuppance in the aftermath of the next market downturn.[4] Meanwhile, optimists saw persuasive evidence in the proportion of institutional investors and numbers of quoted companies, staking their fortunes on AIM's long-term survival.

Whatever the fate of the current market leader, the intense regional competition continues. In this respect, AIM exemplifies a striking paradox concerning the City's resurgence as a leading (if not the leading) international financial center. Despite constant complaints by London financiers about encroaching Brussels bureaucrats and rules and a palpable ambivalence toward European integration, the EU polity—because of its role in fomenting cross-border competition—is a primary source of the City's revitalization. In the case of AIM, London's financial establishment, securities regulators, and politicians have reason to cheer but not to boast. The British market was created in spite of the LSE's opposition to market innovation, not because of its leaders' farsightedness or ingenuity. While the survival of London's new market was in many respects accidental, its early success in attracting local companies, is, like its genesis, as much about Brussels-induced cross-border competition as about British acumen. The possibility that capital-market financing for smaller companies might flourish in Germany or France spurred the UK exchange to support AIM.

Subsequent developments, however, were responsible for the young market's meteoric rise in international appeal.[5] With the long list of complementary reforms associated with the FSAP and Lamfalussy process (see Chapter 7) and the help of the U.S. Sarbanes-Oxley Act (which increased the cost of raising capital in New York), London's new market not only outperformed Nasdaq in attracting foreign companies in 2005 but also prompted continental exchanges to create competing AIM copies of their own. The sequence of events is reminiscent of how the U.S. financial system, in the 1990s, developed a capacity to allocate capital to untested companies and became a magnet for the world's technology, innovation, brains, and high-risk investment. Nasdaq became a core and perhaps necessary institution in this capacity only after the confluence of pension and tax reforms in the 1970s and 1980s with the emergence of a new breed of entrepreneurs commercializing computer-related technologies.[6] It was created in 1971 for unrelated reasons buried in the past.[7] The accelerated pace of EU financial reforms and Sarbanes-Oxley, likewise, are turning AIM and perhaps its rivals into essential institutions in an emerging regional financial system that increasingly competes with that of the United States and Asian financial centers. Similar to the developments that submerged the politics behind Nasdaq's origins, subsequent events eclipsed fifteen years of background bureaucratic action by Brussels civil servants, action that shaped the political battle behind the formation of Europe's new stock markets. Without these cumulative effects, so pervasive in the EU's development, it is unlikely London or another European city would have become an international center of high-risk finance.

As recently as 1995, the idea that Europe was about to rival U.S. capital markets for the world's entrepreneurial companies would have seemed farcical. The same can be said about a host of other European financial sectors—including exchange-traded derivatives, sovereign and corporate bonds, and merger and acquisitions markets—that today compete for internationally mobile capital, companies, and talent.[8] Certainly, the development of Europe's various financial markets evolved gradually and unevenly along different paths and involved separate sets of interests and characters. And a single, regional financial market, however defined, still remains a goal.[9] Nevertheless, the euro's introduction, the FSAP and Lamfalussy process, the resultant increased concentration of European financial activity in London, and the Sarbanes-Oxley Act combined to pull together the new stock markets and the threads of earlier integrationist efforts into a single project that garnered support from the highest levels.

Implications for Europe

Because of the centrality of finance to political economies, change of this magnitude almost by definition affects the performance of companies, work environments, household wealth, and ultimately, as previous chapters have discussed, the share of risks borne by governments and citizens. As the new century's first decade comes to an end, the European Central Bank (ECB), European Commission, and others have reported some of the expected economic efficiencies. They found significant regional integration in money, government and corporate bond and equity markets (though still comparatively less in retail markets) and evidence of lower costs of capital, especially for corporations.

Many observers attuned to existing national barriers and unevenness in the legal overhaul of financial regulation were surprised by the extent and speed of less predictable and indirect effects. The smaller-company stock market sector is an early example. As Chapter 1 has detailed, without the regional legal foundations that many deemed necessary to sustain a pan-European sector for entrepreneurial finance, the creation of new markets nonetheless changed expectations about potential profits and triggered an inflow of venture capital into Europe.

Another class of private equity investment with equally important economic and social implications followed suit. Stiff resistance to harmonizing key aspects of corporate governance (that is, company law, in Europe) did not prevent the region from becoming a favorite destination of internationally mobile capital looking for mergers. Mirroring the trend in venture capital statistics, buy-out investments soared from €3.2 billion in 1996 to €48.9 billion in 2006.[10] Even Germany, where some politicians made vituperative attacks against private equity companies, was not immune. Investments there reached €2.5 billion in 2006 from a minuscule €0.15 billion in 1996. Like venture capitalists, managers of buy-out funds in Europe must adjust their business models to fit different legal contexts, and their investments are unlikely to have the same effects as in the United States. Corporate governance and other national laws, for instance, prevent investors in several countries from raising resale values through large-scale firings. Still, these financiers did not flock to Europe for the climate, and their efforts to increase profitability promise far-reaching social and economic change, even if the exact reverberations are difficult to predict.

Altering the arrangements that allocate financial resources, especially when it means greater reliance on markets, may offer indisputable benefits but is unlikely to spread equally among all members of society. The opening chapters have explained how financial rules reflect choices that can create winners and losers and raise questions about who should make these decisions and by what means. The role of relatively autonomous Brussels civil servants in the creation of the new stock markets, in this regard, deserves sober consideration. Their seemingly small-scale interventions helped to connect European households to the gyrations of international equity markets and added to already intense pressures on EU governments and national social programs. The civil servants' actions contributed to making venture capital investment an established feature of European finance—improving the prospects of upstart companies and their founders; providing societal benefits such as wealth creation, jobs, and technological innovation; but also exposing average citizens and workers to new risks and uncertainties. Because of EVCA, a pressure group with Brussels' imprint, venture capitalists were, moreover, well positioned to protect and lobby in favor of their interests when EU decision-makers launched the late-1990s legislative program.

The core legitimacy issues turn on the procedures that generate the rules underpinning and governing markets. If the European Commission's influence over the market-creation process described in this book is troubling, it is because of the means by which the actions were carried out. Unelected bureaucrats took advantage of the difficulty in discerning the effects of financial change or chose to ignore them. They promoted stock markets as a way to stimulate entrepreneurial activity in part because doing so circumvented politically sensitive issues more typically associated with social welfare reform. Unlike labor markets and corporate governance, equity markets do not typically evoke images of painful adjustments to social safety nets. The civil servants were thus able to sell the stock market idea as a costless, technical, and neutral necessity that would stimulate U.S.-style economic activity and job creation. There was little public discussion about the effects of exposing households to the unpredictable oscillations of global finance. Even after the fact, few made the association between these actions by bureaucrats and their impact. Only ten years later did a handful of European politicians begin to ask whether the benefits of risk capital outweigh the challenge it poses to underlying societal values.[11]

In 2002 European policymakers implicitly acknowledged misgivings about informal Brussels influence in financial matters. These policymakers infused the Lamfalussy process with new political controls and transparency requirements meant in part to function as safeguards against undesirable byproducts of bureaucratic autonomy. The EP and the Council delegated to the European Commission new powers to be carried out in conjunction with bodies of experts and infused the procedures with oversight mechanisms. Seeking transparency, policymakers created new arrangements that institutionalize open consultations and public hearings.

The objective behind the Lamfalussy process was to balance the need for flexible financial rule-making with hierarchical procedures that ensure democratic controls.[12] Early research on the securities sector hints at continued tensions rooted in part in the unintended influence of Brussels civil servants through informal processes. Too heavy a reliance on rigid procedures in the past led to outcomes few wanted to repeat: EU financial arrangements that were unable to adjust to global market changes, undermined internal economic policy goals, and encouraged Brussels civil servants to circumvent formal channels. Some argue, especially in the EP, that in striving to find the right balance, the authors of the adopted solutions went too far, erring on the side of efficiency and leaving behind a democratic deficit. The newly developing informal processes, by this line of thinking, have taken the European Commission's rule-making role and the powers of the committees of national regulators beyond what the originators had envisioned.

Even if current arrangements represent a workable balance, the new transparency requirements introduced an additional dilemma, all too familiar to Americans. Despite their inherent appeal, open consultation processes and public hearings do not automatically or necessarily deliver fair and prudent outcomes. Nor do they eliminate backroom bargains between the most powerful political actors. In the United States, small groups of financial firms whose bottom lines can depend on minute regulatory reforms disproportionately participate in public deliberations.[13] Observers of the early years of the Lamfalussy process see a similar pattern developing in the EU.[14] The essential question in twenty-first-century Europe is the same one that haunts

U.S. financial rule-making procedures. At the very moment in history when public policies force individuals to prepare for their own retirements by investing in capital markets, who will advocate their interests? In the United States, the SEC historically filled this role by keeping the loudest voices in check and making sure they played by the rules. Yet in recent decades, the politicization of the agency, on the back of an ideologically driven budget squeeze, appears to have diminished its effectiveness.[15]

Who in the EU will play this role? At the moment, the answer is not clear. National supervisors organized under CESR are themselves all too aware of the limitations of coordinated actions, given the asymmetrical powers of its members, and external observers see little distance between CESR and the largest financial services companies.[16] This book's analysis suggests that future answers lie in inconspicuous actions, perhaps already taken, by supranational bureaucrats. In a classic European Commission act, Brussels addressed criticisms about lopsided participation in open consultations by creating a new political voice and lobby, the Financial Services Consumer Group (FSCG).[17] Some analysts always saw CESR as an interim solution halfway to a regional securities regulator. Are Brussels bureaucrats constructing a political environment amenable to a more autonomous CESR or even a European SEC? To find out, we might have to get through the financial crisis of 2007/2008.

International Effects

The politics of financial markets used to be an arcane subject for academic specialists. At the beginning of the twenty-first century, however, it lies at the center of discussion about global imbalances and international politics. At issue is the destination of capital flows, which now more than ever are intimately tied to geopolitics. As Beijing commences to diversify its official portfolio away from U.S. Treasury securities, will it continue to invest substantially in the United States, and if not, how would such a decision affect Sino-American geopolitical and economic relations? In light of the post-9/11 campaign against terrorism and the war in Iraq, what will Middle Eastern oil-producing countries do with their excess dollars? In the past, portfolio owners invested in the United States, knowing that there were no comparable jurisdictions to supply a similar combination of a stable political system, panoply of assets, and liquid and well-regulated capital markets. It was largely hypothetical (and usually with reference to China's potential) to ponder the effects on U.S. deficits and the dollar if another jurisdiction were to offer the same combination. With the EU's financial transformation, it is no longer mere speculation to discuss the extent to which the United States is still in a league of its own. The risky shares made available through AIM and the other new markets are but one example of how far Europe has come toward matching the menu of dollar-denominated securities. Moreover, episodes such as the extension of the NYSE-Nasdaq rivalry to the other side of the Atlantic confirm that some of the most important financial service providers expect Europe to be a world center of financial activity.

Whereas the impact of the EU's allure on imbalances and geopolitics promises to unfold slowly, the effects of the polity's financial regulatory overhaul on global governance arrangements were immediate. The legal and procedural reforms encompassed in the FSAP and Lamfalussy process led to new levels of cooperation in bilateral and multilateral forums.[18] Through the end of the 1990s, U.S. financial supervisors jealously guarded their regulatory sovereignty in handling a growing number of transatlantic disputes, which ranged from the governance of cross-border competition for stock exchanges to the merits of a mutual recognition of accounting standards to the regulation of conglomerates. American officials typically exported U.S. solutions by pressuring, persuading, or outmaneuvering their European counterparts and resisted making accommodations to European demands and proposals. If adjustments were going to occur, European national regulators tended to make them.

After 2001, in contrast, U.S. authorities made significant concessions in several high-profile transatlantic conflicts. By 2007, American officials had accepted mutual recognition regimes in some areas of securities regulation and were contemplating them for others.[19] Many of these U.S. regulatory changes met long-standing goals of European firms and authorities. There were also indications that the new relationship between U.S. and European authorities would lead to joint initiatives to further the liberalization of financial services at the multilateral level.[20] The EU-U.S. Financial Markets Regulatory Dialogue launched in May 2002, the Norwalk Agreement of September of that year, and other related new forums, moreover, institutionalized this pattern of cooperation in financial services. European regulators are not achieving all their goals but are doing much better than in the past.

What brought an end to U.S. financial regulatory dominance? Largely, the EU's posteuro legal and procedural transformation revealed the extent to which U.S. financial services companies had already earned a significant amount of their revenues from European markets and increased the bargaining power of European officials in relatioin to their U.S. counterparts. Outside the domain of trade, scholars find little guidance for understanding the EU's influence on the rules managing the international economy. The new transatlantic financial relationship underscores the role of shifting jurisdictional boundaries within the EU polity under conditions of interdependence.

Transferring regulatory authority from the national to the regional level led to a more accommodative U.S. stance, because American firms had to comply with a single set of European rules. Major pieces of EU legislation (for example, those governing conglomerates and accounting standards) contained clauses that gave the European Commission and other EU bodies the power to determine whether foreign standards and regulations were equivalent. U.S. firms, including Wall Street's best-known investment banks, had much at stake in the shape of the embryonic regional financial system. Everyone involved on both sides of the Atlantic quickly figured out that EU decisions had the capability to affect the pan-European businesses of Wall Street banks in ways similar to American authorities' influence over European financial firms with U.S. businesses. While European choices might have benefited U.S. investment banks by promoting transatlantic regulatory harmonization, these choices might just as readily have harmed them through retaliatory responses. To ensure that the interests of U.S. firms were protected under the emerging EU financial system, the U.S. Congress, SEC, and Treasury sought better transatlantic coordination, which translated into less U.S. unilateralism and more cross-Atlantic compromises. The construction of a European-level legal regime thus triggered new U.S. regulatory positions and altered transatlantic and multilateral relations in financial services. Introducing this legal regime had these international effects because changes inside Europe, like the development of the new stock markets, had already drawn so many U.S. financial services companies to the EU.

The first posthegemonic phase yielded EU-U.S. cooperation—as opposed to a conflict between equals—in large part because of common underlying regulatory principles developed during decades of American leadership. What will happen in later phases if U.S.-style financial regulatory practices lose their luster? Will alternate approaches emerge for governing international finance? The EU's new regulatory capabilities are likely to be among the most critical variables.

NOTES

INDEX

Notes

1. Europe's New Stock Markets

1. The Paris, Amsterdam, and Brussels stock exchanges combined in 2000 to form Euronext. In 2001 Euronext acquired the London International Financial Futures and Options Exchange (LIFFE) and in 2002 added the Lisbon Stock Exchange. The new entity is NYSE Euronext. "The Battle of the Bourses," *Financial Times*, May 23, 2006, 23; "Revelling LSE Launches £250m Buy-Back," *Financial Times*, February 13, 2007, 18; "NYSE Says It Could Set Up London Exchange," *Financial Times*, June 18, 2006, 1; "NYSE and Euronext Recast an International Dynamic," *Financial Times*, December 23, 2006, 31. After the LSE rebuffed its offer, the Nasdaq made a successful offer to purchase OMX, the Nordic exchange that runs markets in Denmark, Estonia, Finland, Iceland, Latvia, Lithuania, and Sweden. "Nasdaq Goes Nordic with Dollars 2.7bn Deal for OMX," *Financial Times*, May 26, 2007, 1.

2. John Zysman, *Governments, Markets, and Growth: Financial Systems and the Politics of Industrial Change* (Ithaca: Cornell University Press, 1983). For the British failure, see chap. 4.

3. Stock exchanges are organizations. In Europe, until the mid-1990s, they were mutually owned by national financial insiders (brokers, market makers, specialists, banks, and other financial intermediaries). Since then, many have demutualized and become publicly listed companies. In the United States, the demutualization began several years later. Stock exchanges supply organized stock markets, sets of rules that provide a regulated arena for the buying and selling of ownership shares in companies (also known as stocks and equities). While stock exchanges rarely had a complete national monopoly over equity trading, today they compete with each other and with electronic trading networks and internalization (i.e., in-house trading between clients of a single financial services company).

4. See www.thomson.com for Thomson Financial league tables and www.sifma.org

for statistics on U.S. investment bank activity in Europe. See www.evca.com for statistics on European venture capital and private equity.

5. U.S. Government Accountability Office, *Sarbanes-Oxley Act: Consideration of Key Principles Needed in Addressing Implementation for Smaller Public Companies*, GAO-06–361 (Washington, D.C.: 2006); "Why Aim Is Foreign Target of Choice," *Financial Times*, September 3, 2005, 3; "Nomad Sarbox Refugees Aims for Low-Cost London," *Financial Times*, March 17, 2006, 22; "Selling the Attractions of Euronext," *Financial Times*, May 22, 2006, 30; David T. Hirschmann, "Getting Implementation Right: Sarbanes-Oxley Section 404 and Small Business," Statement of the U.S. Chamber of Commerce, testimony before the House of Representatives Small Business Committee, Washington, D.C., June 5, 2007; Charles E. Schumer and Michael R. Bloomberg, "To Save New York, Learn from London," *Wall Street Journal*, November 1, 2006, A18.

6. Daniel Mügge, "Reordering the Market Place: Competition Politics in European Finance," *Journal of Common Market Studies* 55, 5 (2006): 991–1022; Elliot Posner, "Financial Transformation in the EU," in Sophie Meunier and Kathleen R. McNamara, eds., *Making History: European Integration and Institutional Change at Fifty* (Oxford: Oxford University Press, 2007), 139–156.

7. The name of the European regional polity has changed several times. Complicating matters, parts of the polity go by separate labels. I use EU except where European Economic Community (EEC) or either the European Communities or the European Community (EC) makes better sense. For statistics on financial integration in Europe, see European Central Bank, *Financial Integration in Europe*, Frankfurt, March 2007, at www.ecb.int, and Commission of the European Communities, *Financial Integration Monitor*, SEC(2006)1057 (Brussels, July 26, 2006), at ec.europa.eu/internal_market/finances/fim/index_en.htm. Some non-EU European countries, members of the European Economic Area, have reformed their financial systems in accordance with EU legislation. See "European Economic Area," ec.europa.eu.

8. Lisa L. Martin and Beth A. Simmons, "Theories and Empirical Studies of International Institutions," in Peter J. Katzenstein, Robert O. Keohane, and Stephen D. Krasner, eds., *Exploration and Contestation in the Study of World Politics* (Cambridge, Mass.: MIT Press, 1999), 89–118.

9. By "institution" I mean a complex of rules (formal and informal) and procedures that govern human interactions in a given domain. This definition differs from usage in the financial press, which sometimes refers to companies, such as banks and asset managers, as institutions and institutional investors, respectively.

10. I use "smaller company" and synonyms in roughly the same way that they are used by UK financiers and officials: to indicate a firm that does not fall under the blue chip category but that might, under appropriate conditions, consider listing equity shares on a stock market. What financiers and policymakers mean by "smaller company" (e.g., size, age, industry) has varied across national borders, depended on the constellation of participants in a particular policy debate, and changed over time. As a rule, however, the phrase includes firms that are

neither among the largest quoted companies nor in the class of tiny neighborhood shops and restaurants. Policy debates have focused, though by no means exclusively, on young enterprises in high-technology industries that need large sums of capital before they are profitable.

11. Statistics are for June 2007. See London Stock Exchange, www.LSE.com. By June 2007, roughly 2,800 companies had traded shares on AIM since its inception in 1995. "Taking AIM for Global Success: London's Junior Stock Market Has Outlasted European Rivals," *Financial Times,* October 6, 2004, 18; "London the Laboratory for Biotechnology Launches," *Financial Times,* January 6, 2005, 18; "Scattering of Seedlings Turns into a Forest," *Financial Times,* March 30, 2006, 23.

12. Zysman, *Governments.*

13. Stock market rules may derive from one or more sources, including privately owned exchanges and subnational, national, and supranational authorities.

14. The Nasdaq principle has roots in the U.S. Securities Act of 1933 and Securities Exchange Act of 1934, as well as in political reactions to scandals of the 1960s. Mark Ingebretsen, *Nasdaq: A History of the Market That Changed the World* (Roseville, Calif.: Prima Publishing, 2002); Joel Seligman, *The Transformation of Wall Street,* 3rd ed. (New York: Aspen Publishers, 2003).

15. John Gerard Ruggie, "International Regimes, Transactions, and Change: Embedded Liberalism in the Postwar Economic Order," in Stephen D. Krasner, ed., *International Regimes* (Ithaca: Cornell University Press, 1983); Barry Eichengreen, *The European Economy since 1945: Coordinated Capitalism and Beyond* (Princeton: Princeton University Press, 2007).

16. These calculations are based on statistics no longer available on the exchanges' Web sites. My estimates are almost identical to those of Laura Bottazzi and Marco Da Rin, in "Europe's 'New' Stock Markets," Center for Economic Policy Research Discussion Papers, no. 3521 (2002). The only significant difference is my inclusion of AIM and additional years.

17. In 2006, U.S.-based Fidelity ranked first among institutional investors with holdings in AIM companies, and Merrill Lynch, Goldman Sachs, and Bank of New York were among the top twenty. See "Institutional Investors in AIM 2006," Growth Company Investor, Teather & Greenwood, London, 2006, www.londonstockexchange.com. Euronext in its newsletter boasts that 45 percent of investors in Alternext companies are domiciled outside the Euronext countries— Belgium, France, Netherlands, and Portugal—and specifically mentions Fidelity. See "Alternext Aims to Conquer City Investors," *AlterNews,* April 2007.

18. On the basis of percentages of institutional versus household buyers, I estimate the following: German households lost approximately 65 billion euros as share prices on the Neuer Markt fell between April 2000 and May 2001. French households lost approximately 20 billion euros on the Nouveau Marché during the same period. Interviews by Elliot Posner with executives of Parisbourse, Paris, May 18, 2000, and with Deutsche Boerse, Frankfurt, May 16, 2000.

19. Interviews with EVCA executive, Zaventem, April 26, 2000, and with venture capitalist, Leuven, April 26, 2000.

20. Depending on corporate governance and other arrangements, outsider investment does not necessarily translate into full company control.

21. See EVCA annual yearbooks, www.evca.com.

22. For reasons why social scientists think that the adoption of foreign forms produces differing outcomes from those of the country of origin, see Paul Pierson, "Increasing Returns, Path Dependence, and the Study of Politics," *American Political Science Review* 94, 2 (2000): 251–267; for a thoughtful work on the continued variation in European varieties of capitalism, see Vivien A. Schmidt, *The Futures of European Capitalism* (Oxford: Oxford University Press, 2002); for a skeptical perspective on the Neuer Markt's ability to produce Nasdaq-like effects, see Sigurt Vitols, "Frankfurt's Neuer Markt and the IPO Explosion: Is Germany on the Road to Silicon Valley?" *Economy and Society* 30, 4 (2001): 553–564.

23. See Chapter 5 for details.

24. The Paris stock exchange was the Société des Bourses Françaises (SBF-Paris Bourse), then the Parisbourse, and Euronext after the 2000 merger with the Amsterdam, Lisbon, and Brussels exchanges. It continues to operate as an independent entity under Euronext since the merger with the NYSE.

25. Chapter 6 discusses the Investment Services Directive of 1993 (Council Directive 93/22/EEC).

26. Josefin Almer, "The Reform of Comitology and the Parallel Reform of the European Financial Services Sector," New Modes of Governance Project, CIT1-CT-2004–506392, 7/D05a rev, December 12, 2006, www.eu-newgov.org.

27. See Chapter 3 for details.

28. Chapter 2 examines debates about institutional convergence, which refers to the narrowing of difference between the rules and procedures for governing a domain of human activity.

29. For a good example of the Europeanization literature, see Maria Green Cowles, James Caporaso, and Thomas Risse, *Transforming Europe: Europeanization and Domestic Change* (Ithaca: Cornell University Press, 2001).

30. Sonia Mazey and Jeremy Richardson, "Institutionalizing Promiscuity: Commission-Interest Group Relations in the EU," in Alec Stone Sweet, Wayne Sandholtz, and Neil Fligstein, eds., *The Institutionalization of Europe* (Oxford: Oxford University Press, 2001), 71–93.

31. Michael Barnett and Martha Finnemore, *Rules for the World: International Organizations in Global Politics* (Ithaca: Cornell University Press, 2004). Chapter 2 discusses the academic literature on international bureaucracies and its application to the European context.

32. Commission of the European Communities (CEC) is the label used on official documents. The 1957 treaty, known as the Treaty of Rome, establishing the European Economic Community, has become the basis for subsequent agreements. In 1968, the original European Communities (including the EEC, the European Coal and Steel Community, and European Atomic Energy Community) merged into the European Community. The Single European Act (1986), the Treaty of Maastricht (1992), the Treaty of Amsterdam (1997), and the Treaty of Nice (1997) were revisions to the Treaty of Rome.

33. Anne Stevens and Handley Stevens, *Brussels Bureaucrats? The Administration of the European Union* (New York: Palgrave, 2001); Nicolas Jabko, *Playing the Market: A Political Strategy for Uniting Europe, 1985–2005* (Ithaca: Cornell University Press), 44.

34. Jabko, *Playing,* 42–47.

35. Mark A. Pollack, *Engines of European Integration: Delegation, Agency, and Agenda Setting in the EU* (Oxford: Oxford University Press, 2003).

36. Barnett and Finnemore, *Rules.*

37. I interviewed stock exchange executives, national government and Commission officials, investment bankers, venture capitalists, and executives with the European Private Equity and Venture Capital Association (EVCA), International Federation of Stock Exchanges (renamed World Federation of Exchanges), the Federation of European Securities Exchanges (FESE), the City Group for Smaller Companies in London (renamed Quoted Companies Alliance), and the European Association of Securities Dealers in Brussels (which merged with APCIMS, Association of Private Client Investment Managers and Stock Brokers). Several of these individuals and organizations gave me access to their private archives, which included communications with Commission and government officials.

38. As Chapters 3–5 show, in the mid-1990s, financial policymaking was still a domestic affair, and the post-SEA (Single European Act) push to integrate the sector was among the least successful. Jonathan Story and Ingo Walter, *Political Economy of Financial Integration in Europe: The Battle of the Systems* (Cambridge, Mass.: MIT Press, 1997).

2. Markets, Politics, and Bureaucrats

1. This section specifies the dependent variable of my study.

2. The literature on the politics of finance is vast. For works on European countries and the EU, see John Zysman, *Governments, Markets, and Growth: Financial Systems and the Politics of Industrial Change* (Ithaca: Cornell University Press, 1983); P. G. Cerny, "The 'Little Big Bang' in Paris: Financial Market Deregulation in a *Dirigiste* System," *European Journal of Political Research* 17, 2 (1989): 169–192; Michael Loriaux, *France after Hegemony: International Change and Financial Reform* (Ithaca: Cornell University Press, 1991); Michael Moran, *The Politics of the Financial Services Revolution: The USA, UK and Japan* (New York: St. Martin's Press, 1991); Andrew C. Sobel, *Domestic Choices, International Markets* (Chicago: University of Chicago Press, 1994); William D. Coleman and Geoffrey R. D. Underhill, "Globalization, Regionalism and the Regulation of Securities Markets," *Journal of European Public Policy* 2, 3 (1995): 488–513; William D. Coleman, *Financial Services, Globalization and Domestic Policy Change* (New York: St. Martin's Press, 1996); Steven K. Vogel, *Freer Markets, More Rules: Regulatory Reform in Advanced Industrial Countries* (Ithaca: Cornell University Press, 1996); Sofia Perez, *Banking on Privilege: The Politics of Spanish Financial Reform* (Ithaca: Cornell University Press, 1997); Jonathan Story and Ingo Walter, *Political Economy of Financial Integration in Europe: The Battle of the Systems* (Cambridge, Mass.: MIT Press, 1997);

Susanne Lütz, "The Revival of the Nation-State? Stock Exchange Regulation in an Era of Globalized Financial Markets," *Journal of European Public Policy* 5, 1 (1998): 153–168; Richard Deeg, *Finance Capital Unveiled: Banks and the German Political Economy* (Ann Arbor: University of Michigan Press, 1999); J. Nicholas Ziegler, "Corporate Governance and the Politics of Property Rights in Germany," *Politics and Society* 28, 2 (2000): 195–221; Daniel Verdier, *Moving Money: Banking and Finance in the Industrialized World* (Cambridge: Cambridge University Press, 2003); Nicole de Montricher, "A National Pattern of Policy Transfer: The Regulation of Insider Trading in France," *French Politics* 3, 1 (2005): 28–48; Daniel Mügge, "Reordering the Market Place: Competition Politics in European Finance," *Journal of Common Market Studies* 55, 5 (2006): 991–1022.

3. For arguments about the sources of disintermediation and the disadvantages for small companies, see Verdier, *Moving Money.*

4. For debates in the United Kingdom, see J. E. Bolton (chairman), "Report of the Committee of Inquiry on Small Firms," Her Majesty's Stationery Office, London (hereafter HMSO), November 1971; Harold Wilson (chairman), "Report of the Committee to Review the Functioning of Financial Institutions," HMSO, June 1980; Confederation of British Industry (hereafter CBI), "Smaller Firms Council Report on Finance for Small and Medium Enterprises," London, 1993; HM Treasury, "Financing of High Technology Businesses: A Report to the Paymaster General," London, November 1998. For France, see Jacques Mayoux (chairman), "Le développement des initiatives financières locales et régionales: Rapport à Monsieur le Premier ministre du Groupe de réflexion présidé," La Documentation française, Paris, 1979; M. David Dautresme (chairman), "Le développement et la protection de l'épargne: Rapport au ministre de l'Économie et des Finances et au ministre délégué, chargé du Budget de la Commission," La Documentation française, Paris, 1982; Robert Chabbal (chairman), "Le système financier français face à l'investissement innovation: Rapport à ministre des entreprises et du développement économique," La Documentation française, Paris, 1995; Jonah D. Levy, *Tocqueville's Revenge: State, Society, and Economy in Contemporary France* (Cambridge, Mass.: Harvard University Press, 1979). For Germany, where public officials, financiers, and industrialists saw public support of the *mittelstand* as an economic success but still wanted to spur entrepreneurial activity, see Graham Bannock and Horst Albach, *Small Business Policy in Europe: Britain, Germany and the European Commission* (London: Anglo-German Foundation, 1991); Oliver Pfirrmann, Udo Wupperfeld, and Josh Lerner, *Venture Capital and New Technology Based Firms: A US-German Comparison* (Heidelberg: Physica-Verlag, 1997); Karen E. Adelberger, "Semi-Sovereign Leadership? The State's Role in German Biotechnology and Venture Capital Growth," *German Politics* 9, 1 (2000): 103–122; Ralph Becker and Thomas Hellmann, "The Genesis of Venture Capital: Lessons from the German Experience," CESifo Working Paper, no. 883 (2003), www.cesifo.de. The success of SMEs (small- and medium-sized enterprises) in industrial districts and later high-technology start-ups in the United States combined with skepticism about the mass-production corporate model also fueled a lively academic literature. For reviews, see Charles F. Sabel, "Turning

the Page in Industrial Districts," in Arnaldo Bagnasco and Sabel, eds., *Small and Medium-Size Enterprises* (London: Pinter, 1995), 134–158, and Jonathan Zeitlin, "Industrial Districts and Regional Clusters," in Geoffrey Jones and Zeitlin, eds., *The Oxford Handbook of Business History* (Oxford: Oxford University Press, 2008).

5. Chapter 4 uses barriers to quoting and informational standards to distinguish among larger-company stock markets as well. Finance economists primarily interested in comparing transaction costs and market quality across different stock markets use other dimensions. See, for example, Hendrik Bessembinder and Herbert M. Kaufman, "A Comparison of Trade Execution Costs for NYSE and Nasdaq-Listed Stocks," *Journal of Financial and Quantitative Analysis* 32, 3 (1997): 287–310.

6. While not designed to explain why some markets succeed or fail in economic terms, this study does sometimes bear on these outcomes, as noted where relevant.

7. For an overview of the 1980s markets and their failure, see Graham Bannock, "European Second-Tier Markets for NTBFs," Graham Bannock and Partners, London, 1994.

8. "Playing by the Rules: How Neuer Markt Gets Respect," *Wall Street Journal*, August 21, 2000, 1; Sigurt Vitols, "Frankfurt's Neuer Markt and the IPO Explosion: Is Germany on the Road to Silicon Valley?" *Economy and Society* 30, 4 (2001): 553–564; Vitols and Lutz Engelhardt, "National Institutions and High Tech Industries: A Varieties of Capitalism Perspective on the Failure of Germany's 'Neuer Markt,'" Discussion Paper SP II 2005–03, *Wissenschaftszentrum Berlin für Sozialforschung* (Berlin, 2005). As Chapter 7 discusses, the main markets have since caught up. In 2005 all publicly listed EU companies were required to report consolidated accounts in accordance with IAS/IFRS.

9. In 2000, the Neuer Markt's success was an important Deutsche Boerse asset in the proposed merger with the LSE. The parties had planned to replace the Neuer Markt with a new cross-border market based in Frankfurt, not London ("The London-Frankfurt Merger," *Financial Times*, May 4, 2000, 34.) For Neuer Markt statistics, see Hans-Peter Burghof and Adrian Hunger, "The Neuer Markt: An (Overly) Risky Asset of Germany's Financial System," in Giancarlo Giudici and Peter Roosenboom, eds., *The Rise and Fall of Europe's New Stock Markets* (Amsterdam: Elsevier, 2004), 295–328.

10. For economic analyses of the new markets, see Giudici and Roosenboom, *The Rise and Fall*.

11. For AIM rules, see www.lse.com. Chapter 6 discusses the history of AIM's rule changes in detail. Following Euronext's creation of Alternext, the Deutsche Boerse created Entry Standard (see Table 1.1, page 4). Euronext, "Euronext Launches NextEconomy and NextPrime Segments," press release, December 18, 2001; Euronext, "Euronext Completes Overhaul of Listing Structure on All Its Markets," press release, Paris, March 23, 2005; Euronext, "Alternext: A Tailor-Made Market for Small and Mid Caps," press release, Paris, April 14, 2005; "Euronext Bullish over Alternext," *Financial Times*, April 15, 2005, 18; "Alternext Aims to Be Serious Alternative to London," *Financial Times*, March 9, 2007, 21.

12. "Nouveau Marché Rule Change," *Financial Times*, October 30, 1996, 28; David Mandell, "Alternative Investment Mood," *CISCO Voice*, December 1997, 8–10.

13. "Business in Silicon Valley Seek a Future on UK's AIM," *Financial Times*, October 9, 2006, 1. In March 2007, 13 percent of AIM's foreign listings were from the United States. See www.lse.com.

14. "Companies UK: Alternext Aims to Be Serious Alternative," *Financial Times*, March 9, 2007, 21; "Davos: NYSE Chief Says Aim Must Raise Standards," *Financial Times*, January 27, 2007, 8; Clara Furse, "US Markets Should Shun Navel-Gazing and Accept Global Capital Flow," *Financial Times*, March 20, 2007, 12; "London's Junior Market a Danger, Says Ross," *Financial Times*, April 20, 2007, 1; "Top SEC Official Claims UK's Aim Is a 'Casino,'" *Financial Times*, March 9, 2007, 1.

15. In terms of moving from the feeder form to foreign organizational principles, Table 1.1 shows two exceptions to the pattern. The 1992 Dutch Participation Exchange (Parex) was an early experiment along the lines of the 1995 AIM. It opened briefly before closing because of a lack of interest. Although the Swedish exchange adopted a name similar to those of the other new markets, its 1998 Nya Marknaden had a feeder form.

16. Exceptions include Peter J. Katzenstein, *A World of Regions: Asia and Europe in the American Imperium* (Ithaca: Cornell University Press, 2005).

17. By "institutional convergence," I mean the narrowing of difference between the rules and procedures for governing a domain of human activity. It is a subset of institutional change. In this book, variance in institutional convergence is an outcome to be explained. See Suzanne Berger, "Introduction," in Berger and Ronald Dore, eds., *National Diversity and Global Capitalism* (Ithaca: Cornell University Press, 1996), 1–28; R. O. Keohane and Helen V. Milner, "Internationalization and Domestic Politics: An Introduction," in Keohane and Milner, eds., *Internationalization and Domestic Politics* (Cambridge: Cambridge University Press, 1996), 3–24. The concept of institutional convergence overlaps with institutional copying (mimesis, mimicry, borrowing, emulation, and imitation), connoting a deliberate action, and isomorphism, though Paul J. DiMaggio and Walter W. Powell use "institutional isomorphism" when a form does not represent technical or functional optimality. See DiMaggio and Powell, "The Iron Cage Revisited: Institutional Isomorphism and Collective Rationality in Organizational Fields," in DiMaggio and Powell, eds., *The New Institutionalism in Organizational Analysis* (Chicago: University of Chicago Press, 1991), 63–82. "Regulatory harmonization" refers to deliberate efforts to create international standards. See David Andrew Singer, "Capital Rules: The Domestic Politics of International Regulatory Harmonization," *International Organization* 58, 3 (2004): 531–565. Beth A. Simmons focuses on regulatory harmonization as market or political process. See Simmons, "International Politics of Harmonization: The Case of Capital Market Regulation," *International Organization* 55, 3 (2001): 589–620. "Diffusion," as used by Simmons and Zachary Elkins, is a process, not an outcome. See Simmons and Elkins, "The Globalization of Liberalization: Policy Dif-

fusion in the International Political Economy," *American Political Science Review* 98, 1 (2004): 171–189.

18. For studies that focus on the effects of institutional investors on national macro-financial and macroeconomic policies, see Michael C. Webb, "International Economic Structures, Government Interests and International Coordination of Macroeconomic Adjustment Policies," *International Organization* 45, 3 (1991): 309–342; John B. Goodman and Louis W. Pauly, "The Obsolescence of Capital Controls? Economic Management in an Age of Global Markets," *World Politics* 46, 1 (1993): 50–82; David Andrews, "Capital Mobility and State Autonomy," *International Studies Quarterly* 38, 2 (1994): 193–218. On the theme that asset managers and other global financial firms influence stock exchanges indirectly, see Henry Laurence, *Money Rules: The New Politics of Finance in Britain and Japan* (Ithaca: Cornell University Press, 2001).

19. Paulette Kurzer, *Business and Banking: Political Change and Economic Integration in Western Europe* (Ithaca: Cornell University Press, 1993); Deeg, *Finance Capital Unveiled;* Levy, *Tocqueville's Revenge;* Sobel, *Domestic Choices;* Verdier, *Moving Money;* and Timothy J. Sinclair and Kenneth P. Thomas, eds., *Structure and Agency in International Capital Mobility* (New York: Palgrave 2001).

20. There are two main EU variants of the mobile capital explanation. When firms, responding to new international price signals, face entrenched relationships in their home countries, Commission officials are expected to recognize so-called latent firm preferences and intervene on the firms' behalf or to respond to direct firm lobbying. Andrew Moravcsik depicts the former as underrepresentation, whereby Commission officials see potential efficiency gains and help firms overcome national "coordination problems." See Moravcsik, "A New Statecraft? Supranational Entrepreneurs and International Cooperation," *International Organization* 53, 2 (1999): 267–306. Alec Stone Sweet and Wayne Sandholtz, in contrast, argue that firms wanting regionwide rules may choose to go directly to the Commission. See Stone Sweet and Sandholtz, "Integration, Supranational Governance, and the Institutionalization of the European Polity," in Sandholtz and Stone Sweet, eds., *European Integration and Supranational Governance* (Oxford: Oxford University Press, 1998), 1–26. According to both approaches, supranational officials respond to company preferences.

21. Institutional sociologists, constructivists, and Gramscian international relations scholars focus on the spread of modern "liberalism" and in the main agree that policymakers follow a set of universally accepted liberal principles, including the primacy of market mechanisms, that represent progressive, rational, and modern change. See George M. Thomas, John W. Meyer, Francisco O. Ramirez, and John Boli, *Institutional Structure: Constituting State, Society, and the Individual* (Newbury Park, Calif.: Sage Publications, 1987); Robert W. Cox, "Gramsci, Hegemony and International Relations: An Essay in Method," in Stephen Gill, ed., *Historical Materialism and International Relations* (Cambridge: Cambridge University Press, 1993); Martha Finnemore, *National Interests in International Society* (Ithaca: Cornell University Press, 1996); Stephen Gill, "Global Structural Change

and Multilateralism," in Gill, ed., *Globalization, Democratization and Multilateralism* (New York: St. Martin's Press, 1997); Margaret E. Keck and Kathryn Sikkink, *Activists beyond Borders: Advocacy Networks in International Politics* (Ithaca: Cornell University Press, 1998); John Boli and George M. Thomas, eds., *Constructing World Culture: International Nongovernmental Organizations since 1875* (Stanford: Stanford University Press, 1999); Kathleen R. McNamara, *The Currency of Ideas: Monetary Politics in the European Union* (Ithaca: Cornell University Press, 1998), and "Rational Fictions: Central Bank Independence and the Social Logic of Delegation," *West European Politics* 25, 1 (January 2001): 47–76.

22. Martha Finnemore and Kathryn Sikkink, "International Norm Dynamics and Political Change," *International Organization* 52, 4 (1998): 887–918.

23. Susan K. Sell and Aseem Prakash, "Using Ideas Strategically: The Contest between Business and NGO Networks in Intellectual Property Rights," *International Studies Quarterly* 48, 1 (2004): 143–175; Nicolas Jabko, *Playing the Market: A Political Strategy for Uniting Europe, 1985–2005* (Ithaca: Cornell University Press, 2006).

24. Simmons and Elkins, "Globalization."

25. DiMaggio and Powell, "The Iron Cage Revisited"; Sobel, *Domestic Choices;* Suzanne Berger, "Introduction"; Andrew Moravcsik, *The Choice for Europe: Social Purpose and State Power from Messina to Maastricht* (Ithaca: Cornell University Press, 1998); Robert Boyer, "The Convergence Hypothesis Revisited: Globalization but Still the Century of Nations?" in Suzanne Berger and Ronald Dore, eds. *National Diversity and Global Capitalism* (Ithaca: Cornell University Press, 1996), 29–59; Peter A. Hall and David Soskice, eds., *Varieties of Capitalism: The Institutional Foundations of Comparative Advantage* (Oxford: Oxford University Press, 2001).

26. Deeg, *Finance Capital Unveiled;* Richard Deeg and Sofia Perez, "International Capital Mobility and Domestic Institutions: Corporate Finance and Governance in Four European Cases," *Governance* 13, 2 (2000): 119–154; Levy, *Tocqueville's Revenge;* Vogel, *Freer Markets;* Verdier, *Moving Money;* Mügge, "Reordering."

27. DiMaggio and Powell, "The Iron Cage Revisited"; Annalee Saxenian, *Regional Advantage: Culture and Competition in Silicon Valley and Route 128* (Cambridge, Mass.: Harvard University Press, 1994).

28. Moravcsik, *The Choice.*

29. Adrienne Heritier, "Overt and Covert Institutionalization in Europe," Stone Sweet and Sandholtz, "Integration," and Stone Sweet, Neil Fligstein, and Sandholtz, "The Institutionalization of European Space," all in Stone Sweet, Sandholtz, and Fligstein, eds., *The Institutionalization of Europe* (Oxford: Oxford University Press, 2001), 1–28.

30. Finnemore, *National Interests;* McNamara, "Rational Fictions"; Kathryn Sikkink, "Human Rights, Principled Issue–Networks, Sovereignty in Latin America," *International Organization* 47, 3 (Summer 1993): 411–441; Alexander Wendt, *Social Theory of International Politics* (Cambridge: Cambridge University Press, 1999); Thomas Risse, "US Power in a Liberal Security Community," in G. John Ikenberry, ed., *America Unrivaled: The Future of the Balance of Power* (Ithaca: Cornell University Press, 2002), 260–283.

31. Michael Barnett and Martha Finnemore, *Rules for the World: International Organizations in Global Politics* (Ithaca: Cornell University Press, 2004).

32. Stone Sweet, Fligstein, and Sandholtz, "The Institutionalization"; Daniel Carpenter, *Forging Bureaucratic Autonomy: Networks, Reputations and Policy Innovation in Executive Agencies, 1862–1928* (Princeton: Princeton University Press, 2001).

33. Ernst B. Haas, *The Uniting of Europe: Political, Social and Economic Forces, 1950–1957* (Stanford: Stanford University Press, 1958).

34. Joseph Weiler, "The Transformation of Europe," *Yale Law Journal* 100, 3 (1991): 2403–2525; Anne-Marie Burley and Walter Mattli, "Europe before the Court: A Political Theory of Legal Integration," *International Organization* 47, 1 (1993): 41–76; Sandholtz, "Membership Matters: Limits of the Functional Approach to European Institutions," *Journal of Common Market Studies* 34, 3 (1996): 403–429; Paul Pierson, "The Path to European Integration: A Historical Institutionalist Analysis," *Comparative Political Studies* 29, 2 (1996): 123–163; Stone Sweet, Sandholtz, and Fligstein, *The Institutionalization of Europe.*

35. For examples of the Europeanization literature, see Maria Green Cowles, James Caporaso, and Thomas Risse, *Transforming Europe: Europeanization and Domestic Change* (Ithaca: Cornell University Press, 2001); Vivien A. Schmidt, *Democracy in Europe: The EU and National Politics* (Oxford: Oxford University Press, 2006), and *The Futures of European Capitalism* (Oxford: Oxford University Press, 2002).

36. On political and social skills, see Fligstein, "Social Skill and Institutional Theory," *American Behavioral Scientist* 40, 4 (1997): 397–405; Neil Fligstein and Iona Mara-Drita, "How to Make a Market: Reflections on the Attempt to Create a Single Market in the European Union," *American Journal of Sociology* 102, 1 (1996): 1–33. On maneuvering within the EU, see Heritier, "Overt and Covert," and Sonia Mazey and Jeremy Richardson, "Institutionalizing Promiscuity: Commission-Interest Group Relations in the EU," in Stone Sweet, Sandholtz, and Fligstein, *The Institutionalization of Europe,* 71–93. On legitimacy, see Andy Smith, ed., *Politics and the European Commission: Actors, Interdependence, Legitimacy* (London: Routledge, 2004); Schmidt, *Democracy,* 25–29.

37. B. Guy Peters, "Bureaucratic Politics and the Institutions of the European Community," in Alberta M. Sbragia, ed., *Euro-Politics: Institutions and Policymaking in the 'New' European Community* (Washington, D.C.: Brookings Institution, 1992), 75–122; Pierson, "Path"; Laura Cram, "The EU Institutions and Collective Action: Constructing a European Interest?" in Justin Greenwood and Mark Aspinwall, *Collective Action in the European Union: Interests and the New Politics of Associability* (London: Routledge, 1998), 63–80.

38. Peters, "Bureaucratic Politics"; Laura Cram, "The European Commission as a Multi-Organization: Social Policy and IT Policy in the EU," *Journal of European Public Policy* 1, 2 (1994): 195–217; Andy Smith, "La Commission européenne et les fonds structurels: Vers un nouveau modèle d'action?" *Revue française de science politique* 46, 3 (1996): 474–496; Jacques E. C. Hymans, "Do Too Many Chefs Really Spoil the Broth? The European Commission, Bureaucratic Politics and European Integration" (working paper, Minda de Gunzburg Center for European Studies, Harvard University, May 8, 1999), www.ciaonet.org.

39. Barnett and Finnemore, *Rules for the World.*
40. Heritier, "Overt and Covert."
41. Wayne Sandholtz and John Zysman, "92: Recasting the European Bargain," *World Politics* 42, 1 (October 1989): 95–128; Fligstein and Mara-Drita, "How to Make a Market"; Nicolas Jabko, "In the Name of the Market," *Journal of European Public Policy* 6, 3 (1999): 475–498, and *Playing the Market: A Political Strategy for Uniting Europe, 1985–2005* (Ithaca: Cornell University Press, 2006); Stone Sweet, Fligstein, and Sandholtz, *The Institutionalization of Europe;* Cram, "The EU Institutions"; Mazey and Richardson, "Interest Groups and EU Policy-Making: Organizational Logic and Venue Shopping," in Jeremy J. Richardson, ed., *European Union: Power and Policy-Making,* 2nd ed. (London: Routledge, 2001); Justin Greenwood, "The Professions," in Greenwood and Mark Aspinwall, *Collective Action in the European Union: Interests and the New Politics of Associability* (London: Routledge, 1988), 126–148; Michael W. Bauer, "Limitations to Agency Control in European Policy-Making: The Commission and the Poverty Programmes," *Journal of Common Market Studies* 40, 3 (2002): 381–400; David Coen, "Empirical and Theoretical Studies in EU Lobbying," *Journal of European Public Policy* 14, 3 (2007): 333–345.
42. Bauer, "Limitations"; Cram, "The European Commission"; Heritier, "Overt and Covert"; Marc E. Smyrl, "When (and How) Do the Commission's Preferences Matter?" *Journal of Common Market Studies* 36, 1 (1998): 79–99; Fligstein and Mara-Drita, "How to Make a Market"; Mark A. Pollack, *Engines of European Integration: Delegation, Agency, and Agenda Setting in the EU* (Oxford: Oxford University Press, 2003); Smith, *Politics and the European Commission.*
43. Heritier, "Overt and Covert"; Stone Sweet and Sandholtz, "Integration"; Bauer, "Limitations."
44. Stephen Jay Gould, *Wonderful Life: The Burgess Shale and the Nature of History* (New York: W. W. Norton, 1990).
45. Carpenter, *Forging Bureaucratic Autonomy.*
46. Liesbet Hooghe, "Several Roads Lead to International Norms, but Few via International Socialization: A Case Study of the European Commission," *International Organization* 59, 4 (2005): 861–898.
47. Peters, "Bureaucratic Politics"; Cram, "The European Commission"; and Liesbet Hooghe, *The European Commission and the Integration of Europe: Images of Governance* (Cambridge: Cambridge University Press, 2001). See arguments for treating the Commission as a unitary actor in Pollack, *Engines,* and as a hierarchy in Jabko, *Playing.*
48. On the dysfunctional character of international organizations, see Barnett and Finnemore, *Rules for the World.*
49. Hymans, "Do Too Many Chefs"; Smith, "La Commission européenne."
50. Pollack, *Engines;* Jonas Tallberg, "The Anatomy of Autonomy: An Institutional Account of Variation in Supranational Influence," *Journal of Common Market Studies* 38, 5 (2000): 843–864; Mark Thatcher and Alec Stone Sweet, "Theory and Practice of Delegation to Non-Majoritarian Institutions," *West European Politics* 25, 1 (2002): 1–22. These applications of the principal-agent framework

have close affinities to intergovernmentalism. See Moravcsik, "A New State-craft?" Bureaucratic or political autonomy need not mean that officials achieve all their goals, face only insignificant constraints in carrying out preferred policies, and are impervious to the influences of others. Rather, following scholarly convention, bureaucratic autonomy implies that Brussels officials develop distinct motivations and interpretations of policy problems and solutions, have resources at their disposal for influencing the behavior of others, and alter the course of events through their actions. See Carpenter, *Forging Bureaucratic Autonomy*, 14.

51. Pollack, *Engines*. Moravcsik explicitly acknowledges the limitations of this approach for explaining institutional outcomes like the ones I observe here. See Moravcsik, "A New Statecraft?" 269n10.

52. See Henry Farrell and Adrienne Héritier, "Introduction: Contested Competences in the European Union," *West European Politics* 30, 2 (2007): 227–243.

53. For good examples, see Bauer, "Limitations"; Cram, "The European Commission"; Jabko, *Playing*; and Sandholtz and Zysman, "1992." Carpenter usefully distinguishes bureaucratic autonomy from discretion. See Carpenter, *Forging Bureaucratic Autonomy*, 17–18.

54. Bauer, "Limitations."

55. See Barnett and Finnemore, *Rules for the World*. Even those who use the principal-agent approach recognize these limitations. See Pollack, *Engines*.

56. For a review of these debates, see Pollack, *Engines*, 49–56.

57. For examples, see Abraham Newman, "Building Transnational Civil Liberties: Transgovernmental Entrepreneurs and the European Data Privacy Directive," *International Organization* 62, 1 (2008) 103–130; Burley and Mattli, "Europe before the Court."

58. Fligstein, *The Architecture of Markets: An Economic Sociology of Twenty-First Century Capitalist Societies* (Princeton: Princeton University Press, 2001); Story and Walter, *Political Economy*.

59. Fritz Scharpf, *Governing in Europe: Effective and Democratic?* (Oxford: Oxford University Press, 1999); Tim Büthe, "The Politics of Competition and Institutional Change in the European Union: The First Fifty Years," in Sophie Meunier and McNamara, eds., *Making History: European Integration and Institutional Change at Fifty* (Oxford: Oxford University Press, 2007), 175–194.

60. On political spaces, see Stone Sweet, Fligstein, and Sandholtz, "The Institutionalization," 13.

61. Chapter 6 discusses the Investment Services Directive.

3. The Early History of a Brussels Initiative

1. London's Big Bang, discussed in Chapter 4, refers to the 1986 government-initiated liberalization of the London Stock Exchange. A simultaneous process led to the reregulation of the British securities sector. See Michael Moran, *The Politics of the Financial Services Revolution: The USA, UK and Japan* (New York: St. Martin's Press, 1991); Steven K. Vogel, *Freer Markets, More Rules: Regulatory Reform in*

Advanced Industrial Countries (Ithaca: Cornell University Press, 1996); Henry Laurence, *Money Rules: The New Politics of Finance in Britain and Japan* (Ithaca: Cornell University Press, 2001). For EU efforts to integrate financial sectors after the 1986 SEA, see William D. Coleman and Geoffrey R. D. Underhill, "Globalization, Regionalism and the Regulation of Securities Markets," *Journal of European Public Policy* 2, 3 (1995): 488–513; Jonathan Story and Ingo Walter, *Political Economy of Financial Integration in Europe: The Battle of the Systems* (Cambridge, Mass.: MIT Press, 1997); Nicolas Jabko, *Playing the Market: A Political Strategy for Uniting Europe, 1985–2005* (Ithaca: Cornell University Press, 2006), chap. 5. See Chapter 2 in this book for examples of the scholarly debate on the impact of the post–Bretton Woods return of global finance. For studies that deal with smaller-company arrangements and policies, see Graham Bannock and Horst Albach, *Small Business Policy in Europe: Britain, Germany and the European Commission* (London: Anglo-German Foundation, 1991); Arnaldo Bagnasco and Charles Sabel, eds., *Small and Medium-Size Enterprises* (London: Pinter, 1995); Richard Deeg, *Finance Capital Unveiled: Banks and the German Political Economy* (Ann Arbor: University of Michigan Press, 1999); Deeg and Sofia Perez, "International Capital Mobility and Domestic Institutions: Corporate Finance and Governance in Four European Cases," *Governance: An International Journal of Policy and Administration* 13, 2 (2000): 119–154; Daniel Verdier, *Moving Money: Banking and Finance in the Industrialized World* (Cambridge: Cambridge University Press, 2003).

2. For background on EU technology policy, see John Peterson, "Technology Policy in Europe: Explaining the Framework Programme and Eureka in Theory and Practice," *Journal of Common Market Studies* 29, 3 (1991): 269–290; Wayne Sandholtz, *High-Tech Europe: The Politics of International Cooperation* (Berkeley: University of California Press, 1992); and Johan Lembke, *Defining the New Economy in Europe: A Comparative Analysis of EU Technology Infrastructure Policy, 1995–2001* (Stockholm: Stockholm University Press, 2002).

3. See Commission of the European Communities (hereafter CEC), *The Community and Industrial Innovation* (Brussels, 1978); CEC, *European Venture Capital Pilot Scheme,* EUR 9082 EN-FR final, Directorate General Information and Innovation (Brussels, 1984); Hermann Burgard, "Welcome Address and Progress Report from the Director," and Robin Miège, "Financing Information-Technology-Based Business: Speech Transcript" (papers presented at Symposium on Improving Venture Capital Opportunities in Europe, New Technologies and Innovation Policy, DG Information Market and Innovation, Luxembourg, October 3–5, 1984), printed in CEC, *Improving Venture Capital Opportunities in Europe,* Eur 9756 En/De/Fr (Brussels and Luxembourg, 1985); Sandholtz, *High-Tech;* interview by Elliot Posner with Commission official, DG Enterprise, Innovation Policy, Luxembourg, May 5, 2000.

4. In 1987, the name of DG13 changed to Telecommunications, Information Industries, and Innovation. See Sandholtz, *High-Tech,* chap. 7. The Commission periodically restructured the directorates general and changed their labeling system from numerals to titles. To avoid confusion, I use the original numbers.

The unit in DG13 discussed here is today part of DG Enterprise and Industry. For a mapping of the old and new titles, see David Spence, "The Directorates General and the Services: Structures, Functions and Procedures," in Spence with Geoffrey Edwards, eds., *The European Commission*, 3rd ed. (London: John Harper Publishing, 2006), 128–154. For the reader's sake, I use Arabic rather than the conventional Roman numerals for labeling DGs.

5. NTBF describes young firms set up to exploit patented technologies and therefore firms facing technological and start-up risks in addition to normal commercial risks.

6. CEC, *European Venture Capital Pilot Scheme*, 12.

7. CEC, *European Venture Capital Pilot Scheme;* CEC, *Draft Resolution of the Council Concerning the Action Programme for SME,* Com(86)445 (Brussels, 1986); CEC, *Proposal for a Council Decision Concerning the Implementation at Community Level of the Main Phase of the Strategic Programme for Innovation Technology Transfer (Sprint), 1989–1993,* COM(88)426 final (Brussels, July 20, 1988).

8. Paul A. Gompers and Josh Lerner, "What Drives Venture Capital Fundraising?" National Bureau of Economic Research Working Paper, no. w6906 (1999), www.nber.org.

9. For example, see CEC, *Towards a European Stock Exchange: Symposium Held in Brussels on 13 and 14 November 1980,* XV/231/81 (Brussels, 1980).

10. Scholars dispute the reasons for this proclivity. See, for example, Liesbet Hooghe, "Several Roads Lead to International Norms, but Few via International Socialization: A Case Study of the European Commission," *International Organization* 59, 4 (2005): 861–898. For general works on the Commission, see Michelle Cini, *The European Commission: Leadership, Organization and Culture in the EU Administration* (Manchester: Manchester University Press, 1996); Neill Nugent, ed., *At the Heart of the Union: Studies of the European Commission* (New York: St. Martin's Press, 1997); Anne Stevens with Handley Stevens, *Brussels Bureaucrats? The Administration of the European Union* (London: Palgrave, 2001); Spence with Edwards, *European Commission.*

11. Examples include Wayne Sandholtz and John Zysman, "1992: Recasting the European Bargain," *World Politics* 42, 1 (1989): 95–128; Sandholtz, *High-Tech;* Neil Fligstein and Iona Mara-Drita, "How to Make a Market: Reflections on the Attempt to Create a Single Market in the European Union," *American Journal of Sociology* 102, 1 (1996): 1–33; Laura Cram, "The European Commission as a Multi-Organization: Social Policy and IT Policy in the EU," *Journal of European Public Policy* 1, 2 (1994): 195–217; Susanne K. Schmidt, "Commission Activism: Subsuming Telecommunications and Electricity under European Competition Law," *Journal of European Public Policy* 5, 1 (1998): 169–184; Marc E. Smyrl, "When (and How) Do the Commission's Preferences Matter?" *Journal of Common Market Studies* 36, 1 (1998): 79–99; Johan Lembke, *Defining;* Jabko, *Playing.*

12. CEC, *The Community and Industrial Innovation;* CEC, *Bulletin of the European Union/European Community,* Bull EC 11–1982, 2.1.24 (1982); CEC, *Amendment of the Proposal for a Council Decision: Promoting a European Infrastructure for Innovation and Technology Transfer,* Com(83)277 (Brussels, 1983); CEC, *European Venture*

Capital Pilot Scheme; CEC, *Improving;* CEC, *Fiscal Environment of, and Corporate Ve-hicles for, Venture Capital in the European Communities,* Eur 11527 En, (authored by Deloitte, Haskins & Sells, Reference Date: December 31, 1987), DG Telecommunications, Information, and Innovation (Brussels, 1990); CEC, *Financial Problems of SMEs,* COM(93)528 (Brussels, November 10, 1993); CEC, "Prospects for the Creation of a European-Level Capital Market for Entrepreneurial Companies: Meeting with the Press in Preparation for June 21," DG23 (Direction B, Unit 3, Brussels, June 16, 1994; CEC, *Reporting on the Feasibility of the Creation of a European Capital Market for Smaller Entrepreneurial Managed Growing Companies,* COM(95)498 final (Brussels, October 25, 1995); Heinrich von Moltke, "The Role of DGXIII with Regard to Easdaq" (paper presented at the "EASDAQ—The European Stock Market for Growing Companies" conference, Brussels, June 26, 1996); interview by Steven Weber with Commission officials from the former DG23, Brussels, June 1997; interviews by Elliot Posner with Commission officials, from the former DG18, Luxembourg, June 7, 1999, from the former DG13, Luxembourg, May 5, 2000, and from the former DG15, Brussels, June 8, 2004; telephone interview with Commission official, former director of unit, DG13, May 4, 2000; letter to Elliot Posner from (L.D.M. Mackenzie, director of Promotion of Entrepreneurship and SME, DG Enterprise official, (May 8, 2001).

13. Hooghe, "Several Roads."
14. For a recent discussion of this assumption, see Mark A. Pollack, *Engines of European Integration: Delegation, Agency, and Agenda Setting in the EU* (Oxford: Oxford University Press, 2003), 35. Also, see Jabko, *Playing,* 47.
15. Andy Smith, "La Commission européenne et les fonds structurels: Vers un nouveau modèle d'action?" *Revue française de science politique* 46, 3 (1996): 474–496; Jacques E. C. Hymans, "Do Too Many Chefs Really Spoil the Broth? The European Commission, Bureaucratic Politics and European Integration" (Minda de Gunzburg Center for European Studies, working Paper, Harvard University, May 8, 1999), www.ciaonet.org.
16. On clashing preferences within the Commission, see B. Guy Peters, "Bureaucratic Politics and the Institutions of the European Community," in Alberta M. Sbragia, ed., *Euro-Politics: Institutions and Policymaking in the 'New' European Community* (Washington, D.C.: Brookings Institution, 1992), 75–122; Cram, "The European Commission;" George Ross, *Jacques Delors and European Integration* (New York: Oxford University Press, 1995); Cini, *The European Commission;* Thomas Christiansen, "Tensions of European Governance: Politicized Bureaucracy and Multiple Accountability in the European Commission," *Journal of European Public Policy* 4, 1 (1997): 73–90; Liesbet Hooghe, *The European Commission and the Integration of Europe: Images of Governance* (Cambridge: Cambridge University Press, 2001).
17. Interviews with official from the former DG15, and with FESE executive, Brussels, June 9, 2004. SFE's notes from meeting between Andrew Sundberg, Eugene Schulman, and SFE and the Commission's Inter-DG Working Group, Brussels, October 11, 1989, ELBAssociates historical files, Geneva.
18. Interview with Commission official, DG Enterprise.

19. The Santer Commission produced a risk capital action plan (SEC [1998] 522), which was endorsed by Ecofin at the Cardiff European Council in June 1998. CEC, *Risk Capital: A Key to Job Creation in the European Union,* SEC(1998)552 final, (Brussels, March 31, 1998).

20. Peters, "Bureaucratic Politics."

21. Jabko, *Playing.*

22. On Davignon, see Sandholtz, *High-Tech,* chap. 7. I discuss Delors' interest in the pan-European stock market later in this chapter.

23. See Bannock and Albach, *Small Business,* chap. 6; letter to Elliot Posner from DG Enterprise official.

24. Peters, "Bureaucratic Politics."

25. See CEC, *Towards;* ELBAssociates and Consultex, "The Feasibility of Creating ECU-EASD: A European Association of Securities Dealers to Trade over the Counter in ECU-Denominated Shares," Geneva, 1985. The ECU-EASD document discusses the dismay of DG15 officials over Hartmut Schmidt's commissioned study, which concluded in favor of dividing national stock markets into segments rather than integrating stock markets across borders. See Schmidt, *Advantages and Disadvantages of an Integrated Market Compared with a Fragmented Market, March 1977,* CEC, Competition—Approximation of Legislation Series, no. 30 (Brussels, 1977).

26. Letter to Elliot Posner from L. D. M. Mackenzie, director of Promotion of Entrepreneurship and SMEs, DG Enterprise, May 8, 2001.

27. For the European Venture Capital Fund Project, see CEC, *European Venture Capital Pilot Scheme,* app. 5 of Commission, 1984. For the European Innovation Loan Fund and a specific reference to the United Kingdom's veto in Ecofin, see Burgard, "Welcome."

28. "Regional" here refer to policies of subnational jurisdictions.

29. DG18's financial operations unit oversaw funds managed by the Commission and later moved to DG2. It does not write financial services legislation.

30. CEC, *European Venture Capital Pilot Scheme,* app. 1, esp. 61. The program involved eight of Europe's most important "venture capital" companies. These were primarily government-supported efforts to stimulate national venture capital industries.

31. CEC, *Bulletin of the European Union/European Community,* Bull EC 12–1981, 2.1.18, (1981); CEC, *Bulletin of the European Union/European Community,* Bull 11–1982, 2.1.24 (1982); CEC, *Bulletin of the European Union/European Community,* Bull 6–1983, 2.1.46 (1983); "Entrepreneurs Come of Age on the Continent," *BusinessWeek,* December 12, 1983, 45; CEC, *Improving;* CEC, *Proposal for a Council Decision Concerning* (Brussels, July 20, 1988), app. 3, 10.

32. Eugene Schulman and Andrew Sundberg worked through their respective companies, ELBAssociates and Consultex. ELBAssociates and Consultex, "The Feasibility of Creating ECU-EASD."

33. They ended up selling about thirty copies and making a small profit. Interview with Eugene Schulman, Berkeley, Calif., July 12, 2000.

34. Christian Hemain, "International Equities: Time for a Euro-Nasdaq?" *International Financial Review,* no. 567 (April 20, 1985); "A Nasdaq for Europe," *Econo-*

mist, April 13, 1985, 18; EVCA, "New Survey Shows Need for European Over-the-Counter Securities Market," *Information Bulletin,* December 23, 1985; "OTC Market for Europe Gains Support," *Wall Street Journal,* December 23, 1985, section 2, 11; "Support Found for Over-the-Counter Market," *Financial Times,* December 24, 1985; "Bringing Europe's Small Companies to Market," *Euromoney,* February 1986, 18. Interview with Eugene Schulman and Andrew Sundberg, Geneva, May 8, 2000.

35. Correspondence between Eugene Schulman and Jacques Delors, president of the Commission, 1985, ELBAssociates historical files, Geneva.

36. CEC, *European Venture Capital Pilot Scheme;* Miège, "Financing Information-Technology Based Business."

37. Interview with Schulman and Sundberg.

38. It was officially killed on June 6, 1986, at a Commission meeting.

39. DG15 was most successful in writing legislation that harmonized listing and prospectus standards. The relevant recommendations and EEC directives are 77/534/EEC, 79/279/EEC, 80/390/EEC, 82/121/EEC, 85/611/EEC, and 85/612/EEC.

40. "Choosing the Stock Market That Fits," *Euromoney,* January 1986, supplement, 126.

41. That Schulman and Sundberg were not EC citizens but Americans living in Switzerland did not help the Brussels bureaucrats make their case.

42. Steven Weber and Elliot Posner, "Creating a Pan-European Equity Market," in Weber, ed., *Globalization and European Political Economy* (New York: Columbia University Press, 2001), 140–196.

43. In 1988 Commission officials hired Deloitte, Haskins and Sells to conduct a study on SMEs and capital markets. I was unable to locate a copy of the study, titled "Access for SMEs to the Capital Markets, Particularly Junior Markets." The study was coordinated by Graham Cole, a partner in Deloitte's corporate finance division in London.

44. Interview with Schulman and Sundberg. Letter between Eugene Sundberg and Mike Foulis of the SFE, August 3, 1999, ELBAssociates historical files, Geneva.

45. In addition to a representative of the secretariat general's office, representatives from six DGs participated: DG2 (Economic Affairs), DG13 (Information and Innovation), DG15 (Financial Institutions and Company Law), DG16 (Regional Policy), DG18 (Credit and Investment), and DG23 (SMEs/Enterprise). CEC, "List of Attendees at a Meeting on June 6, 1989," Secretariat General (Brussels), ELBAssociates historial files, Geneva; SFE's notes from meeting between Sundberg, Schulman, and SFE and the Commission's Inter-DG Working Group, Brussels, October 11, 1989, ELBAssociates historical files, Geneva.

46. ELBAssociates and Consultex, "Creating EASD & EOTC: The European Association of Securities Dealers Who Will Create a European Over-the-Counter Market to Trade Securities Demominated in ECUs, July 1989," Geneva; ELBAssociates, Consultex, and Scottish Financial Enterprise, "Creating the European Association of Securities Dealers and an Integrated European Securities

Market: A Proposal to Manage a Programme for the European Commission, September 1989," Geneva.

47. SFE's notes from meeting between Sundberg, Schulman, and SFE and the Commission's Inter-DG Working Group.

48. The Nasdaq model appealed to those with a regional agenda because, as an electronic quotation system, the U.S. market purportedly enabled financial firms throughout the United States to participate on an equal basis. ELBAssociates, Consultex, and Scottish Financial Enterprise, "Creating."

49. SFE's notes from meeting between Sundberg, Schulman, and SFE and the Commission's Inter-DG Working Group.

50. Arguments made by Mr. Wolff, DG15, are quoted in SFE's notes from meeting between Sundberg, Schulman, and SFE and the Commission's Inter-DG Working Group. Interview with Schulman and Sundberg.

51. For larger companies, the main example of cross-border trading in Europe was the shifting of markets to London, an experience that no doubt informed the opposition to cross-border schemes from continental banks, exchanges, and governments. See Chapter 6.

4. Creating Feeder Markets

1. J. E. Bolton (chairman), "Report of the Committee of Inquiry on Small Firms," Her Majesty's Stationery Office, London (hereafter HMSO), November 1971; Harold Wilson (chairman) "Evidence on the Financing of Industry," vols. 1 and 3, Committee to Review the Functioning of Financial Institutions, HMSO, 1977; Wilson, "Progress Report on the Financing of Industry and Trade," vol. 3, Committee to Review the Functioning of Financial Institutions, HMSO, 1977; Wilson, "Report of Committee to Review the Functioning of Financial Institutions," HMSO, June 1980.

2. John Zysman, *Governments, Markets, and Growth: Financial Systems and the Politics of Industrial Change* (Ithaca: Cornell University Press, 1983).

3. Susanne Lütz, "The Revival of the Nation-State? Stock Exchange Regulation in an Era of Globalized Financial Markets," *Journal of European Public Policy* 5, 1 (1998): 153–168, esp. 156.

4. Zysman, *Governments*, 123–124.

5. The "Official List," "Main List," and "Main Market" all refer to the LSE's main market. "Official List" technically means that quoted companies have the "listed" status, which is now codified in a series of EU directives. Some investors are restricted to investments in the shares of listed companies. On stock markets as social bargains, see Michael Moran, *The Politics of the Financial Services Revolution: The USA, UK and Japan* (New York: St. Martin's Press, 1991).

6. Jonathan R. Macey and Maureen O'Hara, "Globalization, Exchange Governance, and the Future of Exchanges," in Robert E. Litan and Anthony M. Santomero, eds., *Brookings-Wharton Papers on Financial Services* (Washington, D.C.: Brookings Institution, 1999), 1–32.

7. On selection bias and asymmetric information, see George Akerlof, "The Market for 'Lemons': Quality, Uncertainty and the Market Mechanism," *Quarterly Journal of Economics* 84, 3 (1970): 488–500; Bruce Greenwald, Joseph E. Stiglitz, and Andrew Weiss, "Informational Imperfections in the Capital Market and Macroeconomic Fluctuations," *American Economic Review* 74, 1 (1984): 194–199.

8. Wilson, "Evidence," vol. 3, 1978, and "Second Stage Evidence," vol. 4, Committee to Review the Functioning of Financial Institutions, HMSO, March 1979, 1–88.

9. Wilson, "Progress Report" and "Report."

10. For a thorough overview of the government and private intermediaries with financing programs for small and medium-sized companies, see Wilson, "Evidence," vol. 1, 1977, 63–78. Also, see Graham Bannock and Horst Albach, *Small Business Policy in Europe: Britain, Germany and the European Commission* (London: Anglo-German Foundation, 1991).

11. Wilson, "Evidence," vol. 3, 1977.

12. Ibid., 110–143.

13. Hartmut Schmidt, *Advantages and Disadvantages of an Integrated Market Compared with a Fragmented Market, March 1977,* Commission of the European Communities, Competition—Approximation of Legislation Series, no. 30 (Brussels, 1977).

14. ELBAssociates and Consultex, "The Feasibility of Creating ECU-EASD: A European Association of Securities Dealers to Trade over the Counter in ECU-Denominated Shares," Geneva, 1985.

15. Zysman, *Governments,* 205.

16. Ibid.; Moran, *Politics;* Steven K. Vogel, *Freer Markets, More Rules: Regulatory Reform in Advanced Industrial Countries* (Ithaca: Cornell University Press, 1996).

17. Wilson, "Evidence," vol. 3, 1978, 263–267, and "Second Stage."

18. Tom G. Wilmot, *Inside the Over-the-Counter Market in the UK* (Westport, Conn.: Quorum Books, 1985), 12.

19. Ibid., 13–15.

20. Joel Seligman, *The Transformation of Wall Street,* 3rd ed. (New York: Aspen Publishers, 2003).

21. Wilson, "Progress Report"; Roger Buckland and Edward W. Davis, *The Unlisted Securities Market* (Oxford: Clarendon Press, 1989), 1.

22. Wilson, "Progress Report," 33–41.

23. Wilmot, *Inside,* 6–16.

24. Moran, *Politics,* 69.

25. For an overview of SME policies, see Bannock and Albach, *Small Business.*

26. Jeremy Pope, managing director, Pope, Eldridge Pope & Co., "The Proposed Enterprise Market: Key Issues and Implications," (speech given at City Group for Smaller Companies [hereafter CISCO], March 16 conference, London, 1994).

27. Buckland and Davis, *Unlisted,* 7–8.

28. Wilmot, *Inside,* 7.

29. CISCO historical documents dated October 28, 1980, October 1981, and March 16, 1994 (private company board deliberations of CISCO member). Hartmut

Schmidt, *Special Stock Market Segments for Small Company Shares: Capital Raising Mechanism and Exit Route for Investors in New Technology-Based Firms*, EUR 9235 EN, Commission of the European Communities, DG Information Market and Innovation (Brussels, 1984).

30. Wilmot, *Inside*, 9.

31. CISCO historical documents dated October 28, 1980 (private company board deliberations of CISCO member); Pope, "Proposed." The LSE made another concession to DTI (Department of Trade and Industry), the British government body that had just implemented the EEC Second Directive on Company Law (77/91/EEC of December 13, 1976) and thereby was concerned about the status of quoted companies. DTI pressed for higher informational standards than the LSE had originally wanted. Correspondence between the LSE executive and DTI undersecretary of Companies Division, July 7, 1981, CISCO historical files, London.

32. Schmidt, *Special*, 60–61; Graham Bannock, "European Second-Tier Markets for NTBFs," Graham Bannock and Partners, London, 1994, 64.

33. Schmidt, *Special*, 53–62.

34. The exchange's Green Paper originally wanted 15 percent, but the CBI successfully argued for 10 percent. It maintained that SMEs would need to adjust to equity finance and that to ask owners to give up too much control would scare them away from the new market. Pope, "Proposed."

35. Buckland and Davis, *Unlisted*, 1–20.

36. Ibid., 46.

37. Ibid., 123–133. In 1988, the LSE allowed members again to make a market in the shares of OTC companies. See Bannock, "European," 64.

38. "A Third Tier For The Stock Market," *Financial Times*, May 29, 1986, 24; Buckland and Davis, *Unlisted*, 131.

39. Commission des Opérations de Bourse (hereafter COB), "Le Second Marché," Paris, 1992.

40. Zysman, *Governments*, 123–124.

41. Ibid., 135–136.

42. Ibid., 147; Peter A. Hall, *Governing the Economy: The Politics of State Intervention in Britain and France* (Cambridge: Polity Press, 1986), 139–163.

43. COB, "Rapport annuel: Rapport au Président de la République," *Journal officiel* (Paris, 1972).

44. Zysman, *Governments*, 144; Jonah D. Levy, *Tocqueville's Revenge: State, Society, and Economy in Contemporary France* (Cambridge, Mass.: Harvard University Press, 1999).

45. Robert Boyer, *The "Regulation" School: A Critical Introduction* (New York: Columbia University Press, 1990); Levy, *Tocqueville's Revenge*, 69–71. Levy shows how these ideas made their way into the leftist decentralization project of the 1980s, which he labels "associational liberalism." The ideas also penetrated technocratic thinking during the rightist governments of the 1970s, at least among those technocrats involved in reforming the financial system.

46. Hall, *Governing*, 174–176; Levy, *Tocqueville's Revenge*, 37.

47. Jacques Mayoux (chairman), "Le développement des initiatives financières locales et régionales: Rapport à Monsieur le Premier ministre du Groupe de réflexion présidé," La Documentation française, Paris, 1979, 118 and app. 19; Michael Loriaux, *France after Hegemony: International Change and Financial Reform* (Ithaca: Cornell University Press, 1991); Loriaux, "Socialist Monetarism and Financial Liberalization in France," in Loriaux et al., *Capital Ungoverned: Liberalizing Finance in Interventionist States* (Ithaca: Cornell University Press, 1997).

48. Mayoux, "Le développement," 267–268.

49. Zysman, *Governments*, 99–169.

50. Hall, *Governing*, 174–176; Levy, *Tocqueville's Revenge*, 35–38.

51. Mayoux, "Le développement"; Loriaux, *France*, 157.

52. For a list of the adopted legislation, see Levy, *Tocqueville's Revenge*, 37; Mayoux, "Le développement," 124 and app. 20.

53. For a list and description of *instituts de participation*, see Mayoux, "Le développement," app. 25. Also, note that "venture capital" had a different meaning in the France of 1979 than in the France of the 1990s.

54. Mayoux, "Le développement," 271.

55. Levy, *Tocqueville's Revenge*, 35–37.

56. Ibid., 10.

57. Mayoux, "Le développement," 119–125 and app. 19; M. David Dautresme (chairman), "Le développement et la protection de l'épargne: Rapport au Ministre de l'Économie et des Finances et au ministre délégué, chargé du Budget de la Commission," La Documentation française, Paris, 1982, app. 69.

58. Gunnar Trumbull, *Silicon and the State: French Innovation Policy in the Internet Age* (Washington, D.C.: Brookings Institution Press, 2004).

59. On the law of July 29, 1961, see COB, "Rapport annuel: Rapport au Président de la République," *Journal officiel* (Paris, 1968), 51.

60. COB, "Rapport," 1968, 74; Mayoux, "Le développement," 121.

61. COB, "Rapport," 1968, 71–74.

62. Mayoux, "Le développement," 121.

63. COB, "Rapport," 1972, 147–152; COB, "Rapport annuel: Rapport au Président de la République," *Journal officiel* (Paris, 1973), 154–155.

64. Schmidt, *Advantages*, 155–157.

65. COB, "Rapport," 1968, 5–6; ELBAssociates and Consultex, "Feasibility," F1–3. COB began functioning in 1968. At the time, the Council of Ministers selected the president of COB's college, and the minister of finance selected its four other members. Significantly, the minister of finance also selected a government representative. The first was Marc Viénot, chief of service at the Trésor. The Ministry of Finance and the COB's president jointly appointed the COB's secretary general. On the COB's evolution, see Nicole de Montricher, "A National Pattern of Policy Transfer: The Regulation of Insider Trading in France," *French Politics* 3, 1 (2005): 28–48.

66. The transactions on the Paris OTC market had fallen from 3 to 1.5 percent of the Official List between 1963 and 1972. See COB, "Rapport," 1972, 151.

67. P. G. Cerny, "The 'Little Big Bang' in Paris: Financial Market Deregulation in a *Dirigiste* System," *European Journal of Political Research* 17, 2 (1989): 169–192.

68. Schmidt, *Advantages*, 155–157.

69. Financial reporting of companies even on the official list was poor during this period and was a primary concern of COB. COB, "Rapport," 1968.

70. COB, "Rapport annuel: Rapport au Président de la République," *Journal officiel* (Paris, 1977, app. 16.

71. COB, "Rapport annuel: Rapport au Président de la République," *Journal officiel* (Paris, 1976), 70, cites p. 33 of the finance committee report for the plan (Rapport du comité).

72. Loriaux, *France,* 203–207.

73. Akerlof, "Market."

74. Loriaux, *France,* 203.

75. Mayoux, "Le développement," 122–123.

76. Dautresme, "Le développement," vol. 1, 321–328, and vol. 2, 197–199. The Dautresme Report is an important source of the policy ideas that were circulating among the financial elite as Mitterrand was deciding whether to remain in the EMS and stick with the socialist program. David Dautresme was administrateur général du crédit du Nord. In addition to leaders in the securities and banking fields, the other members included Dominique Strauss-Kahn, at the time a professor at the Université de Paris X et chef du service de financement du plan, and officials from the Ministry of Finance, including the Treasury, the Bank of France, COB, and the Budget Ministry. See Dautresme, "Le développement," vol. 1, xvi.

77. COB, "Rapport annuel: Rapport au Président de la République," *Journal officiel* (Paris, 1982), 50–52 and 203–218; *L'année politique, économique et sociale en France,* Éditions du Moniteur (Paris, 1982), 447; Schmidt, *Special,* 324.

78. Loriaux, *France,* 223, and "Socialist," 141; Levy, *Tocqueville's Revenge,* 53.

79. Levy, *Tocqueville's Revenge,* 37–39.

80. Interview with Dominique Strauss-Kahn, Stanford University, April 23, 2001.

81. COB, "Rapport," 1982, 55.

82. Interview with Strauss-Kahn.

83. Dautresme himself presided over this working group (Groupe de travail sur la liquidité des participations financières dans les Petites et Moyennes Entreprises), giving weight to its conclusions. See Dautresme, "Le développement," vol. 1, xvii.

84. Zysman, *Governments,* 135–136 and 151.

85. Dautresme, "Le développement," vol. 2, 192.

86. In the Dautresme Report's appendixes 67, 69, and 70 of vol. 2 are special reports that discuss the Compartiment Spécial, Nasdaq, and the USM. See Dautresme, "Le développement," vol. 2, 180–205.

87. Ibid., vol. 2, 192.

88. ELBAssociates and Consultex, "Feasibility," F9.

89. COB, "Rapport," 1982, 208–210.
90. Ibid., 50–52.
91. COB, "Rapport," 1977, 226–227.

5. Capital Mobility, Politics, and New Financial Interests

1. Age F. P. Bakker, *The Liberalization of Capital Movements in Europe: The Monetary Committee and Financial Integration, 1958–1994* (Dordrecht, Neth.: Kluwer Academic Publishers, 1996), chap. 9; Tommaso Padoa-Schioppa, *The Road to Monetary Union in Europe: The Emperor, the Kings, and the Genies* (Oxford: Oxford University Press, 2001).

2. Benn Steil, *The European Equity Markets: The State of the Union and an Agenda for the Millennium* (London: The Royal Institute of International Affairs and European Capital Market Institute, 1996), 52–53; Ian Domowitz and Steil, "Automation, Trading Costs, and the Structure of the Securities Trading Industry," in Robert E. Litan and Anthony M. Santomero, eds., *Brookings-Wharton Papers on Financial Services* (Washington, D.C.: Brookings Institution Press, 1999).

3. I use Dennis Quinn's and Carla Inclán's measure of openness in combination with Scott L. Kastner and Chad Rector's. While Quinn and Inclán's measure gives annual openness scores for each country, Kastner and Rector's measure, also based on IMF data, identifies by month and year any major changes in government policies. Quinn and Inclán, "The Origins of Financial Openness: A Study of Current and Capital Account Liberalization," *American Journal of Political Science* 41, 3 (1997): 771–813; Kastner and Rector, "International Regimes, Domestic Veto Players, and Capital Controls Policy Stability," *International Studies Quarterly* 47, 1 (2003): 1–22. Bakker's thorough study confirms the pattern that emerges from these quantitative measures. Bakker, *Liberalization*.

4. The indicator I used was gross private-capital flows as a percentage of GDP from the IMF Balance of Payments Database.

5. One prominent exception is 3i, today a private firm, with origins in government programs designed to redress problems identified in the 1931 MacMillan Report.

6. Interview with Ronald Cohen, chairman, Apax Partners & Co. Ltd., London, April 1999.

7. For assessments of reasons (unrelated to the USM's collapse) why the 1980s Cambridge "miracle" flopped, see Annalee Saxenian, "The Cheshire Cat's Grin: Innovation, Regional Development and the Cambridge Case," *Economy and Society* 18, 4 (1989): 448–477, and Jonathan Zeitlin, "Why Are There No Industrial Districts in the United Kingdom?" in Arnaldo Bagnasco, eds., *Small and Medium-Size Enterprises* (London: Pinter, 1995), 98–114.

8. British Venture Capital Association, "Report on Investment Activity," www.bvca.co.uk; William D. Bygrave and Jeffry A. Timmons, *Venture Capital at the Crossroads* (Boston: Harvard Business School Press, 1992).

9. Roger Buckland and Edward W. Davis, *The Unlisted Securities Market* (Oxford: Clarendon Press, 1989).

10. Ibid., 19.

11. LSE, "Primary Markets Smaller Companies Study," London, May 1992.

12. "Is the Small Company Sector Subsidized?" *CISCO Voice,* February 1994, 5; interviews with Morgan Stanley Dean Witter managing director, London, March 25, 1999, with LSE executive, London, April 14, 1999, and with *Financial Times* reporter, London, April 21, 1999.

13. Buckland and Davis, *Unlisted;* Simon Mollett, "The Closure of the USM," *Financial Focus,* no. 6, Faculty of Finance and Management of the Institute of Chartered Accountants in England and Wales, May 1993).

14. Interview with former European Association of Securities Dealers (EASD) official, London, April 26, 1999.

15. Speech delivered by LSE official to the Guildhall Dinner, June 15, 1993 (name of speaker illegible), transcript found in City Group for Smaller Companies (hereafter CISCO) historical files, London (hereafter CISCO historical files).

16. LSE, "Primary."

17. Letter to a CBI official from an official of a USM-quoted company, February 16, 1993, CISCO historical files.

18. The three CISCO founders were Andrew Beeson (of Beeson Gregory, a boutique investment bank specializing in entrepreneurial finance), Brian Winterflood (of Winterflood Securities, the leading market-maker in small-company stocks), and Graham Cole (of Coopers & Lybrand, an international accounting firm).

19. Tradepoint, OM, and Nasdaq International all acquired RIE status but failed to compete effectively with the LSE. For an argument that the LSE's markets continued to dominate because of network effects, see Domowitz and Steil, "Automation."

20. In 2000, the Treasury removed this function from the LSE and gave it to the newly consolidated FSA, thus bringing the United Kingdom into line with United States and the rest of Europe. "London Stock Exchange Is Set to Lose Most Regulatory Powers," *Financial Times,* October 4, 1999.

21. National laws and the statutes of institutional investors often limit investment to listed companies. The term is confusing because a "listed stock" in everyday language sometimes refers to any stock traded on an equity market.

22. CBI, "Report on Finance for Small and Medium Enterprises," London, 1993; Bank of England, *Finance for Small Firms, January 1994* (London, 1994).

23. *CISCO Voice,* February 1994, 4.

24. LSE, "Unlisted Securities Market Review," London, December 21, 1992. Other studies also supported this finding. A Price Waterhouse, Nottingham, study, for instance, found 55 percent of its respondents believed the United Kingdom needed a second market, one that was independent of the Official List. Price Waterhouse, "The Future of USM Companies," Nottingham, February 2, 1992.

25. *CISCO Newsletter* 2 (April 1993).

26. Buckland and Davis, *Unlisted,* 43.

27. Jeremy Pope, managing director, Pope, Eldridge Pope & Co., "The Proposed Enterprise Market: Key Issues and Implications," Company Viewpoint (speech given at CISCO's March 16 conference, London, 1994) CISCO historical files.

28. *CISCO Newsletter* 2 (April 1993).

29. Bygrave and Timmons, *Venture*, 66–99.

30. Jos B. Peeters, "A European Market for Entrepreneurial Companies," in William D. Bygrave, Michael Hay, and Peeters, eds., *Realizing Investment Value* (London: Financial Times/Pitman Publishing, 1994), 199.

31. *EVCA Yearbook* (Brussels, 1992).

32. George Akerlof, "The Market for 'Lemons': Quality, Uncertainty and the Market Mechanism," *Quarterly Journal of Economics* 84, 3 (1970): 488–500.

33. *CISCO Voice*, February 1994, 4.

34. Interview with a Working Party member, London, April 1999.

35. Letters between chancellor of the exchequer and CISCO official, March 1993, CISCO historical files.

36. Various letters dated 1993 or 1994 between CISCO leaders and the chancellor of the exchequer, DTI officials, members of Parliament, and other public officials, CISCO historical files.

37. *CISCO Voice*, May 1994.

38. Ibid.

39. COB, "Le Second Marché," Paris, 1992, 48.

40. Ibid., 51. The CAC 40 index took its name from the now-defunct electronic trading system, Cotation assistée en continue, introduced in 1986.

41. "Le président de la NASDAQ à Paris: Le marché financier de demain," *La Tribune de l'économie* (Paris), July 2, 1987; Michel Turin, "Faites-vous coter à New York," *La Vie française*, July 6–12, 1987; "L'avis d'un spécialiste: NASDAQ, le second marché américain," *Nouvel économiste*, July 10, 1987, 600; "Multiplication des plaintes d'investisseurs à Wall Street: La rançon du succès," *Tribune de l'économie*, July 24, 1987.

42. See P. G. Cerny, "The 'Little Big Bang' in Paris: Financial Market Deregulation in a *Dirigiste* System," *European Journal of Political Research* 17, 2 (1989): 169–192.

43. Steil, *European*.

44. I was unable to find a copy of the report in COB's archives, but its findings were reported in COB, "Second," 1.

45. Part'Com's first fund, for example, opened in 1986. Interview with executive of Part'Com, Groupe Caisse des Dépôts, Paris, October 7, 1998.

46. In its early years AFIC used "the French Venture Capital Association" as the English translation. See www.afic.asso.fr.

47. COB, "Second."

48. Graham Bannock, "European Second-Tier Markets for NTBFs," Graham Bannock and Partners, London, 1994; Bygrave, Hay, and Peeters, *Realizing*.

49. "Une mesure de la rentabilité établie par Ernst and Young-Capital investissement," *Les Echos*, June 1, 1994, 34; "Nouveau recul en 1993," *Les Echos*, June 8, 1994.

50. COB, "Second," 63–64.

51. SBF, "1991 Annual Report," Paris, 1991, 18–19.

52. "Le Nasdaq va ouvrir pendant la nuit pour attirer les investisseurs européens," *l'Agence France-Presse*, January 17, 1992. On the influence of U.S. financial models

on the COB, see Nicole de Montricher, "A National Pattern of Policy Transfer: The Regulation of Insider Trading in France," *French Politics* 3, 1 (2005): 28–48.

53. COB, "Second," 7 and 69.
54. "La SBF met en place un contrat d'animation de marché," *Le Monde,* August 5, 1992.
55. Interview with SBF executive, Paris, May 18, 2000.
56. Michel Deprost, "Le Second Marché: Dix ans d'exercice," *Le Progrès de Lyon,* June 23, 1993, 10.
57. Interviews with SBF executive.
58. "Fonds propres: Un bilan dressé par les fondateurs de l'AFIC-Capital investisse-ment: deux défis majeurs à relever," *Les Echos,* June 17, 1994, 37.
59. Denis Mortier, "Relancer le capital-investissement pour soutenir le PMI," *Banque* 542 (1993): 62; Mortier, "Nécessité d'orienter l'épargne longue vers les PME à fort potentiel: Exemple français, solution européenne," note used for lobbying French ministers, December 2, 1993, EVCA historical files.
60. As an example of the different nature of venture capitalism of the time, Sofinnova, the best-known of the French "venture capital" firms, did not invest in risky entrepreneurial companies—a core characteristic of U.S.-style venture capitalism. See CEC, *European Venture Capital Pilot Scheme,* EUR 9082 EN-FR final, Directorate General Information and Innovation (Brussels, 1984).
61. Part'Com, at least in principle, operates like a private company. Interview with executive of Part'Com, Groupe Caisse des Dépôts, Paris, October 7, 1998.
62. Mortier, "Sous-capitalisation des PME: Organiser la liquidité au niveau européen," *Plus-values,* September-October 1994, 12.
63. "Le capital-risque cherche un second souffle avec un Nasdaq européen," *Agence économique et financière,* June 17, 1994.
64. If there was an exception, it was the Dutch venture capitalists, who had together with the government and stock exchange created the ill-fated Parex (Participation Exchange) market.
65. Mortier, "Relancer"; Mortier "Nécessité"; Mortier, "Sous-capitalisation."
66. Chapter 6 discusses the ISD.
67. Pierre Lafitte (chairman), "Réunion du 13 avril 1994. Les entreprises innovantes et l'emploi. Le problème des fonds propres: vers la création d'un NASDAQ européen (ref. no. 2464 BS/CJ)," Groupe d'étude "Innovation et Entreprise," Sénat, République française, Paris, May 4, 1994; "PME: Rapport Chabbal—Quinze mesures proposées pour les PME innovantes," *Les Echos,* July 11, 1994.
68. COB, "Mesures de l'effet des contrats d'animation sur la liquidité du Second Marché," *Bulletin COB* 280 (May 1994); "Second Marché: Un dynamisme raisonnable," *Option Finance,* December 19, 1994, 39; Daniel Szpiro, "Mesure de l'effet des contrats d'animation sur la liquidité du Second Marché," *Analyse financière* 100 (September 1994): 73; Jean Telagre, "Small-Caps Resuscitated: The Second Marché Gets a Second Wind," *AGefi,* special edition, June 1994, 14.
69. "Pour faire contrepoids au Nasdaq américain," *Les Echos,* November 15, 1994, 36.

6. A Brussels Intervention

1. Former chief of division Daniël Janssens of DG13, for example, was active in the 1990s intervention as well as in the one of 1989. In an a telephone interview on May 4, 2000, he did not recall participating in the 1989 decisions, even though his name was listed among the attendees at June 6, 1989, and October 11, 1989, inter-DG meetings on the subject. There was also continuity in the DG13 director of the Strategic Programme for Innovation and Technology Transfer (SPRINT). Albert S. Strub held this position from 1987 to March 1994.
2. Interview by Steven Weber with Commission officials from the former DG23, Brussels, June 6, 1997.
3. On the introduction of the mutual-recognition strategy, see Karen J. Alter and Sophie Meunier-Aitsahalia, "Judicial Politics in the European Community: European Integration and the Pathbreaking Cassis de Dijon Decision," *Comparative Political Studies* 26, 4 (1994): 535–561.
4. Benn Steil, *Regional Financial Market Integration: Learning from the European Experience* (London: RIIA, 1998).
5. The Prospectus Directive created minimal standards for the prospectuses of publicly traded companies not seeking official listing and introduced the mutual-recognition mechanism for prospectuses.
6. Benn Steil, *The European Equity Markets: The State of the Union and an Agenda for the Millennium* (London: RIIA and ECMI, 1996). Interview with Jos B. Peeters, Leuven, April 26, 2000.
7. Jonathan Story and Ingo Walter, *Political Economy of Financial Integration in Europe: The Battle of the Systems* (Cambridge, Mass.: MIT Press, 1997), 21–22, 266–269.
8. Council Directive 93/22/EEC, Title V, Article 15, paragraphs 4 and 5.
9. Josefin Almer, "The Reform of Comitology and the Parallel Reform of the European Financial Services Sector," New Modes of Governance Project, CIT1-CT-2004–506392, 7/D05a rev, December 12, 2006, www.eu-newgov.org.
10. Alec Stone Sweet, Neil Fligstein, and Wayne Sandholtz, "The Institutionalization of European Space," in Stone Sweet, Sandholtz, and Fligstein, *The Institutionalization of Europe* (Oxford: Oxford University Press, 2001), 12.
11. Steven Weber and Elliot Posner, "Creating a Pan-European Equity Market: The Origins of EASDAQ," *Review of International Political Economy* 7 (2000): 545.
12. CEC, *Reporting on the Feasibility of the Creation of a European Capital Market for Smaller Entrepreneurial Managed Growing Companies*, COM(95)498 final, Brussels, October 25, 1995, 7.
13. Telephone interview with Commission official, formerly with DG13, May 4, 2000. Interview by Steven Weber with Commission officials from the former DG23.
14. CEC, *Growth, Competitiveness, Employment: The Challenges and Ways Forward into the 21st Century*, White Paper, COM(93)700 (Brussels, December 5, 1993).
15. Graham Cole, "Access for SMEs to the Capital Markets, Particularly Junior Mar-

kets," Deloitte, Haskins & Sells, 1988; Graham Bannock, "European Second-Tier Markets for NTBFs," Graham Bannock and Partners, London, 1994; Coopers & Lybrand, "Corporate Finance: EASDAQ—a New Opportunity?" London, 1995; Coopers & Lybrand, "EASDAQ, the Nouveau Marché, AIM: An Update," London, 1996.

16. CEC, *Financial Problems of SMEs,* COM(93)528 (Brussels, November 10, 1993); CEC, "Prospects for the Creation of a European-Level Capital Market for Entrepreneurial Companies: Meeting with the Press in Preparation for June 21," DG23, Direction B, Unit 3, Brussels, June 16, 1994; CEC, *Reporting;* letter to Elliot Posner from L. D. M. Mackenzie, director, Promotion of Entrepreneurship and SMEs, DG Enterprise, May 8, 2001.

17. Correspondence between Eugene Schulman and Jacques Delors, president of the Commission, January 14, 1985 ELBAssociates historical files, Geneva. ELB Associates and Consultex, "The Feasibility of Creating ECU-EASD: A European Association of Securities Dealers to Trade over the Counter in ECU-Denominated Shares," Geneva, 1985; interview with Schulman and Andrew Sundberg, Geneva, May 8, 2000.

18. See ELBAssociates, Consultex, and SFE, "Creating the European Association of Securities Dealers and an Integrated European Securities Market: A Proposal to Manage a Programme for the European Commission," Geneva, September 1989; SFE, "Notes from Meeting between Sundberg, Schulman, SFE, and the Commission's Inter-DG Working Group," Brussels, October 11, 1989 ELBAssociates historical files, Geneva.

19. Telephone interview with Daniël Janssens, May 4, 2000.

20. At the time of the Easdaq debates, Paul Goldschmidt was the director of the Financial Operations Service, which was inside DG 18 but later moved to DG2.

21. Interview with Paul Goldschmidt of DG18, Luxembourg, June 7, 1999.

22. Compare Peeters' plans to EVCA, "Venture Capital Special Paper: Capital Markets for Entrepreneurial Companies—a European Opportunity for Growth," Zaventem, 1994, produced by EVCA's Exits Committee.

23. Interview with Peeters. Telephone interview with former EVCA secretary general, April 27, 2000.

24. These figures come from EVCA's General Assembly Report, June 9, 1994, 15.

25. Accounts of this interaction from interviews with Peeters and with Commission official, Luxembourg, June 7, 1999, as well as from telephone interview with former EVCA secretary general.

26. Council Decision 93/379 OJ L 165 of July 2, 1993.

27. Peeters' third goal, to propose a pan-European stock market, was still a source of controversy within EVCA.

28. Jos B. Peeters, "A European Market for Entrepreneurial Companies," in William D. Bygrave, Michael Hay, and Peeters, eds., *Realizing Investment Value* (London: Financial Times/Pitman Publishing, 1994). As early as February 1993, independent reports from EVCA's business seminar in Venice show that Commission officials were welcoming proposals for a Nasdaq-like project. "Visit to the European Commission," August 8, 1993, CISCO historical files, London (here-

after CISCO historical files). Interview with DG13 official, Luxembourg, July 5, 2000.

29. Officials from DG13 had discretion over funds from SPRINT, which was merged into the Fourth Framework Programme at the end of 1994. The officials from DG23 had discretion over funds from the Action Programme for SMEs.

30. Bannock, "European;" Coopers & Lybrand, "Corporate."

31. Telephone interview with former EVCA executive, April 27, 2000.

32. EVCA, "Expert Meeting, European Capital Markets for Entrepreneurial Companies: List of Attendees," dated April 18, 1994, EVCA historical files, Zaventem (hereafter EVCA historical files).

33. Peeters met privately at least once in early 1994 with Albrecht Mulfinger (DG23) and Albert S. Strub (DG13). Interview by Steven Weber with DG23 official, Brussels, June 6, 1997.

34. Letter to continental stock exchange executive, dated April 22,1994, from European Capital Markets for Entrepreneurial Growth Companies Working Group, EVCA historical files.

35. The executives of the Paris exchange were notable exceptions. They pulled out of the project later, as I discuss below.

36. Interviews with former EASD official, Schwalbach, May 12, 1999.

37. Steil, *European.*

38. "Le capital-risque cherche un second souffle avec un Nasdaq européen," *Agence économique et financière,* June 17, 1994; "Vers un marché européen des valeurs de croissance," *Le Figaro/L'Aurore,* June 18, 1994; "Nasdaq Holds Talks on Forming European Exchange," *Financial Times,* June 23, 1994; Richard Evans and Paula Dwyer, "Nasdaq with a European Accent?" *Business Week,* June 30, 1994, 20.

39. The financial problem already existed before the French departure. According to its budget proposal, Peeters' working group had already asked the Commission for an additional 956,804 ECUs in October 1994, to subsidize EASD in its first three years.

40. ECU-EASD (1985), EOTC (1989), ESM (1989), MESEC (1994), and Easdaq (1996); Nasdaq Europe (2001) is the name of the revamped Easdaq after Nasdaq purchased it.

41. Interview with anonymous source in Germany, May 12, 1999.

42. FIBV, "Workshop: Financing Small and Medium-Sized Businesses for Future Growth: Proceedings," Milan, July 6–7, 1995, EASD historical files, Brussels.

43. Interview with official, DG Enterprise, Luxembourg, May 5, 2000.

44. Interviews with Trésor official (Bureau du Marché financier), Paris, June 6, 1999, and with Commission official from DG Enterprise. Letter to Elliot Posner from Mackenzie.

45. Letter to Elliot Posner from Mackenzie.

46. The commissioners in charge of enterprise policy, Raniero Vanni d'Archirafi (January 1993 to January 1995, Italy) and Christos Papoutsis (January 1995 to September 1999, Greece), staunchly supported DG23's director general Dr. Heinrich von Moltke (who had held this position since March 1990) and the

Easdaq project. See Council of the European Union (CEU), "Conclusions," 1880: Council—Industry, Press:310, Nr:111 72/95, November 7, 1995.

47. CEC, *Towards a European Stock Exchange: Symposium Held in Brussels on 13 and 14 November 1980*, XV/231/81 (Brussels, November 13–14, 1980).

48. The figures and other information in this paragraph come from correspondence between EASD and Commission officials, which I found in the EASD historical files in Brussels.

49. CEC, *Bulletin of the European Union/European Community*, Bull EC 7/8–1993.

50. EASD was incorporated in Belgium as an international ASBL *(association sans but lucratif)*, an international nonprofit organization, before it merged with APCIMS, several years later. The idea for EASD was first mentioned publicly on June 16, 1994, in CEC, "Prospects."

51. On Easdaq's legal status, see Dirk Tirez, "Easdaq Benefits from European Framework," *International Financial Law Review* 16, 11 (1997): 11–15; Dana T. Ackerly II, Philipp Tamussino, and Wesley S. Williams Jr., "Easdaq—The European Stock Market for the Next Hundred Years?" *Journal of International Banking Law* 12, 3 (1997): 86–91.

52. Written correspondence to Elliot Posner from Mackenzie.

53. Moltke, "The Role of DGXXIII with Regard to Easdaq" (paper presented at the "EASDAQ—The European Stock Market for Growing Companies" conference, Brussels, June 26, 1996) EVCA historical files.

54. Telephone interview with Commission official, formerly with DG13.

55. Interview with former EASD official, London, April 26, 1999.

56. As detailed below, after the June 1994 meeting of Peeters' working group, Nasdaq, Apax, and the SBF had pledged financial contributions. By November, however, Nasdaq and the SBF had pulled their support for the project, leaving only the Commission, EVCA and Apax. Interview with former EASD official, London.

57. Interview with Peeters.

58. Various documents from the CISCO historical files; interviews with Ronald Cohen, London, April 16, 1999, and with Peeters.

59. Ronald Cohen, "Special Care for Young Companies," *Financial Times*, March 8, 1994, 20; Peeters, "A European Market."

60. Telephone interview with former EVCA secretary general; interview with Peeters.

61. CEC, "Prospects"; Katie Morris (CISCO CEO), "The Development of Competing Stock Exchanges: Speech Given to the Institute of Economic Affairs," London, June 1995, CISCO historical files.

62. Interview with Cohen.

63. See Chapter 5 for SEAQ International and Chapter 1 for the NYSE-Euronext merger. In 1997, LIFFE lost domination of the ten-year German government bond *(bunds)* market to the newly automated Deutsche Terminbörse (DTB).

64. Even though this concession did not withstand a change in LSE chief executives, AIM has remained substantially independent.

65. David Mandell, "Alternative Investment Mood," *CISCO Voice,* December 1997, 8–10.
66. "The London-Frankfurt Merger," *Financial Times,* May 4, 2000.
67. The other two were the Nasdaq and Apax Partners, Cohen's company. Until that point, the Easdaq project had been funded entirely by the Commission and EVCA. Interview with former EASD official, London.
68. "Vers un marché européen."
69. They hired George Hayter, former LSE chief executive, to help with trading and settlement systems and Trevor Smith in London to develop the legal framework. Interviews with former EASD official, London, and with Peeters.
70. George Hayter, "EASDAQ: A Concept Paper," EVCA, EASDAQ-UK, Nasdaq, SBF-Bourse de Paris, London, November 1994, EVCA historical files.
71. Interviews with former EASD official, London, and with Peeters.
72. By 1993, one-third of SBF member firms were subsidiaries of foreign corporations. See AFSB, "Rapport annuel 1993," Paris, 14–15.
73. Interview with SBF executive, Paris, May 18, 2000.
74. Ibid.
75. Telephone interview with former Easdaq official, May 24, 1999.
76. Interview with former French finance minister Dominique Strauss-Kahn, Stanford University, April 23, 2001.
77. Bruno Roger and Pierre Faurre, "Rapport du groupe de travail 'Nouveau Marché,'" SBF–Bourse de Paris, Paris, February, 1995. Interview with French Trésor official, who used the phrase "co-decision," Paris, June 6, 1999. Strauss-Kahn said the creation of the Nouveau Marché was more more a state-led action than a co-decision. Interview with Strauss-Kahn.
78. Interviews with former Deutsche Boerse executive, Nuremberg, May 11, 2000, and with SBF executive, Paris, May 18, 2000.
79. Interviews with former Deutsche Boerse executive, Nuremberg, May 11, 2000; with Deutsche Boerse official, Frankfurt, May 12, 1999; and with SBF executive, Paris, May 18, 2000.
80. Susanne Lütz, "The Revival of the Nation-State? Stock Exchange Regulation in an Era of Globalized Financial Markets," *Journal of European Public Policy* 5, 1 (1998): 153–168.
81. Interviews with former EASD official, Schwalbach, and with Peeters.
82. Karen E. Adelberger, "Semi-Sovereign Leadership? The State's Role in German Biotechnology and Venture Capital Growth," *German Politics* 9 (2000): 103–122; Ralph Becker and Thomas Hellmann, "The Genesis of Venture Capital: Lessons from the German Experience," CESIFO, Working Paper, no. 883 (2003), www.cesifo.de.
83. I was unable to find a copy of this frequently mentioned letter. Deutsche Boerse, "Spotlight," *Vision and Money,* January 1996, 17. Interview with former Deutsche Boerse official, Nuremberg, May 11, 2000.
84. Deutsche Boerse, "Spotlight."
85. Interview with former Deutsche Boerse official.
86. Ibid.

87. "Nouveau Marché Rule Change," *Financial Times*, October 30, 1996, 28.

88. Hans-Peter Burghof and Adrian Hunger, "The Neuer Markt: An (Overly) Risky Asset of Germany's Financial System," in Giancarlo Giudici and Peter Roosenboom, ed., *The Rise and Fall of Europe's New Stock Markets*, vol. 10: *Advances in Financial Economics* (Amsterdam: Elsevier, 2004).

89. Figures from the now-defunct Euro.NM.

90. "Think Nasdaq: Now Double the Pain," *New York Times*, January 28, 2001, section 3, 1.

91. Burghof and Hunger, "Neuer," 309–310.

92. For interpretations, see Sigurt Vitols and Lutz Engelhardt, "National Institutions and High Tech Industries: A Varieties of Capitalism Perspective on the Failure of Germany's 'Neuer Markt,'"Discussion Paper SP II 2005–03, *Wissenschaftszentrum Berlin für Sozialforschung*, (Berlin, 2005); Burghof and Hunger, "Neuer."

93. The economics of the new market's demise is covered in Giudici and Roosenboom, *Rise and Fall*.

94. Burghof and Hunger, "Neuer," 314–315.

95. "The London-Frankfurt Merger," *Financial Times*, May 4, 2000.

96. "Germany's Investors Dig In for the Long Term," *Financial Times*, March 15, 2001, 3; "Analysts to Face Toughest Set of Rules Yet," *Financial Times*, May 21, 2001, 21; "Bourse Tightens Rules on Market," *Financial Times*, July 23, 2001, 16.

97. "Nasdaq Is Set to Control Counterpart in Europe," *New York Times*, March 28, 2001, B1; "Nasdaq Puts High Hopes on New European Trading System," *New York Times*, June 9, 2001, B3; "Nasdaq Europe Makes Debut," *Financial Times*, June 10, 2001, 9; "Nasdaq Sells European Stake," *Financial Times*, November 29, 2003, 8. Peeters purchased Nasdaq's controlling interest in Nasdaq Europe in December 2003 and sought to revive the Easdaq idea under a new label, Equiduct.

98. Euronext, "Euronext Launches NextEconomy and NextPrime Segments," Amsterdam, Brussels, Paris, December 18, 2001.

99. "AIM Rules for Companies, February 2007" and "AIM Rules for Nominated Advisors, February 2007," www.londonstockexchange.com.

100. "Euronext Bullish over Alternext," *Financial Times*, April 15, 2005, 18; Euronext, "Alternext: A Tailor-Made Market for Small and Mid Caps," Amsterdam, Brussels, Lisbon, London, and Paris, April 14, 2005; Euronext, "Euronext Completes Overhaul of Listing Structure on All Its Markets," Brussels, 2005. Alternext was created as part of a complete overhaul of Euronext's market structure, including the closure of the Nouveau Marché. See Euronext, "Euronext Completes Overhaul of Listing Structure on All Its Markets," Brussels, March 23, 2005.

101. "Davos: NYSE Chief Says Aim Must Raise Standards," *Financial Times*, January 27, 2007; "Top SEC Official Claims UK's Aim Is a 'Casino,'" *Financial Times*, March 9, 2007, 1; "London's Junior Market a Danger, Says Ross," *Financial Times*, April 20, 2007, 1.

102. As of 2007, the LSE has mandated AIM companies incorporated in the European Economic Area to use IFRS and non-EEA companies to choose one of five

sets of respected standards. See "AIM Rules for Companies, 2007," www .londonstockexchange.com. International asscounting standards produced by the International Accounting Standards Board (or IASB) nd its predecssor, the International Accounting Standards Committee (or IASC), are now commonly referred to as International Financial Reporting Standards (or IFRS). In the past, they were known as International Accounting Standards (or IAS).

103. Mark Ingebretsen, *Nasdaq: A History of the Market That Changed the World* (Roseville, Calif.: Prima Publishing, 2002).

7. Taking Stock

1. Maurice Anslow, "'EPEE,' 'PAREX,' 'NASDAQ' or 'EASDAQ'?" and *European Venture Capital Journal* 26, 1 (1993), 2; and "Two Ideas for a Private Equity Exchange," *European Venture Capital Journal* 26, 1 (1993), 14–17. "Nasdaq Holds Talks on Forming European Exchange," *Financial Times*, June 23, 1994; Jos B. Peeters, "A European Market for Entrepreneurial Companies," in William D. Bygrave, Michael Hay, and Peeters, eds., *Realizing Investment Value* (London: Financial Times/Pitman Publishing, 1994). Telephone interview with former EVCA secretary general, April 27, 2000; interview with Peeters, Leuven, April 26, 2000.

2. Interviews with Paris stock exchange executive, Paris, May 18, 2000; with Commission official from the former DG15, Brussels, June 8, 2004; and with FESE executive, Brussels, June 8, 2004. Also, see the comments of Jose Fombellida, DG15, in FIBV, "Workshop: Financing Small and Medium-Sized Businesses for Future Growth," Milan, July 6–7, 1995, EASD historical files, Brussels.

3. William G. Christie and Paul H. Schultz, "Why Do NASDAQ Market Makers Avoid Odd-Eighth Quotes?" *Journal of Finance* 49, 5 (1994): 1813–1840; SEC, "Report Pursuant to Section 21(a) of the Securities Exchange Act of 1934 Regarding the NASD and the NASDAQ Market," Washington, D.C., August 8, 1996; "Collusion in the Stockmarket," *Economist*, January 17, 1998, 71.

4. I found a copy of the 1985 proposal in EASD historical files.

5. Robert Chabbal (chairman), "Le Système financier français face à l'investissement innovation: Rapport à ministre des entreprises et du développement économique," Paris, La Documentation française, 1995.

6. Beth A. Simmons, "International Politics of Harmonization: The Case of Capital Market Regulation," *International Organization* 55, 3 (2001): 589–620.

7. For evidence of a changed stance on the part of the Brussels officials, see CEC, *Reporting on the Feasibility of the Creation of a European Capital Market for Smaller Entrepreneurial Managed Growing Companies*, COM(95)498 final (Brussels, October 25, 1995).

8. "Why AIM Is Foreign Target of Choice," *Financial Times*, September 3, 2005, 3; LSE, "London Stock Exchange AIMs for Europe," press release, April 10, 2005, www.londonstockexchange.com.

9. Mark A. Pollack, *Engines of European Integration: Delegation, Agency, and Agenda Setting in the EU* (Oxford: Oxford University Press, 2003).

10. Interviews with French Trésor official (Bureau du Marché financier), Paris, June 6, 1999, and with Commission official from the former DG15.

11. Letters between chancellor of the exchequer and CISCO leader, March 1993, CISCO historical files, London.

12. Interviews with French Trésor official; with Commission official from the former DG13, Luxembourg, May 5, 2000; and with former French finance minister Dominique Strauss-Kahn, Stanford University, April 23, 2001. DG15's and the stock exchanges' opposition to the Easdaq initiative came out in the open during a conference in Milan on July 6 and 7, 1995. See FIBV, "Workshop."

13. CEU, "Conclusions," 1880: Council—Industry, Press:310, Nr:111 72/95, November, 7 1995.

14. Council Decision 94/5/EC.

15. Council Decision 93/379/EEC, app. 1, II.B.

16. In a letter in response to my questions, L. D. M. Mackenzie of the Commission (director, Promotion of Entrepreneurship and SMEs, DG Enterprise) argued that he and his colleagues acted with the approval of the Industry Council and that the multiannual program for SMEs (1993–1996) provided the legal basis. Mackenzie to Elliot Posner, May 8, 2001. See Council Decisions 89/286/EEC, 93/379/EEC, and 94/5/EC.

17. CEC, *Reporting;* ELBAssociates and Consultex, "The Feasibility of Creating ECU-EASD: A European Association of Securities Dealers to Trade over the Counter in ECU-Denominated Shares," Geneva, 1985; Josefin Almer, "The Reform of Comitology and the Parallel Reform of the European Financial Services Sector," New Modes of Governance Project, CIT1-CT-2004–506392, 7/D05a rev, December 12, 2006, www.eu-newgov.org.

18. The commissioners who backed career bureaucrats were Raniero Vanni d'Archirafi (Italy) and Christos Papoutsis (Greece).

19. Heinrich von Moltke, "The Role of DGXXIII with Regard to Easdaq" (paper presented at the "EASDAQ—The European Stock Market for Growing Companies" conference, Brussels, June 26, 1996), EVCA historical files, Zaventem.

20. EU experts use the term "institutionalization" for this phenomenon. See Alec Stone Sweet, Wayne Sandholtz, and Neil Fligstein, eds., *The Institutionalization of Europe* (Oxford: Oxford University Press, 2001); Michael E. Smith, *Europe's Foreign and Security Policy: The Institutionalization of Cooperation* (Cambridge: Cambridge University Press, 2004).

21. Fritz Scharpf, *Governing in Europe: Effective and Democratic?* (Oxford: Oxford University Press, 1999).

22. For an excellent example of recent work, see Neil Fligstein, *The Architecture of Markets: An Economic Sociology of Twenty-First Century Capitalist Societies* (Princeton: Princeton University Press, 2001).

23. Tim Büthe, "Taking Temporality Seriously: Modeling History and the Use of Narratives as Evidence," *American Political Science Review* 96, 3 (2002): 481–494; Paul Pierson, *Politics in Time: History, Institutions, and Social Analysis* (Princeton: Princeton University Press, 2004); Kathleen Thelen, *How Institutions Evolve: The*

Political Economy of Skills in Germany, Britain, the United States and Japan (Cambridge: Cambridge University Press, 2004).

24. U.S. Government Accounting Office, *Financial Regulation: Industry Changes Prompt Need to Reconsider US Regulatory Structure,* GAO-05–61 (Washington, D.C., October 2004).

25. For analyses of the relationship between financial and monetary integration, see Tommaso Padoa-Schioppa, *The Road to Monetary Union in Europe: The Emperor, the Kings, and the Genies* (Oxford: Oxford University Press, 2000); Kathleen R. McNamara, "Making Money: Political Development, the Greenback, and the Euro" (Center for German and European Studies, working paper, University of California, Berkeley, October 2004).

26. CEC, *Financial Services Action Plan,* COM(1999)232 (Brussels, 1999). For related documents, go to ec.europa.eu/internal_market.

27. Interviews with Delegation of the European Commission official, Washington, D.C., May 4, 2004, and with European Parliament official (Committee on Economic and Monetary Affairs), Brussels, June 8, 2004.

28. CEC, *Financial Services: Building a Framework for Action* ip/98/941 (Brussels, October 28, 1998), ec.europa.eu/internal_market.

29. Interview with Commission official (DG Internal Market), Brussels, June 9, 2004.

30. CEC, *Risk Capital: A Key to Job Creation in the European Union,* SEC(1998)552 (March 31, 1998).

31. Interview with former UK Treasury official, Washington, D.C., November 4, 2005.

32. Huhne's writings on the subject are available at chrishuhne.org.uk/.

33. Nathaniel W. Lalone, "An Awkward Partner: Explaining France's Troubled Relationship to the Single Market in Financial Services," *French Politics* 3, 3 (2005): 211–233.

34. For a contrasting view, see Daniel Mügge, "Reordering the Market Place: Competition Politics in European Finance," *Journal of Common Market Studies* 55, 5 (2006): 991–1022.

35. European Financial Services Round Table, www.efr.be/index.asp.

36. Eurofi, www.eurofi.net.

37. "Synthesis of Responses [to COM(2000)729]", ec.europa.eu/internal_market.

38. FESE changed its name but not its acronym. (The Federation of European Stock Exchanges became the Federation of European Securities Exchanges.) "Securities exchanges" used to be "stock exchanges."

39. Interview with FESE secretary-general in Brussels, June 9, 2004.

40. Compare recommendations for the structure of securities regulation cooperation in these documents: CEC, *Financial Services: Building a Framework for Action,* FESE, *Report and Recommendations on European Regulatory Structures,* (Brussels, September 2000); Alexandre Lamfalussy (chairman), "Final Report of the Committee of Wise Men on the Regulation of European Securities Markets," Brussels, February 15, 2001.

41. "Presidency Conclusions," Cardiff European Council, June 15 and 16, 1998, 9.

42. CEC, *Financial Services: Building a Framework for Action,* 2.

43. Ibid., 3.

44. Interview with Delegation of the European Commission official.

45. CEC, *Financial Services: Building a Framework for Action,* 2.

46. Interview with Delegation of the European Commission official.

47. See CEC, *Financial Integration,* COM(83)207 (Brussels, April 1983); CEC, *Completing the Internal Market,* COM (85) 310 (Brussels, June 1985).

48. Interview with Delegation of the European Commission official.

49. CEC, *Single Market in Financial Services Progress Report, 2004–2005,* SEC(2006)17 (Brussels, January 5, 2006).

50. International accounting standards produced by the International Accounting Standards Board and its predecessor, the International Accounting Standards Committee, are now commonly referred to as International Financial Reporting Standards, or IFRS. In the past, they were known as International Accounting Standards (IAS).

51. The regulation applies to consolidated accounts only. See Karel van Hulle, "From Accounting Directives to International Accounting Standards," in Christian Leuz, Dieter Pfaff, and Anthony Hopwood, eds., *The Economics and Politics of Accounting: International Perspectives on Research Trends, Policy, and Practice* (Oxford: Oxford University Press, 2004), 364–365.

52. The Federation of European Securities Commissions (FESCO) became CESR under the new Lamfalussy regime. See the following section of this chapter for more details.

53. Van Hulle, "From Accounting."

54. Ian P. Dewing and Peter O. Russell, "Accounting, Auditing and Corporate Governance of the European Listed Countries: EU Policy Developments before and after Enron," *Journal of Common Market Studies* 42, 2 (2004): 289–319.

55. Van Hulle, "From Accounting," 352–353.

56. Marc Barber, "EU Veto on Derivatives Standard Threatens Move to IAS by 2005," *The Accountant,* June 30, 2004, 1; "Lex: IAS 39," *Financial Times,* July 7, 2004; "When Politicians Write Accounting Rules, Reality Can Be Forgotten," *New York Times,* July 23, 2004, C1.

57. Interview with Commission official (DG Internal Market).

58. Van Hulle, "From Accounting," 253.

59. Ball (2004).

60. CEC, *Accounting Harmonisation: A New Strategy vis-a-vis International Harmonisation,* COM95(508)EN (Brussels, 1995).

61. Ibid.; CEC, *EU Financial Reporting Strategy: The Way Forward,* COM(2000)359 (Brussels, 2000); Van Hulle, *From Accounting;* interview with Commission official, Washington D.C., May 5, 2004.

62. Simmons, "International."

63. In the final years of IASC 1997–2000, five of thirteen board members chosen by country were European. The rest were from Australia, Canada, India, Japan, Malaysia, Mexico, South Africa, and the United States. In addition, at least one and sometimes two of the industry organization members were European.

Liesel Knorr and Gabi Ebbers, "IASC Individual Accounts," in Dieter Ordelheide and KPMG, *Transnational Accounting* (New York: Palgrave, 2001), 1457–1458. Under IASB's new constitution, six of nineteen International Accounting Standards Committee Foundation (IASCF) trustees must be from European countries; see www.iasb.org.

64. For example, see Pervenche Berès, "La Consruction d'un Marché Financier intégré: Le Rôle du Parlement Européen," January 16, 2007, 18, www.pervenche-beres.fr.

65. Knorr and Ebbers, "IASC."

66. Originally, the Lamfalussy process applied only to the securities sectors. In December 2002 it was extended to the entire financial services industry, including banking, pensions, and insurance.

67. The committee was comprised of seven members. The rapporteur and secretariat were representatives of the Commission.

68. Alexandre Lamfalussy, "The Four-Level Approach to Financial Regulation in Europe: Origins, Main Features, Achievements, Concerns" (paper delivered at the "Euro: Once Currency, One Financial Market" conference, New York, April 19–20, 2005); Carl Fredrik Bergström, Josefin Almer, Frédéric Varone, and Christian de Visscher, "Final Report," New Modes of Governance Project, CIT1-CT-2004–506392, 7/D06 (Report), August 31, 2006, www.eu-newgov.org.; Inter-Institutional Monitoring Group, "Second Interim Report Monitoring the Lamfalussy Process," Brussels, January 26, 2007, Part III, ec.europa.eu.

69. Pollack, *Engines*, 143.

70. "A Ragbag of Reform," *Economist*, March 3, 2001, 63–65.

71. Lamfalussy, "Final," 7–8.

72. Almer, "Reform"; Pollack, *Engines*.

73. CEC, *Financial Services: Building a Framework for Action;* Josefin Almer and Matilda Rotkirch, *European Governance: An Overview of the Commission's Agenda for Reform,* Swedish Institute for European Policy Studies, 2004, www.sieps.se; Charles F. Sabel and Jonathan Zeitlin, "Learning from Difference: The New Architecture of Experimentalist Governance in the European Union," *European Law Journal* 14, 3 (May), 2008, 271–327.

74. Almer, "Reform"; Carl Fredrik Bergström, Josefin Almer, Frédéric Varone, and Christian de Visscher," Governance and the EU Securities Sector," New Modes of Governance Project, CIT1-CT-2004–506392, 7/D1 (Report), November 30, 2004, 7–10, www.eu-newgov.org.

75. Almer, "Reform."

76. Lamfalussy, "Final," 86.

77. "Ragbag."

Conclusion

1. John Gerard Ruggie, "Territoriality and Beyond: Problematizing Modernity in International Relations," *International Organization* 47, 1 (1993): 139–174.

2. David S. Evans, "The New Trustbusters: Brussels and Washington May Part

Ways," *Foreign Affairs* 81, 1 (2002): 14–20. On how the European Commission's guardian role combines with the ECJ to produce regional markets along the liberal model, see Fritz Scharpf, *Governing in Europe: Effective and Democratic?* (Oxford: Oxford University Press, 1999).

3. As of January 2006, AIM listed companies from twenty-two countries. See www.londonstockexchange.com.

4. "Top SEC Official Claims UK's AIM Is a 'Casino,'" *Financial Times*, March 9, 2007, 1; "London's Junior Market a Danger, Says Ross," *Financial Times*, April 20, 2007, 1; Telephone interview with former SEC chief accountant, July 8, 2007.

5. "Nomad Sarbox Refugee Aims for Low-Cost London," *Financial Times*, March 17, 2006, 22; "Scattering Seedlings Turns into a Forest," *Financial Times*, March 29, 2006; U.S. Government Accountability Office, *Sarbanes-Oxley Act: Consideration of Key Principles Needed in Addressing Implementation for Smaller Public Companies*, GAO-06–361 (Washington, D.C.: 2006); "Selling the Attractions of Euronext," *Financial Times*, May 22, 2006, 30.

6. Bernard S. Black and Ronald J. Gilson, "Venture Capital and the Structure of Capital Markets: Banks versus Stock Markets," *Journal of Finance Economics* 47, 3 (1998): 243–277; Paul A. Gompers and Josh Lerner, "The Determinants of Corporate Venture Capital Successes: Organizational Structure, Incentives, and Complementarities," National Bureau of Economic Research Working Paper, no. w675 (September 1998); Mark Ingebretsen, *Nasdaq: A History of the Market That Changed the World* (Roseville, Calif.: Prima Publishing, 2002), chaps. 4 and 5.

7. The SEC first broached the idea of an electronic quotation system as a solution to the unruly and corrupt OTC market. See Ingebretsen, *Nasdaq*, chap. 5; Joel Seligman, *The Transformation of Wall Street*, 3rd ed. (New York: Aspen Publishers, 2003).

8. Diana Farrell, Susan M. Lund, and Alexander N. Maasry, "Mapping the Global Capital Markets, January 2007: Europe Rising," *McKinsey Quarterly* (January 2007).

9. European Commission, *Financial Integration Monitor*, europa.eu; ECB, *Financial Integration in Europe*, www.ecb.int.

10. EVCA yearbooks with statistics and legislative agenda are available at www.evca.com. EVCA's 1990s figures were denominated in ECUs. The yearbooks used a one-to-one conversion rate into euros. See *EVCA Yearbook* (Brussels, 2000).

11. "Germany Bristles at Capitalist 'Locusts,'" *New York Times*, May 5, 2005, 1.

12. Alexandre Lamfalussy (chairman), "Initial Report of the Committee of Wise Men," September 11, 2000, and "Final Report of the Committee of Wise Men on the Regulation of European Securities Markets," February 15, 2001, europa.eu.

13. For comments to SEC proposed rules, see www.sec.gov.

14. Lamfalussy, "The Four-Level Approach to Financial Regulation in Europe: Origins, Main Features, Achievements, Concerns" (paper presented at the "Conference on the Euro: Once Currency, One Financial Market," New York, April 19–20, 2005).

15. Seligman, *Transformation;* telephone interview with former SEC chief accountant.

16. CESR, "Which Supervisory Tools for the EU Securities Markets? Preliminary Progress Report [Himalaya Report]," www.cesr-eu.org; Daniel Mügge, "Reordering the Market Place: Competition Politics in European Finance," *Journal of Common Market Studies* 55, 5 (2006): 991–1022.

17. See ec.europa.eu/internal_market/finances/fscg/index_en.htm.

18. Elliot Posner, "Global Financial Rule-Making after Hegemony: Explaining Change in Transatlantic Regulatory Cooperation," unpublished paper.

19. SEC, "Acceptance from Foreign Private Issuers of Financial Statements Prepared in Accordance with International Financial Reporting Standards without Reconciliation to U.S. GAAP: Proposed Rule" (Release No. 33–8818, July 2, 2007), www.sec.gov; Ethiopis Tafara and Robert J. Peterson, "A Blueprint for Cross-Border Access to US Investors: A New International Framework," *Harvard International Law Journal* 48, 1 (2007): 31–68.

20. Marc E. Lackritz, "The US-EU Economic Relationship: What Comes Next," testimony before the U.S. House of Representatives Financial Services Committee, Washington, D.C., June 16, 2005, financialservices.house.gov.

Index